GROWTH MANAGEMENT

KEEPING ON TARGET?

DOUGLAS R. PORTER, Editor

ULI–the Urban Land Institute,
in association with
the Lincoln Institute of Land Policy

ABOUT ULI–THE URBAN LAND INSTITUTE

ULI–the Urban Land Institute is an independent, nonprofit educational and research organization that, from its incorporation in 1936, has been dedicated to improving the quality of land use planning and development, and to creating an atmosphere within which reasonable approaches to problem solving will prevail. ULI believes that these objectives can be achieved by conducting practical research to establish creditable information, and by using education to communicate this information to public and private professionals in the many disciplines active in land use and development.

James A. Cloar
Executive Vice President
Urban Land Institute

ABOUT THE LINCOLN INSTITUTE OF LAND POLICY

The Lincoln Institute of Land Policy offers intensive courses of instruction in the fields of land economics and property taxation. It provides a learning environment for students, policy makers, and administrators, as well as challenging opportunities for research and publication. The goal of the Institute is to improve theory and practice in those fundamental areas of land policy that have significant impacts on the lives and livelihoods of all people.

Arlo Woolery
Executive Director

ULI PROJECT STAFF

Douglas R. Porter, Director of Development Policy Research, Project Manager
Frank H. Spink, Jr., Director of Publications
Robert L. Helms, Staff Vice President, Operations
Ann Lenney, Manuscript and Production Editor
M. Elizabeth VanBuskirk, Art Director
Tawanda R. Queen, Word Processing Specialist
Kim Rusch, Artist
Helene Youstra, Artist

RECOMMENDED BIBLIOGRAPHIC LISTING

Porter, Douglas R., ed. *Growth Management: Keeping on Target?* Washington, D.C.: ULI–the Urban Land Institute, with the Lincoln Institute of Land Policy, 1986.

ULI Catalog Number G06
Library of Congress Catalog Number 86-50332
International Standard Book Number 0-87420-655-3
Lincoln Institute Monograph # 86-1

TABLE OF CONTENTS

FOREWORD

G rowth management, a term and concept popularized in the 1970s, soon acquired a certain mystique in the land use and development field. In some
circles, growth management programs suggested broadly comprehensive
and meticulously detailed direction by public entities of the pace, location, and
quality of development—the classic "management" scenario. In other circles,
growth management techniques were seen, quite simply, as means to slow growth
or stop it altogether. Whatever the perspective, growth management techniques
transcended the traditional boundaries of planning, zoning, and other forms of land
use regulation, thereby stirring up new issues of equity and balance between public
and private interests.

The great tide of community experimentation with growth management techniques in the 1960s and 1970s was reflected in a surge of litigation in the courts.
Hundreds—perhaps thousands—of cases and court decisions have helped to place
growth management practices squarely in the mainstream of contemporary land
use regulation, so that communities now routinely enact and administer such techniques. Even the early torrent of articles and research papers on the topic has
slowed to a trickle, since the mystique of growth management has been slowly
swept away.

Now, in 1986, it seems timely to reflect on the whole experience, to take stock of
what has happened in those communities that adopted these techniques in the
1970s, and to consider the appropriateness of such techniques for the present and
future.

This publication, it is hoped, gives such an overview: a pragmatic, mid-1980s report on current practices, techniques, and issues of growth management. The collection of papers and articles covers a wide range of experiences in 11 distinctly
differing parts of the United States, and at local, regional, and state government levels. Some of these programs have evolved over many years, while others have just
begun. All show the common interest shared by public entities in managing the effects of growth through the exercise of the police power.

Growth management techniques have long been a concern of the Urban Land Institute. Beginning in 1975, and continuing through 1980, ULI produced a series of

five publications under the general title of *Management & Control of Growth.* These publications furnished a unique source book for practitioners seeking to learn about this rapidly expanding and fast-changing field. The present book builds on that foundation by describing what has transpired since the halcyon days of the early growth management programs.

This publication began with the organization of a professional development seminar, to be cosponsored by ULI and the Lincoln Institute of Land Policy. This seminar, held in Washington, D.C., in October 1985, brought together speakers who reviewed some of the notable growth management programs of the past one and one-half decades, and examined some of the issues surrounding the theory and practice of such programs. Following the seminar, the speakers' presentations were transcribed, edited, and (sometimes) excerpted, to produce a series of papers; to these has been added a selection of germane articles previously published in periodicals and in other sources.

This probing of past and current experiences and issues is meant to give the reader a fresh look at practices in this field, and to provide timely information to those considering revisions or adoptions of growth management techniques. Perhaps, the best way to conclude this Foreword is with an excerpt from the introduction to the first volume of *Management & Control of Growth,* published in 1975. These words remain as cogent today as they were then:

> To the extent that the "ethic of growth" of years past has been replaced by an Ethos of Managed Growth, the mood and effort are to be applauded. But the rationality of such an approach must not obscure the fact that complex systems often have untoward consequences . . . and that, as a result, the repercussions of our failures and our attempts at managing and controlling growth must come under far more careful scrutiny than before.

Douglas R. Porter
Editor

INTRODUCTION

PAUL R. NIEBANCK

I n the fall of 1984, the *Journal of the American Planning Association* published a special symposium issue on growth management. As editor of the issue, the present writer is proud to report that the managing editor of the *Journal* described the symposium as "the best we've had, and the best we've got in the works."

The words of the *Journal's* editor were salve to ears that had been burnt several times, as we sought scholars willing to contribute articles to the symposium. More often than not, they said, "I'm not doing work in that area anymore."; or, "The growth management issue is dead."; or, "Everything that might have been said has already been said."

Our personal experience with growth management in California had suggested a different conclusion. Apparently, growth management, whether as a land use tool, a social issue, or a reflection of the national mood, was at its height. It was worrisome, therefore, to hear these negations.

One year after the publication date of the symposium issue of the *Journal,* leaders in the land use field met to discuss growth management. The ULI/Lincoln Institute seminar on the topic was proof positive that the growth management phenomenon is anything but dead, that the land use leaders are staying on top of the situation, and that there is a great deal of worthwhile subject matter to share.

In trying to reconcile 1984's reactions with those voiced at 1985's seminar, we have decided that the academics were simply reacting to what might now be called "growth management, phase I." They had grown accustomed to it, expected nothing more from it, and had stopped writing about it. Generally, their assessment was that the right of a local jurisdiction to control the size of its population had become firmly entrenched. So, apparently, had the tendency of many localities to use that right for purposes of exclusion and avoidance—clouded in the rhetoric of environmental protection and fiscal necessity as these purposes were. The busywork of growth management had, moreover, aided in the bureaucratization of local government and in the formalization of its planning function. Objective analysts were turned off by the persistence of all these negative side effects of growth management efforts, discouraged by the refusal of growth control advocates to do anything about these side effects, and unwilling to wade through the volumes of extant self-justification to ferret out any more insights.

Meanwhile, professionals with courage and perspective were working to change these negative stereotypes for growth management. In the courts, in the city halls, and in discussions with peers, these leaders were helping to shape growth management so it could promote real societal and environmental advances. Growth management, they began to demonstrate, could give operational meaning to such ideals as social inclusiveness, environmental self-discipline, and ecological stewardship. It could also help knit together a new fabric of local autonomy and accountability. These professionals were setting the stage for growth management, phase II, right in front of the academics' noses.

Alas, we have all known phase I pretty well. At its dead-end worst, it has meant the denial of entry into a community to all but the most affluent population groups; the relegation of local planners to the role of border guards; the conversion of the natural environment into an article of private consumption; and the abandonment of the idea of responsible membership in the larger society. David Dowall sees a large potential for "regional gilded ghettos." The picture is an unsatisfying one to study, much less to identify with professionally.

Growth management, phase II, promises to be something else again. In it, the tools are sharpened. Their uses are more precise and more laudable. In response to persistent criticism and to freshly expressed professional commitments, growth management now stands a chance of rejuvenating the entire land use planning enterprise. The level of participation in the ULI/Lincoln Institute seminar burst with evidence of this vitality.

Part of the promise of phase II comes from a stronger and more defensible goal structure. Part ensues from the invention of more refined instruments. Yet another part emerges from the new professional standards and the willingness to stand by them. And finally, part has to do with a redefinition of all citizens' collective understanding of their responsibilities to the larger society.

At this transitional point, an opportunity offers itself to compare notes on the experimentation with phase II that is now occurring, and to evaluate its content. How far have communities moved toward higher performance levels? Is the new growth management strong enough now to be extended? Can it operate on a larger scale?

The title of the 1985 seminar—"Growth Management: Keeping on Target?"—brings to mind a basis for a visual representation of growth management, phase II. For instance, one might take the word "target" quite literally, and picture the target as looking like a dart board. The board might be divided into a number of sectors, each one standing for a consideration of importance within growth management, phase II. Twelve such considerations seem to exist:

Substantive
1) The operational condition of the environmental systems in any given locality.
2) The satisfaction of that community's members with private and public life there.
3) The levels of social diversity and inclusiveness.
4) The degree of efficiency and restraint with which natural and material resources are used.
5) The physical attractiveness of the locality.
6) The extent of its active regard for its natural and historical features.

Procedural
7) The community's awareness of both its limitations and its capacities for service.
8) The presence of a community consensus on substantive goals.
9) The existence of a nonstereotyped community identity.

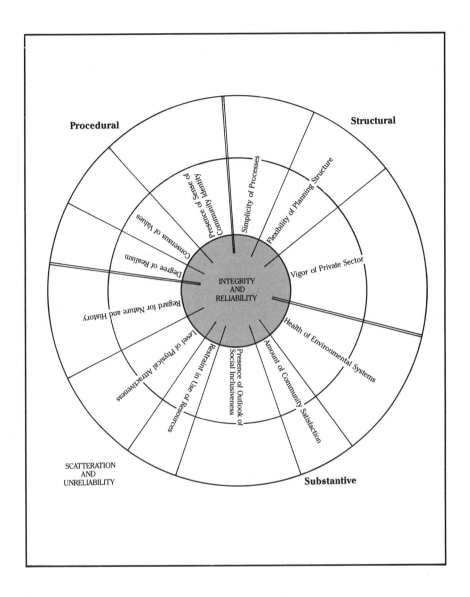

Procedural   **Structural**

Simplicity of Processes

Presence of Sense of Community Identity

Consensus of Values

Flexibility of Planning Structure

Degree of Realism

INTEGRITY AND RELIABILITY

Vigor of Private Sector

Regard for Nature and History

Health of Environmental Systems

Level of Physical Attractiveness

Restraint in Use of Resources

Presence of Outlook of Social Inclusiveness

Amount of Community Satisfaction

SCATTERATION AND UNRELIABILITY

Substantive

Structural
10) The simplicity and accessibility of the decision-making processes.
11) The capacity of the local planning structure for change, invention, and imagination.
12) The health and competitive vigor of the private sector.

Each of these considerations is inextricably linked to a community's performance in the face of the challenge of growth management. Each consideration invites a dart, and the distances at which the darts land from the center indicate the success of that community's growth management enterprise.

If the darts land at the circumference or beyond, a locality's performance might be regarded as primitive, with comprehension, commitment, and active engagement existing only at low levels. If they land at the center, the reverse is true: the locality is, in this case, aware of its situation, willing to do what it realistically can do, and actively doing it. The greater the number of darts landing near the bull's-eye, the more vigorous, respectful, and productive are the interactions among the local sectors.

The dart board, being only a symbol, is, of course, open to suggested additions or substitutions. The relative importance of some of the dart board's sectors—as indicated by the lengths of their arcs—might need adjustment. And some of the wording may be unacceptable or in need of editing. But the idea is a sound one. This is the kind of target that should spring to mind when asking the question, "Are we keeping growth management on target?"

A crucial element, implicit in the diagram, is the matter of maturity. Growth management, as a concept, is a magnificent one. Would that each of us, as individuals, could arrive at a point of maturity at which we could declare, "I am the manager of my own growth." So it is with localities. Land use professionals remain outside the bounds of the real business of growth management until and unless they can think in terms of the facets of communal life that together make for mature representations of their communities. These include, for instance, a certain community's self-knowledge with respect to its own capacities and limitations; its confidence about what it really is and what it can do; its leaders' habit of active engagement in each daily encounter; its ability to define itself as would an accountable member of a larger whole; its assertiveness and responsiveness, which permit it to change; and the degree of its poise—its persona—which reflects the level of its inner maturity.

Some existing U.S. communities stand close to the bull's-eye position. These places enjoyed good representation at the seminar. Here, then, follows the substance of the presentations made by those attendees who know such communities well. We hope that the seminar, and this publication, will help to realize the promise of growth management, phase II. The greater the maturity of a locality, the nearer its approach to a dawning awareness of society as a whole. There is no other way.

Paul R. Niebanck is professor of environmental planning at the University of California at Santa Cruz. This material is drawn from an address Niebanck made at the ULI/Lincoln Institute seminar on growth management.

PART I.

GROWTH LIMIT MECHANISMS

A mong the early manifestations of growth management techniques were attempts by many rapidly growing communities to slow or even to stop growth, usually by rationing building permits. Petaluma, California; Boca Raton, Florida; and Boulder, Colorado, were—and remain—three of the best-known examples of such communities.

Boca Raton led other entries in the field by a good three years, when it voted to cap growth in 1969. Petaluma's program, enacted in 1972, became the most noted—or notorious—example, after a series of well-publicized and still-controversial court cases established the city's right to limit growth to 500 residential units per year. Meanwhile, over several years, Boulder had steadily solidified its interest in controlling growth, despite the defeat in 1971 of its proposed population limits. The city's interim growth policy, adopted in 1972, called for a rate of growth "substantially below that experienced in the 1960s."

In each case, the experience in a given city is described in this book by three papers or articles. Petaluma's planning history since the events of 1972 is summarized by its current planning director, Warren Salmons, who concludes that positive results have been achieved, although the level of development has anyway remained lower than that set by the growth cap. Schwartz, Hansen, and Green, however, present an analysis of housing prices in Petaluma that demonstrates that growth controls have contributed to high housing prices in the city. And the mid-course report, made in 1980 by ECO Northwest, Inc., indicates that growth management remained a source of controversy in Petaluma, even eight years after its instigation.

Boulder's program is described by Paul Danish, author of the legislation that established the threshold for building permits there. His perspective on the overall success of Boulder's efforts is largely supported by James Leach, a local builder, who finds fault, however, with the way in which the program has been administered. Sandra Cooper's article presents yet another view:

she maintains that the program may have aggravated the rise in housing prices without achieving its growth limitation objectives.

The workings of the growth control program in Boca Raton, both before and after the 1975 court decision that nullified the building cap, are described first by Marie York, a planner in the city's community development department, and then by Charles Cobb, a developer. The two commentators reach basically the same conclusion—that Boca Raton's program has raised housing prices, excluded lower-income residents, and deflected development pressures toward other jurisdictions. The 1980 report of ECO Northwest's review also supports this conclusion.

Taken together, these reports on three growth control programs show both the possibilities and the perils of setting arbitrary limits on growth; they also reveal the constant tinkering that even these communities have had to do to adjust their management mechanisms to changing conditions and political perceptions.

Douglas R. Porter

PETALUMA'S EXPERIMENT

WARREN SALMONS

Petaluma's growth management program is in its teenage years. And teenagers can be really hard to deal with. They struggle with subtle yet profound internal changes, and discover that the simplistic responses that carried them through childhood will not meet the complex and ever-changing demands of adult life. Petaluma's growth management system is on the verge of such a change, but its direction is as yet unknown.

CONTROLS FIRST CONSIDERED

The Reasons

Four major influences were at work in Petaluma when the community was forced to consider the institution of a growth management system:

- Location. The city stood in the path of rapid suburban growth pushing outward from San Francisco. The freeway (U.S. 101) provided fairly short commuting times to jobs in San Francisco and Marin County. The city lay in an attractive rural valley, adjacent to large tracts of flat, easily buildable, agricultural land across the freeway.
- Services. The city offered a full complement of public and commercial services. But by the time the growth pressures of the late 1960s and early 1970s were abruptly slowed by a one-year moratorium, the city's sewage treatment plant would only have had one year's additional growth capacity; the water supply was stretched, while awaiting the completion of a two-county water project; and, to the distress of parents, elementary schools in the newer parts of the city were on double sessions.
- Growth. In spite of already overtaxed services, the city's general plan, in place since 1962, clearly anticipated and encouraged continued wide-scale residential growth. From 1968 to 1972, locational and economic circumstances brought an average of 2,000 new residents per year to a community that claimed a population of only 15,000 in 1960.

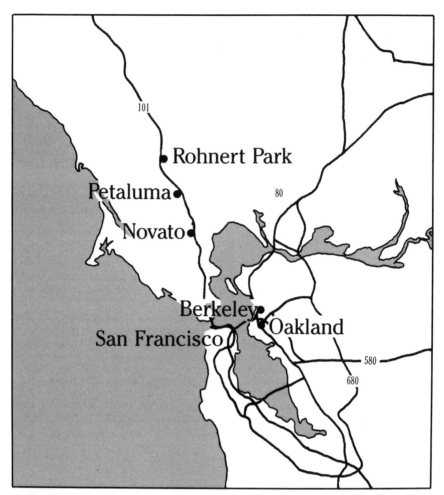

Petaluma is located in the growth corridor along Highway 101 north of San Francisco. City offi-cials are now reexamining and updating their growth control policies.

- Preservation of Quality of Life. Apologies to those who mistrust, as trite, attempts by a community to preserve its "small-town feeling." But the efforts to maintain quality of life and small-town feeling were important determinants in Petaluma's decision to institute a radical new planning tool—growth management—in 1972.

It is worth a moment here to establish the character of the community. John Hart wrote, in an article for *Cry California,* at the time the community was struggling in court to legitimize its growth management system, that Petaluma was for 100 years a rural market town, a place of business for the ranches of southern Sonoma and northwestern Marin Counties. The local wealth was largely in cattle and poultry.
Set in the large, flat drainage basin of the San Francisco Bay, surrounding a slough called the Petaluma River, the town was for decades a busy secondary port.

Petaluma has never been a picture-postcard town. But with its Victorian houses, its tall silver grain elevators, even its long-unused river landings, it has a character that is distinct, valuable, and vulnerable.

The City's Evolution before Controls

Petaluma today shows the evidence of two different eras of development. Generally, for instance, the west side represents the era before growth management. The freeway snakes through the section lying west of the center of town, as does the river. Housing ranges from the simple to the elaborate. And the older parks and tree-lined streets radiate west from the center. Clearly, the west side could be said to have developed organically.

Today, the town as a whole passes for "old" by California standards. It had already become well established, and grown to about 10,000 in population, within its first 100 years. It grew compactly. It spread from just beyond the river to the feet of the nearby western hills—a town tied to the land and to the people who worked the land.

The residents, especially the new residents who came just before growth management started, and who live in the single-family tracts that cropped up in the fields flanking the freeway, understood the type of "aw, shucks" values that the community represented. In addition, they obviously understood the priorities of a tolerable commuting time and of affordable housing. Both old and new residents clearly understood that growth was fast outstripping the city's capacity to provide services, and was moving faster than the value systems of the community—either those of the old or the new contingent—could accept.

CONTROLS INITIATED: EARLIEST EFFORTS

In 1969 and 1970, the community began to wake up to and be alarmed by the magnitude of recent growth. Conferences and discussions went on between builders, community residents, professional staff members, and decision makers. But these meeetings failed to produce an alternative course. In 1971, there was a moratorium, intended to give the community time to plan for action. Then, in 1972, the five-year environmental design plan, which was really a short-term general plan, was adopted. It called for a cap of 500 new housing units per year, which represented the average annual growth during the immediately preceding years.

Later in 1972, the city adopted, by resolution, what has since been named the residential development control system. Among its features were the 500-unit-per-year limit, applicable to any project in excess of four units; and a 17-member evaluation board, whose members were chosen at large from the community by the city council.

The 1972 control system incorporated a once-a-year competitive evaluation of projects, quotas for housing types and geographic distribution, and evaluation criteria. The criteria included consistency with the environmental design plan, availability of services, urban design features, and provision of needed public facilities.

In 1973, the city of Petaluma was sued. The issue was the annual cap on new dwelling units. The Supreme Court settled the matter in 1976, when it refused to review the appellate court decision, and let stand the "Petaluma Plan" and the residential development control system. In the following year, when the city had been operating the original management system for five years, it decided the time had come to reevaluate its efforts.

THE ORDINANCE

In 1977, a second environmental design plan, or short-range general plan, was adopted that ran largely along the lines of the first (1972) plan. The 1977 plan's adoption led to a revised residential development control system, adopted, not by resolution, but as an ordinance. This was an important change: an ordinance is much less flexible and much less easy to administer.

The ordinance called for an annual maximum of 5 percent population growth, which, at the time, in 1978, equalled about 500 new limits per year. Because of increased population growth in the intervening years, the cap is now around 700 units per year. Since 1977, housing production has rarely approached the 5 percent limit.

Other features of the 1977 system included exemptions: for housing for low-income persons, the elderly, and the handicapped; for developments with fewer than 10 units; and for infill projects under five acres. The ordinance also introduced the new concept of reservations for future-year allocations. This feature applied particularly to larger projects of more than 100 units. This move was indicative of a changed development community, in which fewer developers chose to work in Petaluma, but those who did, tended to undertake larger projects.

Mandatory environmental review, which had come into being in California in 1973, now formed part of the process and had to be completed after evaluation by the review board, yet, of course, before the onset of construction. This new environmental review could and did lead to problems. Projects passed board review, only to be found later to have serious environmental problems.

OTHER RECENT MEASURES

Also in about 1978, the city land division and zoning regulations were modified, in order to require that projects evaluated under the management system would have to have their building permit allotments granted by the city council before its tentative (land division) map could be filed. Sites had to be rezoned as planned unit developments (PUDs). And in some cases, this was an unnecessary procedure.

In 1981, additional revisions were made to the evaluation criteria of the residential development control system, to focus more heavily on design features. Also, the composition of the evaluation board was modified, to include only the appointed planning commission and the city's architectural review committee. This gave the appointed commissioners an advantage when they later had to rule officially on the projects. Exemption from review now applies to projects having fewer than 15 units, rather than the earlier 10 units. Projects are rated all year long, instead of only once a year, on a competitive basis, and environmental review has to occur *before* project evaluation.

The process today is: environmental review; technical evaluation under this revised residential development control system; PUD rezoning for all residential projects subject to the management system; planning commission and city council review for all land division projects; and architectural committee review for all projects. This process takes between six and 18 months and still does not award to applicants their building permits.

LOOKING BACK

Disadvantages

What lessons has Petaluma learned? Some of the drawbacks might easily be listed first. The system is simplistic, given the complexity of the greater system by which housing is produced. It has proved cumbersome and much less effective in the current housing market, dominated as this market is by cautious investment rather than by rampant speculation. The process adds time and, therefore, cost to housing production—especially when developers ask to revise a project to meet changing market demands.

The system has tended to reduce the number of developers willing to participate in our market and, thereby, the variety of housing in the market. Nor has the program resulted in geographic balance or balance of housing opportunities.

Advantages

The system has not been all bad. Benefits have included reductions in leapfrog development. A fairly compact growth pattern has resulted—one that is economical to service. And the system has helped moderate growth over the years. The city has had, over the past 10 years, an average rate of about 2.5 percent average annual growth.

The system gives early opportunities for staff and decision makers to review projects. We can review projects earlier and react earlier, before details are locked in. To builders, the system offers the chance to understand the community's development criteria, as they are spelled out in advance.

The program did promote an image that the community is willing to go to great lengths to preserve its character and livability. This is a significant benefit from this kind of system.

Also, the program has allowed the city to promote certain types of housing by offering exemptions from the system. When, for instance, developers were building only single-family houses, multifamily units were exempted, and developers responded by proposing condominium projects. When apartments were needed, apartments were exempted.

One last positive benefit: the program bought the city some time during which its policy planning, municipal management, and decision making functions could become more sophisticated in response to growth pressures.

Litigation

Of considerable interest is the real impact of the system, with respect to the alleged or expected impacts suggested during the protracted litigation of the 1970s.

One allegation was that the community was violating the U.S. Constitution by limiting the "right to travel," with "right to travel" measured in terms of housing demand. If a city provided any fewer units than were actually demanded, it was limiting the public's right to travel. In spite of Petaluma's 500-unit limit, and its later 5 percent limit, its average population growth has actually been about 2 percent, and its housing unit production has remained around 2.5 percent. There has not been the demand for as many units as are now available through the system.

Second, it was charged that the city's management system would upset the regional housing market. This did not happen. Petaluma's 1978 environmental design plan anticipated a population of some 55,000 by 1985. In fact, the current population is about 37,000. Since 1970, Petaluma has grown about 4 percent faster than its closest neighbor to the south, i.e., nearer San Francisco.

LOOKING FORWARD

In 1985, Petaluma is updating its 1962 general plan. The city's second short-range environmental design plan expired in 1985. Civic leaders are rethinking the whole program. The development control system, in its present form, has probably reached the end of its useful life. It will be restructured. The concept will remain, but with a new focus—not on quantity, but on quality.

Warren Salmons is director of community development and planning for the city of Petaluma, California. Salmons's contribution to this book is drawn from an address he made at the ULI/ Lincoln Institute seminar on growth management.

THE EFFECT OF GROWTH CONTROL ON THE PRODUCTION OF MODERATE-PRICED HOUSING

SEYMOUR I. SCHWARTZ, DAVID E. HANSEN, AND RICHARD GREEN

INTRODUCTION

G rowth control programs that restrict the supply of new housing, and hence the rate of population growth in a community, can be expected to increase the prices of new and existing housing in the growth control community. Our study of the growth control community of Petaluma, California (Schwartz, Hansen, and Green, 1981), detected statistically significant price increases for new houses by comparing price changes for standardized houses in Petaluma with price changes in two nearby communities.[1] This statistical analysis did not, however, tell the entire story about the effects of the program on housing production and on housing opportunities, expecially for moderate-income homebuyers.

To many policy makers, the distributive consequences of growth control, especially those affecting lower-income households, are of great concern. The important questions these policy makers want answered are: What is the effect of the growth control program on the availability of lower-priced housing, and how are the housing prospects of moderate-income families affected? To provide the information with which to answer these questions, we examined the characteristics (prices and floor areas) of the houses actually built in Petaluma and in a neighboring comparison city—Santa Rosa—between 1970 and 1976. In this note, we present the results of this analysis and discuss the reasons for the observed differences between cities. First, we describe the characteristics of Petaluma's growth control program and discuss our methods.[2]

---

[1] A hedonic model of house price was used for the comparison of price changes. The standardized houses were statistical composites, using the average of each of six house characteristics. Price changes were compared for several combinations of house and lot size. See Schwartz, Hansen, and Green (1981) for details.

[2] A detailed discussion of the growth control program is contained in Schwartz, Hansen, and Green (1981).

PETALUMA'S GROWTH CONTROL PROGRAM

Petaluma was a small agricultural trading center (14,035 population in 1960) until the mid-1960s, when rapid suburban growth from San Francisco (40 miles to the south) and Marin County spread to Petaluma. This growth, which increased Petaluma's population to 24,870 by 1970, strained the capacity of the sewerage system and caused serious overcrowding in the schools—events that were largely responsible for Petaluma's adoption of a pioneering growth-rate limitation program in 1972.

Petaluma sought to limit its growth rate by establishing a housing quota of 500 new units per year (single-family plus multifamily) from 1973 through 1977 (City of Petaluma, 1972). Developers competed in an allocation process in which a citizens' review board evaluated subdivision proposals according to two major sets of criteria: one to ensure that adequate public services were provided by the developer, and the other to ensure that house and subdivision quality and other goals sought by the city were attained. Housing allocation and building permit data indicate that the growth control program reduced the number of housing units built. In the first three years of the program, only 37 percent of the single-family units proposed by developers received allocations (permissions to build). Also during this period, the number of building permits issued was 67 percent less than the number issued during the three years before growth control.

The comparison city of Santa Rosa is 15 miles north of Petaluma—that is, at the outer limits for most commuters to San Francisco. Santa Rosa is larger than Petaluma (1960 population of 31,027) and has a considerable industrial and commercial base of employment. Santa Rosa did not change its policy of encouraging growth during the period of this analysis, nor did it experience any other changes that would rule it out as a suitable control for this comparison between cities.

DATA AND METHODS

Sales prices and physical characteristics of new houses sold in Petaluma and Santa Rosa between 1970 and 1976 were obtained from the Society of Real Estate Appraisers. Our sample included approximately 75 percent of all sales during this period. The total number of cases was 597 for Petaluma and 784 for Santa Rosa. Sales prices were deflated to 1970 values by means of the Boeckh construction cost index,[3] which closely followed the consumer price index.

We calculated the annual cumulative distribution of sales prices and floor areas for houses sold in the two cities between 1970 and 1976. To determine what percentage of the houses could have been purchased by moderate-income households (or lower-income households), we calculated the maximum price that such households could have afforded to pay. California's Department of Housing and Community Development defines the moderate income range as between 80 percent and 120 percent of the county's median income for a household of four people. To calculate the maximum price that a household in this income range could have paid, we assumed that the household spent 30 percent of its gross income for housing and that the buyer made a 20 percent downpayment and took a 30-year, constant-payment loan at the interest rate that prevailed in that year (in the range of 9.00 percent to 9.75 percent for FHA loans). Under these assumptions, the maximum price that a moderate income household could have paid is approximately $25,000 in 1970 dollars. Taking this as the cut-off (criterion) price, we compared the results in

---

[3]The Boeckh index is published in U.S. Department of Commerce, Bureau of Industrial Economics, *Construction Review.*

Petaluma with those in Santa Rosa. Comparing Petaluma with another city was necessary to eliminate outside events (other than Petaluma's program) as possible explanations for the result.[4] If the pattern of changes in Petaluma differed from that in Santa Rosa, and in the direction predicted by theory, we could conclude that the changes were due to growth control. The degree of confidence in such a conclusion would always depend, of course, on the appropriateness of the comparison city.

It is important to note that new houses built under the growth control program in Petaluma did not appear on the market until 1974, so we considered the period 1970 through 1973 as pre–growth control, and the period 1974 through 1976 as post–growth control.

RESULTS

In Petaluma, the percentage of houses that sold for less than $25,000 ($1970) was between 48.3 percent and 56.7 percent before growth control; after growth control, it dropped to 15.2 percent in 1974, 2.3 percent in 1975, and 3.3 percent in 1976. In 1976, 68.2 percent of Petaluma houses sold for more than $30,000, whereas before growth control, no more than 21.7 percent sold for more than $30,000 ($1970): in

---

[4]Since a true experiment using random assignment was impossible in this situation we used a quasi experiment, wherein the comparison city of Santa Rosa served as a control. See Cook and Campbell (1979) for a detailed discussion of quasi-experimental methods.

FIGURE 1
DISTRIBUTION OF SALES PRICES OF NEW HOUSES: CUMULATIVE PERCENTAGE OF HOUSES SOLD AT OR BELOW THE STATED PRICE[1]

Cumulative Percentage[2]

Sales Price Less than	1970	1971	1972	1973	1974	1975	1976
			Petaluma				
$20,000	9.1	12.5	13.3	6.7	4.4	0.0	0.0
25,000	52.1	54.2	48.3	56.7	15.2	2.3	3.3
30,000	97.8	92.5	78.3	96.2	58.7	51.2	31.8
35,000	99.9	100.0	98.3	98.1	93.5	88.4	74.7
			Santa Rosa				
$20,000	26.2	21.5	7.1	5.1	10.4	5.8	10.7
25,000	43.1	38.7	32.9	36.5	39.9	37.4	37.5
30,000	66.2	68.8	78.6	69.4	66.4	67.8	59.8
35,000	78.5	95.7	94.3	88.3	85.3	87.9	74.1

[1]Prices are in constant 1970 dollars.

[2]We do not show the remaining price category, which results in an entry of 100 percent in the last row, because our interest is in the lower-priced houses. The reader can easily calculate the remaining percentage of houses that sold for more than $35,000 (the difference between the last entry and 100 percent).

three of the four years before growth control, fewer than 8 percent of Petaluma houses sold for more than $30,000 ($1970).

The contrast to Santa Rosa is striking. There, between 32.9 percent and 43.1 percent of the houses sold for less than $25,000 over the entire period (1970 through 1976). From 1974 through 1976 (the postcontrol period), between 37.4 percent and 39.9 percent of Santa Rosa houses sold for less than $25,000. Thus, the percentage of "affordable" housing dropped from about 50 percent to less than 5 percent in Petaluma, but it remained high—nearly 40 percent—in Santa Rosa. These data provide strong evidence of the shift in Petaluma's housing away from the low end of the market after growth control.

The data for floor areas document the disappearance of the small house in Petaluma after growth control. This is not surprising since hedonic price studies have repeatedly shown that floor area is the most important determinant of variation in house price. If we consider 1,400 square feet to be a small house, we see that the percentage of small houses built in Petaluma dropped from about 39 percent in 1970 and 1971, to 11.0 percent in 1976. The percentage of very small houses (fewer than 1,200 square feet) dropped from about 20 percent in 1970 through 1972, to 1.1 percent in 1976.

Again, the results from Santa Rosa were in sharp contrast. The percentage of Santa Rosa houses smaller than 1,400 square feet averaged 32.1 percent before growth control and 32.8 percent after growth control. The percentage of very small houses was greater in 1975 and in 1976 than in any one previous year except 1970.

FIGURE 2
DISTRIBUTION OF FLOOR AREAS OF NEW HOUSES: CUMULATIVE PERCENTAGE OF HOUSES WITH FLOOR AREAS AT OR BELOW THE STATED SIZE
(Square Feet)

Cumulative Percentage[1]

Floor Area Less than	1970	1971	1972	1973	1974	1975	1976
			Petaluma				
1,200	20.4	22.5	20.0	10.6	6.5	2.3	1.1
1,400	38.7	39.2	28.3	27.9	23.9	18.6	11.0
1,600	58.4	56.7	43.3	43.3	28.3	25.6	23.1
1,900	81.0	77.5	71.7	68.3	73.9	55.8	39.6
			Santa Rosa				
1,200	4.6	6.5	10.0	11.0	14.0	17.2	16.1
1,400	36.9	34.4	25.7	31.4	34.3	35.6	28.6
1,600	52.3	57.0	51.4	54.0	62.9	57.5	55.4
1,900	70.7	84.9	82.9	86.9	86.7	81.0	81.3

[1]We do not show the remaining price category, which results in an entry of 100 percent in the last row, because our interest is in the lower-priced houses. The reader can easily calculate the remaining percentage of houses that sold for more than $35,000 (the difference between the last entry and 100 percent).

It is clear that small, lower-priced new houses nearly vanished from Petaluma after it imposed growth control, but that did not happen in the comparison city of Santa Rosa during this same period. There are two major reasons why the disappearance of low-priced houses in Petaluma could be attributed to its growth control program. First, the criteria for evaluating development proposals and awarding housing permissions (allocations) were heavily weighted toward quality and amenity items. More than 50 percent of the maximum number of points awarded in the rating of subdivision proposals were for such items as architectural design quality, site design quality, character of landscaping and screening, provision of foot or bicycle paths *and equestrian trails,* and provision of usable open space (City of Petaluma, 1972, General Plan, Housing Element). Second, the city council made it clear to builders in the first year's allocation process that it wanted subdivisions of high quality. Proposed subdivisions of modest quality were rapidly eliminated from consideration (Tarr, 1978). We concluded, therefore, that Petaluma's growth control program effectively eliminated the production of lower-priced housing in that city.

POLICY IMPLICATIONS

Many local government decision makers perceive important benefits to their communities from growth control, including enhanced environmental quality and amenities, maintenance of "small town character," and better public services and fiscal status[5] (Rosenbaum, 1978; Johnston, 1980). However, local decision makers may not be aware of, or concerned about, the costs of growth control because most of the costs fall upon individuals who live outside the growth control community or on renters in the community. Since the losers are usually in lower-income groups than the beneficiaries of growth control, such programs have potentially serious equity consequences (Schwartz, 1982). To the extent that the losers lack political power to influence decisions within the growth control jurisdictions, the stage is set for confrontation between state and local policy makers over the acceptability of growth control programs. Recent actions by some local governments, as well as by state legislatures and state courts, are evidence of growing concern for the equity consequences.

In California and New Jersey, the state supreme courts have held that it is not enough for a growth control program to provide benefits only to residents of the enacting community.[6] If challenged in court, a community must show that its program does not create negative *regional* impacts on the supply of lower-priced housing; if it cannot do so, the program will be considered exclusionary. In California, the legislature mandated that local governments act affirmatively to meet their fair shares of regional housing needs for all income groups (Chapter 1143, California Statutes of 1980). The legislature further placed the burden of proof on local governments that enact growth control ordinances to show, in any court challenge, that the ordi-

---

[5]Less socially acceptable reasons for restricting growth may exist, but are not usually expressed. For example, Ellickson (1979) asserts that suburban growth controls are designed to enrich existing homeowners, who, in effect, form a housing cartel to restrict the supply of new single-family houses. The large literature on exclusionary land use practices points to the protection of property values as the primary motive for such practices (Delafons, 1969; Babcock and Bosselman, 1973).

[6]In California, the relevant case is *Associated Homebuilders of Greater East Bay* v. *City of Livermore,* 18, Cal 3d 582, 557P. 2d at 483, 135 Cal Reporter 41 (1976); in New Jersey, the relevant case is *Southern Burlington NAACP* v. *Township of Mount Laurel,* 161, N.J. Super. ct. Law Div. 317, 391, A.2d 935 (1978).

nance "is necessary for the protection of the public health, safety, or welfare of the population" (Chapter 1144, California Statutes of 1980).[7]

Although California and New Jersey are at the forefront of efforts to eliminate exclusionary land development practices and provide affordable housing, other states seem likely to follow suit. Consequently, stringent growth control programs may not be able to withstand legal challenges unless the enacting communities also make special efforts to provide affordable housing to lower-income households. Petaluma's program withstood a legal challenge shortly after it was adopted, based largely on the city's goal of providing between 8 percent and 12 percent of new housing in a price range affordable to low- and moderate-income households. Our analysis shows, however, that Petaluma failed to achieve this goal. Instead, its growth control program nearly eliminated new, lower-priced single-family housing. Petaluma's only incentive for encouraging affordable housing was awards, in its evaluation of proposed developments, of up to 15 points out of a total of 130 points for the provision of affordable housing. This incentive was insufficient because most of the remaining points were awarded for house and subdivision quality and amenities. A stronger commitment must be made by the local government if affordable housing is to be built. Other jurisdictions—for example, Davis, California—have combined a stringent growth control program with stronger incentives for providing affordable housing (Schwartz and Johnston, 1983). However, the ability of even these stronger incentives to overcome the adverse impacts of growth control programs on affordable housing is very much in doubt.

REFERENCES

Babcock, Richard F., and Bosselman, Fred P. *Exclusionary Zoning: Land Use Regulation and Housing in the 1970s.* New York: Praeger Publishers, 1973.

Delafons, John. *Land-Use Controls in the United States.* Second Edition. Cambridge, Mass.: The MIT Press, 1969.

City of Petaluma, California. General Plan, Petaluma Housing Element (July 10, 1972).

Cook, Thomas T., and Campbell, Donald T. *Quasi-Experimentation: Design and Analysis Issues for Field Settings.* Chicago, Ill.: Rand McNally College Publishing Co., 1979.

Ellickson, Robert. "Suburban Growth Controls: An Economic and Legal Analysis." *The Yale Law Journal,* 86, January 1977, pp. 385–511.

Johnston, Robert A. "The Politics of Local Growth Control." *Policy Studies Journal 9* (Special #1), 1980, pp. 427–439.

Rosenbaum, Nelson. "Growth and Its Discontents: Origins of Local Population Controls." *The Policy Cycle,* eds. Judith May and Aaron Wildavsky. Beverly Hills, Calif.: Sage, 1978.

Schwartz, Seymour I., and Johnston, Robert A. "Inclusionary Housing Programs." *Journal of the American Planning Association* 49, January 1983, pp. 3–21.

————— . "Equity Implications of Local Growth Management."*Environmental Policy Implementation,* ed. Dean E. Mann. Lexington, Mass.: Lexington Books, 1982.

—————; Hansen, David E.; and Green, Richard. "Suburban Growth Controls and the Price of New Housing." *Journal of Environmental Economics and Management* 8, December 1981, pp. 303–320.

Tarr, Fred. Interview with Maureen Newby. Petaluma, Calif.: City of Petaluma, November 1978.

---

[7]Chapter 1143 in the Statutes of 1980 is at *California Government Code,* sections 65580 ff.; Chapter 1144 in the Statutes of 1980 is at *California Evidence Code,* section 669.5.

Seymour Schwartz is a professor in the division of environmental studies, University of California, Davis, and David Hansen and Richard Green are professors in the department of agricultural economics of that university.

This article is excerpted from *Land Economics* for February 1984. Reprinting is by permission.

GROWTH MANAGEMENT STUDY OF PETALUMA, CALIFORNIA

ECO NORTHWEST, INC.

I n August 1972, a residential development control system was adopted as the implementation arm of the "Petaluma Plan." Now, as then, the system establishes numerous single- and multifamily quotas, and provides for the spatial distribution of these units in various sectors of the city. Developers compete for allotments. To be considered, their proposals must conform to the general plan, the environmental design plan, and the housing element. Each proposal is then rated by the residential development evaluation board (a citizens' committee) using the following criteria:[1]

1) Utilities and public services (as evaluated by agencies)
   a) The ability and capacity of the water system to provide for the needs of the proposed development without system extensions beyond those the developer will consent to provide. (Based upon comments from Petaluma's city engineer)
   b) The ability and capacity of the sanitary sewers to dispose of the wastes of the proposed development without system extensions beyond those the developer will consent to provide. (Based upon comments from Petaluma's city engineer)
   c) The ability and capacity of the drainage facilities to dispose adequately of the surface runoff of the proposed development without system extensions beyond those the developer will consent to provide. (Based upon comments from the Sonoma County Water Agency)
   d) The ability of the fire department of the city of Petaluma to provide fire protection according to the acceptable response standards of the city without the necessity of establishing a new station, or of requiring the addition of

---

[1] These are the criteria as revised by ordinance in September 1978. Previously, the board had evaluated the several criteria for public facilities. These are now considered by the planning staff and by appropriate agencies, as part of the process ensuring the proposal's conformance with the environmental design plan.

major equipment to an existing station. (Based upon comments from the Petaluma Fire Department)

e) The capacity of the appropriate school or schools to absorb the children expected to inhabit a proposed development—without necessitating or aggravating double-session scheduling, other unusual scheduling methods, or classroom overcrowding. (Based upon comments from the appropriate school district)

f) The ability and capacity of major street linkages to provide for the needs of the proposed development—without substantially altering existing traffic patterns, overloading the existing street system, or hurting the ability of other public facilities (parks, playgrounds, etc.) to meet the additional demands for vital public services without the city's extension of those services beyond those provided by the developer. (Based upon comments from the appropriate department heads)

2) Quality of design, and contribution to public welfare (as evaluated by the board)

a) Architectural-design quality, as indicated by the architectural elevations of the proposed buildings, and as judged in terms of architectural style, size, height, and innovation (10 points).

b) Innovative site-design quality, as indicated by lot layout, orientation of units on the lots, blending of construction to the natural landscape, and similar site-design considerations (20 points).

c) Site- and architectural-design quality, as indicated by the amount and character of the landscaping, screening, and colors of the buildings (10 points).

d) Site- and architectural-design quality, as indicated by the arrangement of the site for efficiency of circulation, on- and off-site traffic safety and privacy (20 points).

e) Site- and architectural-design quality, as indicated by the amount of private safety and security provided in the design of the development and of its individual structures (five points).

f) The provision of usable public and/or private open space and, where applicable, of the greenbelts provided for in the environmental design plan (15 points).

g) Provision of foot or bicycle paths, equestrian trails, or pathways, in accordance with adopted plans of the city (five points).

h) The extent to which the proposed development accomplishes an orderly and contiguous extension of existing development, rather than "leapfrog" development—by being either within the present city limits or contiguous to urban development within the city limits (15 points).

i) The provision of needed public facilities such as critical linkages in the major street system, schoolrooms, or other vital public facilities (15 points).

j) The provision of on- or off-site units that meet the city's policy goal of an 8 to 12 percent proportion of low- and moderate-income dwelling units annually. (Developments proposing to provide these units shall file a detailed statement indicating the location and means of provision. For the purposes of this ordinance, the terms "low-" and "moderate-income" shall refer to those income ranges and correlative price ranges established by the U.S. Department of Housing and Urban Development on an annual basis.) (15 points)

THE PROCESS

The evaluations of each board member are combined and averaged. All developments receiving a minimum score of 70 are ranked.

After evaluation, the ratings are published, and an appeal hearing is provided for applicants who disagree with the ratings given their proposals. Final ratings are sent to the city council, which allots permits on the bases of the quota for each sector of the city, and of the ratings earned by the proposals within each sector. If a developer fails to begin construction within six months, then his allotted number of units may be withdrawn and either given to the next highest-rated applicant or added to the quota for the ensuing year.

Exempt from the allocation system are develpments of 10 or fewer units, on five or fewer acres, in existing urban areas, or approved by the city because they provide housing for the elderly, the handicapped, or low-income households. The city council is currently considering allowing all developers who receive initial plot approval and prezoning to construct at least 25 units, even if they did not receive an allocation from the board. Total units allocated in any year would still be less than 5 percent of existing units.

REACTIONS TO THE PROGRAM

According to the planning department, the citizens are generally pleased with the system and its results. (In 1973, 82 percent of the voters responded affirmatively to a ballot question asking whether they approved of the way the city council was attempting to control growth rationally.) Planner Fred Tarr indicates that the majority of residents do not know that the city has a growth management strategy, but that those who do know, tend to support it. This is probably because of a "last one in, close the door" philosophy. Though the construction industry did and still does grumble, Lawrence Burrows's study has stated that developers should be pleased because the Petaluma system differs from the traditional city decision-making process: it lists explicitly the criteria by which a proposal will be accepted or rejected, rather than allowing a city council to make a decision without ever specifying the standards used in making its determination.[2] Burrows's study did, however, note two important defects. First, too much weight is given to the less precise, aesthetic variables and not enough to public facility variables. Second, simply singling out the western sector of the city for development does not assure that construction will occur. In 1973, two-thirds of the units proposed for the east side were not even approved; but on the west side, even though every proposal submitted was approved, only 72 percent of the west-side quota was actually allocated. Since that time, the number of permits issued has never reached the maximum permissible. The city council is considering changing the locational requirement.

John Joslyn of Quantas Development has no good words for the Petaluma Plan. Time delays are extreme: three or four years may pass before groundbreaking may take place. Subdivision requirements are excessive: in the last 15 months, Petaluma has added $3,000 per unit of fees. Echoing Burrows, Joslyn feels that the acclaimed evaluation criteria are useless: they are so vague that they change every time the members of the evaluation board change. He believes that the growth management policies have increased the price of housing, but not that of raw land. He explains this paradox by noting that residential development is such a difficult and uncertain proposition in Petaluma that developers' demands for land have dropped off.

[2]Lawrence B. Burrows, *Growth Management* (New Brunswick, N.J.: Center for Urban Policy Research, Rutgers University, 1978), p. 87.

ECO Northwest, Inc., prepared this report in 1980 for the planning department of the city of Eugene, Oregon. The article appearing here is excerpted from that report.

BOULDER'S SELF-EXAMINATION

PAUL D. DANISH

T he "Danish Plan" got its name through the nature of my present trade—journalism. For me, this includes, among other functions, that of headline writing. Have you ever tried to fit "Petaluma" into a headline? It isn't easy. And that is really what happened.

In fact, the plan was originally known as the "slow-growth ordinance," a handle that necessarily distinguished it from the several basic laws, charters, amendments, and ordinances that the city adopted over a 20-year period, and that collectively formed what might be termed the community's environmental constitution. That is the first and perhaps most important point to keep in mind—the ordinance didn't stand alone. Thus, taking a look at some of those other city measures seems worthwhile, in order to get a better view of how growth control and environmental protection have worked in Boulder.

EARLIER PRESCRIPTIONS

First, then, Boulder does have a highly detailed comprehensive plan, adopted in 1970, extensively revised in 1977, and updated subsequently. The plan indicates where growth may occur, where it may not occur, and, in very rough terms, when it may occur. One of the plan's most important aspects is its identity as a contractual relationship between the city of Boulder and the county of Boulder. So, enforcement of the plan probably carries much more weight than does the enforcement of such plans in many other communities.

The city has an 18-year-old program that acquires municipal open space. Adopted in 1967, the program is funded by a 0.4 percent, earmarked sales tax that has so far been used to secure some 12,000 acres of greenbelt around the city of Boulder. In fact, the city has been acquiring land for several open space purposes almost from the turn of the century (using nonearmarked funds before 1967), and it now has close to 14,000 acres in greenbelt. And several thousand more acres are scheduled for acquisition. The open space program has done much to prevent urban sprawl and leapfrog development, while maintaining the city's mountain backdrop. Boulder lies hard by the Rocky Mountains. For many years, I lived four blocks from the Rockies. And maintaining the foothills as open land has proved a high priority for the community. (The alternative to taking this action may be seen in Berkeley, California, where the Berkeley Hills have been built out, to their very tops.) In

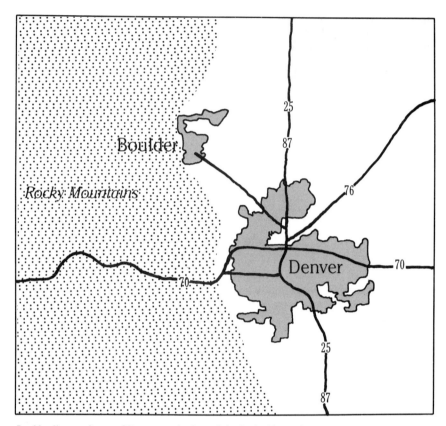

Boulder lies northwest of Denver, at the foot of the Rocky Mountain range.

Boulder, at present, some 3,000 to 4,000 acres of additional land are scheduled for acquisition by the locality. The greenbelt program is probably the single most popular local program. And in every political poll conducted within the last 10 years, this measure has gained 80 percent or more of the support of those polled.

In 1971, Boulder adopted a 55-foot height limitation, which was written into the city charter. Today, this ceiling lacks the popularity it had in 1971, although not for the reason one might expect. The citizens would like to see a lower height limitation. Probably, a cap of 35 feet would garner wider support. This phenomenon partly results from the recent completion of several 55-foot buildings that are seen as excessively massive. Indeed, these structures have quite literally become lightning rods.

The city has made a strong commitment over the past 10 years to keeping its existing commercial areas healthy. In the early 1970s, this commitment manifested itself in the building of a downtown mall with a $2 million investment that came out of the CE funds in the assessment district. The city closed four blocks of its main street and soon had a highly successful mall in its historic business district.

In the late 1970s, the same commitment showed itself in a $20 million investment, made through an urban renewal authority, using tax increment financing, to upgrade an existing shopping center inside the city to regional shopping-mall standards. This project came about only after two lacerating public votes on the subject, and only after several regional shopping centers were rejected that had been planned for the city's fringes. (Ironically, in recently looking over the Forbes "400" list, which names the 400 richest individuals in the United States, I found at least two people listed whom Boulder had kicked out of town for their proposals of shopping center projects in the 1970s. Money talks, but Boulder doesn't always listen.)

Quite possibly, this drive to keep existing commercial areas healthy began with a 1967 charter amendment that repealed the 60 years of prohibition in Boulder (and that took all of 11 tries to pass). The city went dry in 1907, and it only went wet again in 1967: this latter decision, of course, had proved a crucial land use decision because downtown revitalization would simply have been impossible in a dry Boulder. Naturally, a great deal of commercial development was occurring immediately over the city line because of that prohibition. Here again, we see the sorts of social issues that can get tied up in land use issues.

Needless to say, beyond its comprehensive land use plan and related commitments, Boulder does have strong land use and development regulations. These cover an astonishing array of topics. Among the regulations that have succeeded most notably have been those that have encouraged developers in the region, which is semiarid, to leave untouched open space in their projects, in the form of native grasses—with critical water conservation implications for residents. Boulder uses some 40 percent less water per capita than Denver does. And this conservation record has arisen out of the city's land use policies, and out of the fact that it metered water use a long time ago. The city has also, of course, adopted controls like solar access ordinances, minimum insulation standards, and so on.

GROWTH LIMITS IN BOULDER

A Primer

Finally, there is the growth control question itself. To draw a brief sketch of its background: the first attempt to pass a growth control ordinance in Boulder came about in 1971, when the Boulder chapter of Zero Population Growth (ZPG) put a proposed dwelling-unit cap of 40,000 to a vote by the initiative process. This move sufficiently frightened the prevailing local establishment that the latter persuaded the city council to put an alternative advisory question on the ballot, urging the city government to keep the growth rate "substantially below the rates experienced during the 1960s." (During the 1960s, the growth rates had averaged about 5 percent per year, rising occasionally as high as 10 percent.) In 1971, a battle arose over this issue. But when the dust had settled, ZPG's measure had been soundly defeated, and the advisory measure had been passed overwhelmingly.

Simultaneously, the city elected the first clearly liberal city council in its history. And this council became, of course, the one charged with carrying out the mandates of the advisory referendum directing city government to keep growth rates well below those of the 1960s. It did what any group of red-blooded 1970s liberals might have been expected to do—it appointed a "blue ribbon" citizens' study commission and gave it a pile of money (in this case, about $200,000) and two years in which to prepare the definitive plan on how to control growth in Boulder. Then, the study commission, called the Boulder Area Growth Study, or BAGS for short, did what any red-blooded "blue ribbon" study panel might have been expected to do— it produced 10 volumes of data; four possible scenarios; 56 recommendations, most of which were eminently sensible; and the final recommendation that the city staff draft the definitive growth management system for Boulder. And by now, it was 1973: while the growth commission had been doing its thing, the local builders had been doing theirs. Indeed, in the two years of the growth study, over 3,000 new units had been put on the ground. And the city's population had already reached 66,000 by 1970.

During the following two years, much the same pattern prevailed. The city staff dutifully labored to produce a growth management ordinance, while the city's builders dutifully labored to produce growth. The finished system duly landed in the city council's lap in early 1976, more than four years after the voters had passed the original mandate, and just in time to be considered by a newly elected, pro-growth, conservative majority of councillors.

The system that had been produced gave no numbers but relied on an extensive review process, during which projects were to be measured against a series of performance criteria whose nonspecificity was in a class by itself. The criteria, I think, could fairly be characterized as owing more to Franz Kafka than to Ebenezer Howard. The new system was promptly denounced as an administrative nightmare by both builders and environmentalists—as, in fact, it was. That program arrived as a dead letter, deservedly.

The Climate Preceding the Danish Plan's Proposal

By now, the date was early 1976. I had been elected to the city council in the previous election, even though a conservative council had come in. And I saw no reason for continued beating about the bush on the growth issue. Very clearly, growth management had earned wide support in the city. The U.S. Supreme Court had just refused to take certiorari in the Petaluma case, which had been won by that city in the appeals court. Moreover, the Colorado Supreme Court had just sharply limited Boulder's ability to use the provision of water and sewer services beyond its borders as a lever for development management and for implementation of its comprehensive plan. And the conservative majority on the city council had just fired the city manager, who had been hired by the liberals to carry out the mandate of growth management.

The result was that I drafted an ordinance patterned after Petaluma's. The Boulder version called for a 1.5 to 2 percent growth rate over the subsequent five years. The numbers were arrived at because, during the previous five years—the early 1970s—the growth rate had averaged higher than 3 percent per year, and the people did want a substantial reduction from that rate. And the people's wishes struck me as reasonable ones.

The new growth rate was to be achieved by allocations of building permits. The ordinance called for the permits to be awarded on the basis of merit: projects would be given points for meeting certain criteria, such as availability of urban services, price, energy efficiency, and so on; and permits would go to those projects with the highest scores. This ordinance went to the city council for consideration in April of 1976, although, really, no possibility existed that it would ever be enacted in any way other than by citizen initiative.

THE DANISH PLAN

To make a long story short, the draft ordinance was in fact placed by petition on the ballot for the 1976 general election. And following a brisk, exhilarating punch-up of a campaign, it passed in November 1976. This particular ordinance provided for a 120-day grace period to precede its taking effect. During that time, some 900 permits were taken out. These permits were for projects already in the mill. Well, this outcome certainly made for a surge of unwelcome additional growth. But, arguably, it did have at least one good effect. It emptied the pipeline of projects that were already underway, providing a fairly clean start for the new system. A reasonable fairness did result from allowing those who had made large investments on going projects to proceed past the starting point without the guillotine crashing down.

Generally, the system called for allocating an average of 450 permits per year for five years. If fewer permits were given in one year, more permits could be given in the next, or vice versa. Also called for were certain exceptions, such as allowing a single house to be built on a single lot without going through the system, if the lot had been platted when the ordinance was passed. In addition, it allowed a single fourplex to be built on a single lot that had existed when the ordinance was passed.

Briefly, the 450-unit figure would have given a 1.5 percent, noncompounded growth rate. The various exceptions were expected to push the rate up to 2 percent. In the event, during the five-year life of the ordinance, growth from all sources came in at almost precisely 2 percent—excluding, of course, the 900-permit surge at the outset.

RESULTS OF THE PLAN

Housing Prices

That initial growth ordinance had four consequences worth mentioning. First, it had no lasting effect on the average price of a housing unit. Historically, Boulder housing prices have run 10 to 15 percent above those in Denver. But in the six months immediately following the enactment of the ordinance, that gap grew to about 25 to 30 percent. The gap, however, closed again almost immediately; the differential dropped back down to its normal 10 to 15 percent; and the two sets of housing prices went up almost in lockstep during the rest of the life of the ordinance.

The ordinance was in effect from 1977 through 1982. And this was a period of fairly high housing inflation in the Denver/Boulder market. Although it was widely perceived that the ordinance did contribute to higher housing prices, the data—looked at closely at the end of the period of the ordinance—showed that the evidence for this perception simply was not there.

Downtown Development

As a second consequence, the fact that the ordinance exempted small projects on existing lots—together with the fact that 175 of the 450 permits given out annually were set aside for central Boulder—gave great impetus to downtown revitalization, which had been proving a problem ever since the 1960s. Today, the widespread feeling is that this revitalization process has gone too far. The present growth ordinance no longer gives the downtown a favored position.

Demographics

A third possible consequence—the effect, if any, of the ordinance on Boulder's demographics—is unclear. The graph of Boulder's income distribution is not a bell-shaped curve. Rather, it looks like a two-humped camel, which is to say that it shows a disproportionate number of people above the average income and a disproportionate number of people below the average income. And this trend did become more pronounced during the time when the ordinance was in effect. Boulder's demographics, however, have always been marked by these disproportions.

Historically, the city has had both a disproportionate number of professionals and a disproportionate number of the "unwealthy-by-choice" (among whom the present writer would certainly count himself). And this is a far-from-trivial factor in the local demographics. Many people live in the community who could be earning more money elsewhere. They have chosen to stay in Boulder and take substantial pay cuts because they like the life there. And they become quite upset when anything degrades the quality of life that brought them there in the first place. This stance largely reflects the fact that Boulder is a university town, with an economy largely dependent on knowledge-based industries.

Critics argued that the ordinance drove the traditional family out of town, but the impact on the local nuclear family is also inconclusive. During the six years before the adoption of the growth ordinance, 80 percent of the units built in Boulder were multifamily units. Now, that suggests that the nuclear family was undergoing a critical "core meltdown" in Boulder well before the building-permit allocation process began.

Neighboring Localities

A fourth and final observation worth making is that the Boulder growth ordinance seems to have had very little effect on the growth rate in surrounding towns. An observer would have intuitively expected some effect. But almost no evidence exists that a departure occurred from the historic growth rates in the surrounding communities during the life of the ordinance. Then again, those communities pursued policies during most of that period that favored the high growth rates that are far more typical of the Denver metropolitan area in general, than they are of Boulder.

There are about seven towns in Boulder County. All of them had comprehensive plans that called for fairly high growth rates. And in fact, all of them were growing fairly rapidly during the period when Boulder had the growth ordinance in place. Probably, the fact that Boulder was controlling its own growth had very little to do with these towns' high growth rates. First of all, their growth was desired. And second, the entire metropolitan area was growing at a fast pace during the late 1970s anyway, partly as a result of the oil boom and partly of the electronics boom. (Incidentally, the county has by now had an oil bust *and* an electronics bust. And those communities that did grow at a fairly fast clip are taking far nastier hammerings than Boulder is.)

IN CONCLUSION

The Boulder growth ordinance was enacted in 1977. Because of its sunset clause, it went out of existence in 1982. On balance, the ordinance may be deemed a success. It has been replaced by another ordinance that has suffered some problems. But the difficulties that have ensued in Boulder would make material for a quite separate and substantially more intricate discussion than the present one. And a discussion that would call, needless to say, for a much-too-long headline.

Paul D. Danish is a columnist and copyeditor on the Boulder, Colorado, *Daily Camera*. Formerly, he was a science writer and a speechwriter for members of Congress and for at least one university president.

Danish's contribution to this book is drawn from an address he made at the ULI/Lincoln Institute seminar on growth management.

A HOMEBUILDER LOOKS AT BOULDER'S CONTROLS:
Stonewalling Growth?

JAMES LEACH

The pressure to "do something" about growth in Boulder came about because of the type of development that Boulder experienced in the 1950s and early 1960s—basically, a matter of wholesale construction of large tracts of housing. Boulder citizens feared that large-scale developers were going to take advantage of the nifty environment and make a bedroom community out of Boulder, which is 20 or 25 miles outside of Denver. This would have made the town grow much faster than the local community wanted it to. Capacity of services, however, was not a problem in Boulder, as it was in Petaluma. At least in Boulder, water, sewer, and other services were generally adequate.

As it happened, the process of adopting a growth management program proved a rather long-winded one. The city tried dealing with the earlier pressures of growth control through the planning department, largely through negotiating with developers. Our firm, for example, took what was for Boulder a major development—a 324-unit development—through that process, and part of our agreement was a buildout rate not to exceed 75 units per year. In fact, this approach probably worked about as well to control growth as anything done in Boulder since that time.

The Danish Plan, of course, formalized growth control in Boulder through a city ordinance. It allocated building permits according to a complex merit system.

The Danish Plan ordinance was not appreciated by the homebuilding community, although I personally supported two components of it. One was the grandfather clause, which let builders start a great many units before the controls really took effect. Besides giving builders something of an open door, that clause took a lot of pressure off the resistance to the adoption of the ordinance. It also avoided some hardships that would have resulted from rapid implementation.

The other feature I liked about the Danish Plan was the sunset provision: the ordinance expired in five years. Unfortunately, the expiration had the effect of polarizing the community and developing a great deal of strength among the town's environmentalists. The city government created a committee that, for a long time before its expiration date, studied a possible extension of the ordinance. The committee came up with a new version that everyone found desirable. From a builder's perspective, the new provisions were better because the merit system, with its confusion and bureaucracy, was no longer triggered until a threshold number of permits had been applied for in a given year.

Indeed, one effect of the new ordinance was to keep growth pressures down. In Boulder, as in Petaluma and some other communities, this type of control needed only to be talked about—it didn't even have to be implemented—to drive away the larger developers. These developers were not interested in dealing with communities with this sort of attitude. Consequently, Boulder's growth rate for the next few years was not much greater than 2 percent.

In any case, for some period of time, the second ordinance had little effect, and high interest rates kept down housing development. Then, all of a sudden, in 1981 or 1982, the development picture improved and homebuilding picked up. Still, building kept considerably below the limits in the ordinance. Then, virtually overnight, a developer walked in and asked for 200 permits. That tipped the scales for everyone. The building threshold was reached; the builders were all cut off from more permits for that year; and the burdensome merit system was triggered for the next year.

It was a really exciting time, if one was in the building business, held contracts with homebuyers, and could not get permits. The city was arbitrary about dealing with such problems. Although the ordinance was changed within six months into something more palatable to the building community, the situation still created hardships for builders. But city hall had little sympathy.

As a consequence, the local builders started a lawsuit against the present ordinance. The case is still being heard. For almost 10 years, the ordinance had not been challenged by the industry because it was tolerable to operate under, even though it increased the amount of hassle in getting permits and raised the cost of housing. Now, however, this ordinance is being challenged on the basis that Boulder is affecting jurisdictions outside its borders.

To a certain extent, Boulder has driven out its middle class through its growth management programs. The middle class in Boulder is the "no-class" class. Supposedly, middle-class people pick houses that are ugly, and live in subdivisions filled with ranch houses and bereft of trees; Boulder does not want this kind of folks. So the middle-class homebuyers have begun to move into the surrounding communities and commute into Boulder—a change that has probably hurt Boulder's traffic situation and environment more even than their staying in the city would have done.

The town's voters are an interesting group. Boulder has a dual bell-curve income graph—with the lower- and upper-income groups predominating. The residents definitely do not want to be branded as elitist, but they do respond to elitist concerns. Basically, they are like sheep that have gone to greener pastures. Any kind of growth control that prevents development around their own houses, allows their own kids to attend smaller classes, or keeps the traffic off their own streets—that is what they will vote for. "I got here and I got mine, and now I'd just as soon the rest of you stay out of here," they are saying.

But I say that the issue of growth control is a lot more complicated than that, and cannot be dealt with simply by pulling a lever in the voting booth. Growth control is really a planning problem, and its impacts are unclear. For instance, it is difficult to show the impact of growth controls on the price of housing in Boulder. But from a builder's perspective, there is no question that the growth ordinance has added to the cost of producing a housing product—by adding to the amount of hassle involved and to the time it takes to process a development, and by slowing the rate at which a development can be built.

Probably, the two main sore points that I, as a developer, find in the Boulder approach to growth control are, first, the method of quality control and, second, the complexity of the ordinances. A community like Boulder is very conscious of development quality. However, the growth control ordinance tries to deal with issues of quality in a quantitative way—by putting numbers on things and saying, "You can only do this and that at this or that rate." It is impossible to deal with qualitative issues in a quantitative way; this practice, quite simply, detracts from good planning. The experience in Boulder has been that the planning department has deteriorated in quality because it has had to concentrate on counting numbers and on administering a highly bureaucratic system. Boulder's is not a lousy planning department— its staff members are good planners. Perhaps under the newest system, they will even be able to get back to planning.

A third problem with Boulder's growth control system is its redundancy, with all of the other controls that are already in place, like the comprehensive plan and the greenbelt program. There are so many controls in place in Boulder that rampant growth would be curtailed even without a growth control ordinance.

In summary: growth controls—from both the builder's and developer's perspectives—can prove very profitable, simply by creating exclusive situations for builders. But such controls also create a lot more work, developments take more time, and the consumers end up paying more money. A development approval system ought to be as simple as possible, consistent with keeping the desired environmental quality.

James Leach is president of D.L. Development Company, and a partner in Downing, Leach Architects of Boulder, Colorado. Leach's contribution to this book is drawn from an address he made at the ULI/Lincoln Institute seminar on growth management.

GROWTH CONTROL EVOLVES IN BOULDER

SANDRA COOPER

O
n November 2, 1976, voters passed a measure to create an ordinance limiting the number of residential building permits issued annually within the
city of Boulder, Colorado, to an average of 450. Known variously as the
"Boulder Growth Limitation Plan," the "Danish Plan" (after its author), and the "No-
Growth Plan" (which it is not, as will become apparent), the voter-initiated referendum aimed to establish a per annum rate of growth in the Boulder Valley comprehensive planning area of no greater than 2 percent, through the limited issuance of
permits allocated on a geographical basis. To many of Boulder's residents, passage
of the ballot measure appeared to give final form and structure to the somewhat
amorphous policies being used by the city to control growth.

Legislatively mandated growth control seems an almost predictable outcome of
this 80,000-member community's past efforts to plan and regulate the use of its
land. Concern for the land is related in part to Boulder's distinctive geographic setting on the Front Range of the Colorado Rockies. Situated 25 miles northwest of
Denver against a dramatic backdrop of mountains, and framed by massive sand-
stone outcroppings, Boulder is home to the University of Colorado, as well as to
numerous government and private research and development installations.

Historical records document an early awareness of land use planning and regulation: a 1910 report, *The Improvement of Boulder, Colorado* by Frederick Law
Olmsted, Jr., one of the country's foremost parks planners, contained recommendations on physical improvements—such as parks and natural areas planning—needed to maintain the city as a place of quality in which to live. Initial regulation was
achieved in 1928, when Boulder adopted its first zoning ordinance and, in so
doing, established itself as a forerunner of land use regulation among western
cities.

PUBLIC UTILITIES EXTENSION

Early attempts at controlling physical expansion were based for the most part on
water and sewer line locations and extensions. The 1959 Blue Line Charter Amend-

ment established an elevation of 5,750 feet along the mountainsides beyond which utility service could not be extended. The "spokes of the wheel" concept guided the introduction of new development: water and sewer utility lines were located along three spokes radiating south, east, and northeast from the city limits. Because of voter disaffection with this concept, the "spokes" plan was never fully implemented. However, the lines laid to the east and, more particularly, to the northeast have continued to hamper the city's attempts to control growth in the unincorporated portion of its planning area.

A case in point is a 1976 Supreme Court decision (*Robinson v. City of Boulder*), which required the city to provide water and sewer service upon request to a proposed development in the unincorporated portion of the Boulder Valley—an area designated on the Boulder Valley Comprehensive Plan for development only after 1990. This judicial opinion ruled that the city of Boulder was acting as a public utility in its role as sole provider of water and sewer service for the area. The ruling effectively ended the city's reliance on utilities extension as a planning tool for controlling growth in the unincorporated portion of the valley.

INTERGOVERNMENTAL PLANNING

In 1968, an effort to accomplish a unified planning program outside Boulder's municipal corporate limits was begun. The city participated with Boulder County in developing a comprehensive land use plan for the Boulder Valley, a land area of approximately 58 square miles that included the 13-square-mile, incorporated municipality. In 1970, the Boulder Valley Comprehensive Plan was adopted jointly by the city and county. It incorporated both the city's greenbelt plan and its utility service-area plan. The greenbelt program, funded by a sales tax approved by the voters in 1967, was already underway, moving toward its intended acquisition of 15,000 acres of land, to be designated as open space in the plan. (To date, the program has acquired some 9,500 acres of open space, either by fee simple or by development rights purchases.) The comprehensive plan did serve as an effective planning guide to future land uses. But it was not totally successful in directing and regulating growth within the unincorporated area because of the ineffectiveness of the implementation tools (for instance, public utilities extension) being used to phase development.

In recognition of the need to seek new methods to control growth and development in the unincorporated planning area, the Boulder Valley Comprehensive Plan was revised in 1977. The revised plan designated areas outside the incorporated limits for annexation to the city within the 15-year period of the comprehensive plan. However, the annexation schedule for that area known as Gunbarrel has met with unexpected opposition from local residents. Thus, residential development continues at a high rate, regardless of the 2 percent annual limit established in the growth limitation ordinance.

Following closely on the heels of adoption of the original Boulder Valley Comprehensive Plan in 1970, the local chapter of Zero Population Growth (ZPG) published a report entitled *Is Population Growth Good for Boulder's Citizens?* The report investigated possible diseconomies of scale in cities that grow beyond certain population sizes. ZPG proposed a 100,000-population limit for Boulder and put the proposal before the voters in 1971, via a citizen-initiated referendum. The measure lost. But two companion ballot items placed by the city—to "take all steps necessary to hold the rate of growth . . . to a level substantially below that experienced in the 1960s . . . in keeping with the policies found in the Boulder Valley Comprehensive Plan," and to "undertake a definitive analysis of the optimum population and growth rate for the Boulder Valley"—were overwhelmingly approved.

GROWTH MANAGEMENT

In March 1971, in response to the ballot items, the Boulder City Council adopted a set of interim growth policies aimed at holding the growth rate in the Boulder Valley to a level substantially below that of the 1960s. The tools selected to control and manage this growth were implementation of the Boulder Valley Comprehensive Plan, and evaluation of potentially adverse economic, social, and environmental impacts on the valley from proposed developments.

A citizens' commission was created by the Boulder City Council and the Boulder County Board of Commissioners in April 1972. The commission was to undertake a study to determine the optimum population and growth rate for the Boulder Valley. In November 1973, the 13-member commission released its 10-volume report. Seventeen recommendations were directed to the state, county, and city; their implementation, it was stated, would result in greater intergovernmental cooperation in enforcing and creating conventional and innovative planning tools for growth control. The commission recommended a growth rate of 3 percent per annum over the Boulder Valley Comprehensive Plan area. Although many of the recommendations were directly or indirectly carried out by city and county governments, the city council—overwhelmed by the enormity of the material (in this writer's opinion)— never moved to replace the interim growth policies with permanent policies reflecting the commission's recommendations.

Meanwhile, the growth rate in the city of Boulder at this time had been slowed substantially, compared with that of the period 1960–1970, when the annual rate of growth was some 6 percent—six times the national annual growth rate. In keeping with the intent of the adopted interim growth policies, growth had been reduced to a rate of 3.7 percent per year for the years 1970–1973. But the issue of a permanent growth policy had still gone unresolved.

Enter Paul Danish, a Boulder city councilman elected to office in 1974. He first introduced a proposed growth limitation ordinance to the council in early 1976. It met with ridicule: "naive and premature," "a head-in-the-sand approach," "potentially harmful to the Boulder Valley Comprehensive Plan revision, now in process," and so on. Danish, undaunted by the council's rejection, went on to head a successful petition drive that resulted in the passage of the "Danish Plan," or growth limitation plan, in November 1976. The ballot measure, which would become Ordinance 2408, required that the following steps be taken to preserve the special environment and high quality of life within the Boulder Valley:
• Limit major residential development projects to an average of 450 dwelling units per year for a period of five years;
• Limit the number of units constructed outside the Boulder inner area to 275 units annually;
• Devise a merit system, or point system, to determine the allocation of building permits to developers; and
• Amend the Boulder Valley Comprehensive Plan to provide for a growth rate of no greater than 2 percent per year within the comprehensive planning area.

The measure exempted projects of four or fewer units (either single or multiple dwellings) to be constructed on lots platted before enactment of the ordinance, as well as projects of the Boulder Housing Authority required to meet low-income housing commitments. The measure also exempted "any existing agreement or commitment of the [c]ity of Boulder explicitly stipulating an annual rate of construction for a subdivision or planned unit development existing at the time of this ordinance's adoption." This last condition had the potential of decreasing the average number of building permits issued in the preceding five-year period (1970–1975) by only a token 93 permits per year! The county was later to determine that

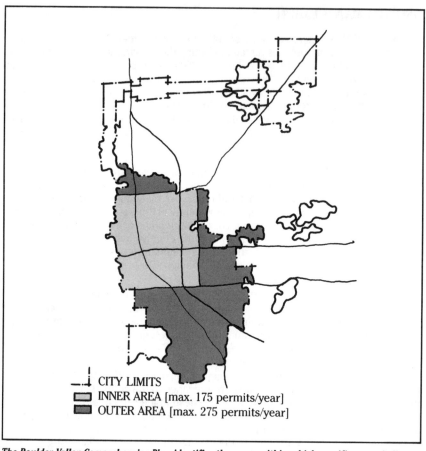

CITY LIMITS
INNER AREA [max. 175 permits/year]
OUTER AREA [max. 275 permits/year]

The Boulder Valley Comprehensive Plan identifies the areas within which specific annual alloca-tions of building permits are to be made.

the allocation limitation would only legally apply to that portion of the Boulder Val-ley within the city's jurisdiction (that is, within its incorporated limits).

Given a "worst case scenario," an average of 1,100 building permits per year might be issued, if total buildout were realized, and if all authorized permits under the growth limitation ordinance had been allocated in this five-year period. Clearly, it was *not* the intent of the measure approved by the voters to continue the high growth rate of the past, but to limit growth even beyond those restraints imposed by the interim policies.

Now, enter the city attorneys, who saved the "growth limitation measure" from becoming the "growth stimulation ordinance." In their opinion, the future status of approved but unbuilt PUDs and subdivisions should be determined by the city council on a case-by-case basis. No automatic exemptions for existing commit-ments should be "grandfathered-in," as in the Petaluma, California, plan, the model for the Boulder plan. Under this advised revision, the council, in making a final de-termination of the status of an existing commitment, would determine if the project was exempt from the allocation limitation and therefore not required to compete for points under the merit system, or, conversely, not eligible for exempt status. Criteria for judging exempt eligibility included performance record, level of development activity on the site, and intent to fulfill past commitments on the part of the applicant. Once exempt status had been awarded by the council, a development schedule had to be agreed upon by the applicant. Noncompliance with the development schedule would result in loss of the exempt status and of the right to build future units. The city council, after determination of each applicant's exempt status, was given the discretionary power to include the exempt building permits among the 450 annual allocations, or to increase the number of allocations accordingly.

This discretionary authority led to a 1979 administrative interpretation of the ordinance revising the limitation of 450 to one of 650 permits per year. It was determined that if a true 2 percent-per-year growth rate was to be reflected, and if the exempt and existing commitments were to be included, 650 permits per year should be the upper limit for all types of allocations. If the average rate of growth since adoption of the ordinance (in March 1977) should exceed 2 percent per year, allocations for existing commitments were to be excluded from the 650-permit base. If, however, the annual rate of growth was found to be less than 2 percent, allocation requests for existing commitments would be included in the 650-permit limitation.

MERIT SYSTEM

The merit system called for in the original ballot measure was developed by the planning staff from requirements in the city's land use regulations, as well as from model merit systems devised by other communities, such as Petaluma, California, and Ramapo, New York. The final document, which incorporated the concerns of numerous city departments, ultimately integrated specific community goals and standards. (The method of awarding points to determine project merit is shown in Figure 2.)

According to the ordinance, only when the projects proposed for a semiannual allocation period exceed the permit allotment for the inner and outer areas is the merit-system review to be invoked. When applications exceed the semiannual limit, projects are reviewed and ranked according to the number of merit points assigned by the staff and by the planning board. Those projects that have received the highest scores—if, together, they do not exceed the allocation limit—are given the blessings of the board and a go-ahead to proceed with the subdivision process. Any dwelling units that have been authorized but awarded neither a building permit nor subsequent final inspection, revert to an unused allocation pool. They become available for later allocation, anytime before March 14, 1982, the expiration date of Ordinance 2408.

Members of the planning staff and planning board who were interviewed agreed that the allocation, or merit, system is neither unmanageable nor unduly time-consuming at their respective levels. However, several land developers, active in large-scale developments in Boulder for the past 10 years, offered different opinions. Tom Hoyt, president of McStain Enterprises, maintained that the merit system's evaluation adds to the already existing burden of documenting compliance with land use regulations: in order to prepare an application for merit review of a sizable project, he must assign two people for a minimum of two weeks to assemble and complete the required information. Depending upon the size of the development, Hoyt felt that an additional 60 days' maximum might be "lost" in the process before building permits are issued. Similarly, Jim Leach, the developer of Wonderland Hill and of other large projects, commented that an average of six to nine months is added to the length of time an application is in process. But he added that on some

FIGURE 2
THE POINT SYSTEM

1) Public Facilities (30 points maximum)

Streets	4 points
Parks	4 points
Fire protection	4 points
Flood control	4 points
Water distributions	2 points
Sanitary sewage collection	2 points
School capacity	2 points
Storm drainage	2 points
Police protection	2 points
Public transportation	2 points
Special facilities and services	2 points

2) Low- and Moderate-Income Housing (20 points maximum)

Rental units with or without rental assistance	20 points

OR

Sales units	20 points

3) Environmental Elements (20 points maximum)

Hazards and engineering constraints	3 points
Natural resources and natural areas	3 points
Project impacts	4 points
Conservation	10 points

4) Site Design and Relationship with Surrounding Areas (30 points maximum)

Open space and landscaping	8 points
Circulation and parking	8 points
Livability	8 points
Relationship to surrounding areas	6 points

5) Approved PUDs (5 points maximum)

PUDs approved before November 10, 1976	5 points
PUDs annexed by the city after November 20, 1976, but approved by the county before that date	2 points

projects—"the right kind at the right time"—no additional time is added, even though other projects might require an extra year.

PERCEIVED RESULTS

It is sometimes tough to come away with a clear consensus in Boulder, a community noted for its active and vocal citizenry. And the public's perception of any impacts from the growth limitation plan on the diversity, quality, and cost of housing, as well as of its ultimate effectiveness, hardly resembles a consensus.

There seems to be little argument that the cost of housing has increased in the city of Boulder. However, there is less agreement on the reasons for the increased cost. Housing demand, improved quality and increased size of new homes, and increased cost of construction are primary reasons for the dramatic rise in housing costs—both nationally and locally. However, in Boulder, increased demand and relatively constant supply of housing, due to the declining growth rate imposed by the interim policies, are seen to have aggravated the situation. Furthermore, compliance with the merit system is blamed for raising housing costs.

The results of a five-county survey of the Denver metropolitan area, conducted in early April 1979 by the Rocky Mountain Research Institute, refuted the contention that housing costs in Boulder had been skyrocketing since enactment of the Danish Plan. The average 1978 price for resale houses in Boulder County rose by 15.5 percent—8.2 percent less than the Denver-area average. Although the highest average resale price did occur in Boulder County, the price of resale houses increased faster during 1978 in Adams County (28.6 percent), Jefferson County (26.5 percent), and Denver County (22.8 percent). In other words, the cost of resale housing in counties surrounding Boulder County—counties where no growth controls were in effect—was escalating at higher annual percentages than in Boulder.

Although a clear consensus may be lacking on the growth limitation plan's effect on local housing costs, there is general agreement that the growth limitation ordinance has generated an increased stock of moderate-priced housing since its inception. The competition for merit points has served as a real incentive to incorporate housing for moderate-income owners into project planning. John Hooyer, executive secretary to Boulder's housing authority, said, "The plan has had the effect of producing more moderate-income housing than anything that has happened in the last five years." The annual income range for housing in this category stands at $14,000–$21,000, with a house priced at $53,700 representing the maximum affordable. Since March 10, 1977, commitments for 216 moderate-income houses have been made. Of these, 63 have been completed, and 35 are under construction, as of November 1979. Although Hooyer suspects that the costs incurred by the developer in producing moderate-income housing are passed along to upper-moderate and upper-income buyers, higher-priced housing is "snapped up" immediately. This buyer phenomenon may be attributed to the higher-than-average incomes characteristic of Boulder.

So far, the success of the allocation system in meeting the low-income housing objectives of the community has been much more modest. The provision of low-income housing largely depends upon the availability of Section 8 federal funds in the form of rent assistance. For this reason, an "in-lieu-of" process is available to the developer within the merit system: he may transact with the housing authority a formal agreement to provide off-site rental units eligible for inclusion into the Section 8 program. John Hooyer reports that approximately 10 low-income rental units have become available through the in-lieu-of program. The prospects for the future of increased low-income units appear brighter, however. According to Hooyer, commitments for 40 more units have been made in the competition for merit points.

Improved site planning was identified in the course of this investigation as a benefit directly accruing to the community from application of the merit system. City of Boulder Assistant Planning Director Ed Gawf observed that site design and planning were good before the merit system came into effect but definitely better now—"better, not so much because of any extra money expended, but because more time has been spent thinking about the details and how they all work." Boulder Planning Board Chairman Chet Winter concurred and said that the merit system has provided specific criteria for future development. Tom Hoyt, on the other hand, was critical of the homogeneity created as a consequence of the merit system because "everyone does what the winner does."

SUCCESS AT LIMITING GROWTH

The question that must be asked finally is, how effective has the growth limitation plan been in limiting growth? Figure 3 lists building-permit information for the years 1970–1979 as a comparison between building activity before the growth limitation ordinance and after the growth limitation ordinance. It should be noted that during the time between approval of the ballot measure (November 2, 1976) and adoption of the ordinance (March 10, 1977), a grace period was extended until mid-February for the issuance of building permits. A total of 824 permits was issued in this period of three and one-half months.

It becomes apparent from the data in Figure 3 that the number of building permits issued has increased since 1975, the year before adoption of the ballot measure. Several factors, including the issuance of permits during the grace period, may account for this increase. The discretionary power of the city council to award allocations in excess of the original 450 units to eligible existing commitments has added an annual average of 162 permits since the ordinance went into effect (that is, from March 15, 1977, through December 31, 1979). The 1979 council decision to increase the average base to 650 allocations per year, to reflect a 2 percent-per-year rate of growth, has obviously increased the allowable number of permits available for annual allocation.

The planning staff, in reviewing the status of the allocation system before the city council in mid-January 1980, reported that the average number of building permits issued each year since inception of the ordinance was fulfilling the intent of the ordinance to limit growth to no more than 2 percent per year. If the council acted to subtract allocations, from the 650 allowed, for existing commitments in 1980, the

FIGURE 3
DWELLING UNITS GENERATED BY THE ISSUANCE OF A BUILDING PERMIT

Year	Single-Family[1]	Multiple-Family	Total
1970	231	807	1,038
1971	372	1,919	2,291
1972	258	786	1,044
1973	210	628	838
1974	166	430	506
1975	206	80	286
1976	409	253	662
1977	395	568	963
1978	371	359	730
1979	397	198	595

[1]Includes duplexes.
Source: Building permit data, building department, city of Boulder, Colorado (February 12, 1980).

rate of growth achieved so far would be 2.08 percent per annum. Future council decisions on the disposal of prior commitments, however, must await the as-yet-unknown activity of approved allocations for which no building permits have been issued.

One of the requirements within the ballot measure adopted on November 2, 1976, was that the city council urge the Boulder County Commissioners to enact procedures to hold growth within the unincorporated portion of the Boulder Valley comprehensive planning area to a level of no greater than 2 percent per year. Because this area is outside the incorporated boundaries of the city, it is not subject to municipal regulation. Upon advice of their legal staff, the county commissioners determined that they lack authority to effect restrictions in one part of the county without applying them to the whole county. Hence, the mandated 2 percent-per-year growth rate has gone without legislative recognition in the unincorporated portion of the Boulder Valley since enactment of the growth limitation plan in March 1977.

Revisions to the Boulder Valley Comprehensive Plan made in 1977 called for annexation by the city of those areas designated as 2a and 2b on the map—for the express purpose of implementing the 2 percent-per-year growth rate. Failure to annex these lands since adoption of the plan revisions has led, according to Boulder County Planning Director Ed Tepe, to the false assumption that the growth rate in the unincorporated portion of Boulder Valley has been 2 percent per year. Only through annexation of these areas, which are served with city utilities, can the restrictions of the growth limitation plan be applied. "In actuality," Tepe observed, "Gunbarrel is growing just as fast as it was and maybe faster." This growth rate is reported to be 6 percent per year.

Few will deny that growth in the unincorporated valley has continued, or perhaps even accelerated, as a result of the growth limitation plan. Former Boulder Planning Director Nolan Rosall likened the current growth control dilemma to a balloon: "You squeeze it in one place, and it pops out in another place." He fears that it will become more and more difficult for the county to hold the line, as growth pressures increase, both in the Boulder Valley and elsewhere in the county.

Many people believe that enforcement of the Boulder Valley Comprehensive Plan plus implementation of the plan policies to phase growth according to the availability of a full range of urban services, would be a better approach to growth control in the total valley than the imposition of a numerical limit. But the growth limitation plan has at least brought the issue into focus. Whether the annual 650-dwelling-unit limit is being applied literally or not, a structure now exists for growth's containment, if not for its total control.

THE NEXT STEP

Boulder is about to initiate another growth study—this one on the recommendation of Planning Director Frank Gray, who feels that some important questions need answering before the present growth limitation ordinance expires in March 1982. Questions like housing supply and demand, housing costs, housing types—and the effects of the ordinance on these issues—must be addressed. Gray has proposed this study in order to develop the successor to the Danish Plan; he envisions it to be a growth management system that will balance employment opportunities and commercial services with housing controls. Meanwhile, it will take into consideration additional variables, such as community energy and transportation needs. The 20-month growth management study is slated to get underway within several months. A citizen's steering committee and a technical advisory committee will oversee data collection and development of a proposed system. The city intends to work closely with the county government—a prudent step, in light of the frustrations already experienced in applying the growth limitation plan to the unincorporated portion of the valley.

Growth management, according to its broadest definition, is a far more sophisticated system for containing growth than the numerical limit imposed by the Danish Plan. The Boulder community has been feeling its way with some available tools, and is now positioned to proceed with more refined growth management ideas.

Sandra Cooper is a planner with Land Counsel, a Boulder, Colorado, consulting firm. She has served in an official capacity on a number of public planning commissions in Boulder.
This article is drawn from one that appeared in *Urban Land* in March 1980.

BOCA RATON'S CHANGING APPROACH

MARIE YORK

Perhaps it's best to begin with statistics.

In 1970, Boca Raton had a population of 30,000. Today, it has 60,000. And in 15 or 20 years, estimates put that number at more like 90,000. That is just within the city limits. If all of the greater area is included, then predictions claim a population of almost 200,000 for Boca Raton by the year 2000.

Twenty-seven square miles in size, Boca Raton is on the east coast of Florida, about halfway between West Palm Beach and Fort Lauderdale, in southern Palm Beach County. It is a predominately white community with a greater-than-median age, a greater-than-median income, and a smaller-than-average household size— compared with the national norms.

THE GROWTH CAP, OTHER MEASURES, AND THEIR AFTERMATH

In 1972, Boca Raton adopted its controversial growth cap. The number of new dwelling units per year was capped at 40,000. The growth cap was a citizen-initiated charter amendment, supported by a rather unscientific five-part report that the citizens had put together without professional input. (Interestingly, later, when the cap was challenged in the courts, that citizens' report became the basis for the city's defense.)

Immediately after the cap's adoption, the community put in force a moratorium, and a 50 percent, across-the-board downzoning of multifamily housing. The developers sued. The case proved very expensive for both sides; it cost the city somewhere between $1 million and $2 million in defense. And the courts eventually ruled that the cap was unconstitutional. But by the time the cap had been repealed, in 1979, the trend of local development had been well established. Basically, in that time frame, the developers had had the choice of waiting for justice to be served, or proceeding with development. Some of them chose not to develop. But those who went ahead were forced to do so under the downzoning.

These conditions were not all bad for the development community, inasmuch as they proved a tremendous sales tool. Boca Raton now has an image of having a

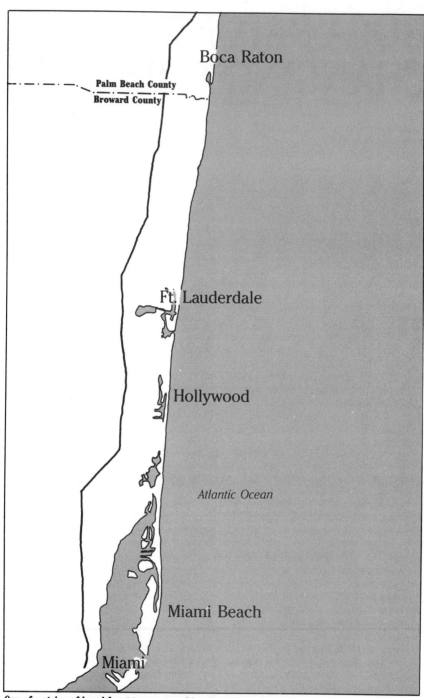

One of a string of beachfront towns stretching north from Miami, Boca Raton has established a reputation as a haven for wealthy residents.

quality difference. Boca has become a prestigious place to live, and developer and investor confidence has risen in the long run.

The effects of the cap have been many. The first effect was that the demand for housing increased. And with the downzoning, the density decreased, which caused a lowered housing supply, which in turn caused increased housing prices. The increased price range then led to a slowdown of growth—the cap's original intention.

Regarding Boca Raton's share of building activity, out of the amount that was occurring in the region before growth controls were adopted: the data showed that the level of building activity in Boca Raton exceeded the regional level. In 1969, 7.5 percent more building permits were issued in Boca Raton than in Palm Beach or Broward County. Throughout 1970 and 1971, Boca grew at about a 4 or 4.5 percent faster rate than its neighbors did.

If the cap slowed the growth, the question, of course, is why? Quite simply, the building activity slowed, first through the moratorium, and then, eventually, through the increase in housing prices. Before 1972, our housing prices were higher than our neighbors' prices but still fairly constant. But after 1974, prices escalated, relative to the rest of the region. And by 1983, the cost of housing was some three times higher in Boca Raton. This rise resulted from the decreased density, but also from the cost of doing business in this city—a subject that will concern me later in this discussion.

GROWTH MANAGEMENT AND THE CITY'S PLANNING TOOLS

Since the cap, the political climate has changed. Development has continued. But now, the city has the tools for growth management in place to allow development to grow, within limits. Of course, we have zoning and land use planning provisions. The new legislation that came out of Tallahassee this year [1985] brings more stringent guidelines for the adoption of comprehensive plans: now, Boca and other Florida cities may only be able to change their comprehensive plans twice a year.

When the city was in such haste to adopt a comprehensive plan to harmonize with the new zoning, which called for the 40,000-dwelling-unit cap, the planning department, basically, put a comprehensive plan on top of the zoning. From then on, every time we wanted to change the zoning, we had to change the comprehensive plan, rather than to change the zoning in the way that the Florida state government would have preferred to see us do it: namely, that we look at the land uses; look at the land availability; determine where the industrial, commercial, and residential development should take place; and *then* change the zoning to match the plan, as the development proposals came in.

Infrastructure Provision

Another move that will now be required is to institute a capital improvements program. Boca Raton has one. But it is almost a wish list of what we think we will have to spend for various capital items within the next 10 years. But now, we are going to be required to determine when capital improvement is to take place, when the infrastructure is to go in, and, most importantly, how it is going to be financed. And development is not to take place until the infrastructure goes in.

The city's lowered housing density *has* resulted in some inefficient provision of services. The city has had an increased demand for water: Boca Raton uses more water than any of the municipalities in its region. Much of this use derives from the demand for open space. And anyone who has lived in Florida and tried to maintain a lawn knows that grass does not grow naturally. It takes a lot of water and is a very high-maintenance item.

Another spin-off of lowered density is that we have been unable to support a mass transit system. We have a large elderly population, who have difficulties with their eyesight. Many of these older folks should probably not be on the roads. But, for lack of a public transit system, they are still driving their Cadillacs like armored cars.

Planned Unit Developments

Other tools of growth management include the planned unit development and its near relative, the planned industrial development. These allow for much flexibility, for the clustering of multifamily units, and for a lot of open space. Boca Raton has planned unit developments that are beautiful—many of them built around golf courses or lakes. And an industrial park that is also beautiful: an observer would never think it was an industrial or manufacturing section of town.

Annexations

Another recently applied tool has been annexation. We have not used this one as effectively as we could have, mainly because of the fear that "bigger is not better." And if land is annexed, then the city will become bigger, and the current residents will have their political base diluted.

Palm Beach County has an area of 2,200 square miles. This is a very large area to service. And the county commission and county staff just cannot cost-effectively enter into the business of providing urban services. They have been generous in their development approvals. But their allowed densities have been higher than what we in Boca Raton would prefer. And the county has also permitted leapfrog development.

Last year, we annexed the last vacant parcel that did not have any development approval applicable to it. That parcel was some 800 acres in extent. And it was given zoning for a lower density than the one that would probably have been approved under Palm Beach County's regulations.

Impact Fees

Another tool of growth management has been the impact fee. These fees have passed the court test of constitutionality, although they do increase the cost of housing and are regressive in nature. They are criticized because the provision of capital is through the government's taxation processes. One of the aspects for which impact fees are criticized is that of their "triple taxation" approach. First, the land is taxed when it's vacant, before it comes in for development. Then, the developer pays the impact fee, which he or she eventually passes on to the consumer. And then, the consumer has to pay for the debt service when the expansion of the facilities actually takes place.

Impact fees are a favorite tool for growth management because, basically, the growth finances itself. But the problem is that the current residents have not had to pay any such fee, directly or indirectly. And their philosophy—"We're here. Pull up the drawbridge. We don't want any more people. And we don't want our town to change."—makes impact fees all too popular a concept.

Environment, Open Space, and Community Appearance

Regulations exist, too, that protect the environment. One of these is the tree preservation ordinance, which is a tough one. If a landowner has a tree that is greater than five inches in diameter, then he or she must get a permit to cut it down. Also, the site-plan approval process requires an environmental survey if the trees on a site exceed a certain size. An environmental officer determines if there are trees involved that should be preserved. And a developer must show that his or her development proposal protects those trees as far as possible. Furthermore, if there are any endangered species involved, the environmental officers will request that the developer provide a habitat for them, or at least devise a suitable relocation plan.

Boca Raton has a land dedication fee. Now one can see why the relative cost of housing in Boca Raton has become so high. The land dedication fee uses a complicated formula that evaluates the amount of open space and recreational facilities provided in a development. And based upon these data, the developer pays a certain amount that is earmarked for acquiring or developing more parkland.

Recently, the planning and zoning board has gone into the business of soliciting "voluntary contributions." This money is earmarked for a beautification program for the median strips in the rights-of-way around the new developments. Although this scheme does enhance the vicinity and does, in turn, produce a sales tool, it also represents something else that the developer has to put out so that a project can be approved in a timely manner.

Some of our other controls entail the work of the city's planning and zoning board, which meets weekly to review all site plan approvals. The staff includes nine full-time planners, plus seven code enforcement officers. This is for a city with a population of 60,000.

In addition, Boca has a community appearance board that reviews all architectural plans. And it also has a tough sign ordinance that really does make Boca Raton distinctive. The requirement for a sign is that it identify, not advertise. It cannot have flashing lights or be unprotected, like the lights in a typical used-car lot. The sign ordinance distinguishes Boca from nearby towns: when visitors leave, they realize they have gone into another jurisdiction because they have lost that quality control and that awareness of image.

The community also has a downtown redevelopment agency, established about two years ago. Its work is based on tax increment financing. Also, we have three historic preservation groups, which is not a bad showing for a city that is only 60 years old.

TAX-BASE CONSIDERATIONS

All of these items do add to the cost of development, and thus to the cost of housing, which is passed on to the consumer. These policies increase the tax base, which is just fine with the residents. There are winners, and there are losers. And the winners in a case like this are the current residents. The losers are the new people who want to move in but cannot find a broad enough range of housing prices to accommodate them. The cap and other growth management policies have indeed underscored our exclusionary image. Affordable housing in Boca is almost unknown.

There is now a $4 billion tax base, and that is increasing each year with growth. This last year, $161 million of taxables were added. Therefore, the municipality has had a decreasing millage rate over some seven years. This outcome has proved possible because the growth is financing itself. But the problem is that we need to plan for the long run. In 15 or 20 years, when Boca Raton reaches buildout, and when the finite land supply can no longer support the rollback tax policy, then we will have some problems. Long-range planning, however, is unpopular with the citizens, and the policy makers have to run for reelection every March.

CITIZENS' INVOLVEMENT

In the early 1970s, a citizens' group formed that called itself Citizens for Reasonable Growth. The CRG was, in fact, the group that brought forth the referendum that adopted the cap. Since then, we at city hall have been thinking that our image had changed. We had gone through many trials. And the faces on the city council had changed, too—such that, although the council was not necessarily prodevelopment, it did welcome industry because the councillors thought they had the planning tools in place to manage development. But the CRG is alive and well and fighting.

In fact, within the last fiscal year, the CRG forced two more referendums. The more recent of these was the defeat of a $125 million financial center that was to go into the downtown. At present, our "100 Percent Corner" in downtown Boca Raton has a strict commercial development: two gas stations and a vacant lot. The community had a developer willing to take a risk and consolidate some property, in order to build a financial plaza comprising 160-foot structures. (Our height limitation in the downtown was 100 feet.) And the Citizens for Reasonable Growth came back, got out the petitions to force a referendum, and defeated the financial plaza.

A CLOSING ESSAY

Boca Raton is a fine place to live. There is a sense of quality: it is a high-quality community. And there is a real sense of community, too. However, as with most local governments, we do often act out of narrow self-interest. We seldom consider the regional impacts of our decisions. We are exclusionary. And we are a microcosm of society.

The growth management policies in effect today derive from several factors. One is quite simply luck. For instance, the Arvida Corporation, with which Boca has had some tugs-of-war over the years, has been a large landholder. But it is also a forward-thinking, imaginative, and high-quality developer. It introduced the concept of the planned unit development/planned industrial development to Boca Raton. The city did not have this kind of legislation on its books at the time that Arvida submitted its proposals. And also for example, Boca has had the good fortune to learn from the problems of its neighbors to the south. It has a citizenry of government watchdogs; government watching is a leisure-time activity in southern Florida.

In addition, the retiree base provides leaders who have held leadership positions around the world. They have retired in Boca, and now it has the benefit of their expertise. But the need for professional staff has also been recognized—which is all to the good. And finally, another important stroke of luck is that Florida's state government has had more vision than have many governments, and has implemented growth management legislation.

In summation, Boca Raton has been highly successful in managing growth and in establishing a quality-minded community. But all this has been based on an unconstitutional cap. And the cap and allied measures have increased the cost of housing. The current growth, however, permits us to enjoy a decreasing tax millage rate that is based on expensive housing characteristics and an increasingly high-tech industrial base.

Perhaps Boca's measures will all work in the long run. Perhaps the rising housing costs and the increasing property values will allow the city to keep its low level of taxation. After all, the lower-income housing is being provided elsewhere. But land is a limited resource, and growth cannot support our expected high level of services indefinitely.

I, personally, have a problem with the exclusionary aspect. If every community chose to emulate Boca Raton, most of us would not have a place to live.

Marie York is an economist and planner with the growth management division of the city of Boca Raton, Florida. In this position, she is in charge of economic evaluations of the impacts of major developments on the city's fiscal structure.

York's contribution to this book is drawn from an address she made at the ULI/Lincoln Institute seminar on growth management.

At the seminar, a question-and-answer session immediately followed York's presentation. In reply to Marie York's closing statement, and in reference to two of Warren Salmons's slides from Petaluma ("before" and "after" pictures), **Frank Schnidman** *maintained that Salmons's slides symbolized the politics of growth control: "My hope was that you would all remember these slides after they had been shown. One photo was of a 'bad' subdivision from the 1950s. And the main feature of that photo was the pickup trucks that were parked in substantial numbers along the street. There were also prominent utility poles and the like. Not too many houses were visible. These are the 'bad' sorts of developments that still occur before growth management. Mr. Salmons's slides showing 'life after growth management' included some shots of spanking-new condos that were like photos that a developer might have taken—that is, they had no parked cars at all.*

"As you know, developers' model homes do not even have driveways. They have grass in front. So developers try to dress the models up. And the latter are the 'good' developments we get after growth management. They are the kinds of developments you would submit for design competitions. Petaluma, like Boulder, had a point competition for developments. And we know which projects are going to come out ahead in these point competitions—these elite, designed condos, not the bad old subdivisions like those built in the 1950s.

"There is a danger. According to Paul Niebanck's introductory remarks, what we have in growth management can be a tool of exclusion. Marie York has explicitly stated that this has been the case in Boca Raton. And basically, a lot of folks in a lot of cities want to keep out those folks who drive pickup trucks, and all sorts of growth management systems will allow them to do just that.

"Let me give you a few data from academic studies. The results of a number of studies of the effects of growth control on housing prices and housing production have appeared in the academic literature. These studies were largely done in California in the late 1970s, during the period when California's housing prices were rising very fast, and also when stringent regulation of development was being carried out. Two studies in particular are worth mentioning briefly, and a study that involved Petaluma is worth examining more closely.

"The first study, basically, makes the important theoretical point that growth management cannot be expected to have much effect on prices, unless it involves a

large part of a metropolitan market. For example, in the Washington, D.C., area, there is a little city called Falls Church. It is unlikely that Falls Church is a powerful enough entity that, if it controlled growth, its controls would have much effect on price. Fairfax County, on the other hand, is a very large county that surrounds Falls Church. And if Fairfax County controlled growth, its controls would likely have a major effect on local prices.

"One of the studies—performed by an associate of MIT's department of city planning, Michael Elliott—confirmed this principle of economic theory: in California, housing prices went up sharply only when both a city and its surrounding county controlled growth. But when both entities did this, prices really soared. This amounts to controlling for house quality. [And, thus, to probable elitist exclusion.]"

Paul Danish *then replied to Schnidman: "Let me just make one response to a point you have made a few times about elitism. And that is that Boulder awarded points not merely on the basis of design. In fact, design, in the original plan, accounted for only about 25 percent of the points that were given for providing moderate-income housing, and 35 percent of the points given for providing urban services. Whether or not this discriminated against people who drive pickup trucks, it certainly did result in a certain amount of moderate-income housing. It is also fair to say that a growth management system (and this was something that the appellate court said in the Petaluma decision) can be used as a tool of inclusion as well as of exclusion.*

"For that matter, growth management in certain communities can also mean growth stimulation. And in some communities, that is the proper goal of it. Heaven knows it is needed in certain places in this country.

"Moreover, I do think that telling towns that they must somehow meet somebody else's expectations of what the proper community balance must be, in terms of demographics, is a little unfair. In Boulder, for instance, a substantial number of people earn less than the national median income. And this fact was discovered by the critics of growth management only after they had complained for several years about the town's being elitist. And then, the 'rap' became that we were driving out the middle class.

"I guess, after having gone through a lot of these arguments over the years, I have simply concluded that, in the nature of things, if a city is going to try to control its growth, it is going to find itself among the few parties in the world ever to be condemned by a board of realtors for raising property values. I do not think [such condemnations] are always made in good faith. And actually, if a town has a set of growth management tools in place, then the town can use these tools for many different purposes. And those purposes are not always going to be elitist ones."

The discussion gathered momentum and went on in this vein:

Warren Salmons: *"If the number of pickup trucks in a neighborhood is any measure of fairness in growth management systems, then Petaluma is doing just fine, thank you. And it has a very fair system. It's astounding, frankly, how many pickup trucks there are. And if you live in Petaluma, you have to have one: one with four-wheel drive is better; and one that rides high off the ground is even better. A dog in the back is perfect."*

Marie York: *"No gun racks?"*

Salmons: *"Gun racks are good, too. And that's really a measure of the nature of Petaluma—of the set of values that I tried to get at by my slides and my discussion. That set of values belongs not only to the long-standing residents, but also to the newer arrivals in Petaluma. And I think all sectors of the community understand that set of values and aspire to it—whether it's achievable or not, and whether it's idealistic or not."—Editor*

A DEVELOPER'S VIEW OF BOCA RATON

CHARLES E. COBB, JR.

When I joined Arvida in 1972, it was with a vision of creating the premiere large-scale community development company, complete with the strongest financial, managerial, and technological capabilities in America. Even though several new towns had been built in the 1960s—such as the Irvine Ranch and two new towns I had developed along with another employer: the Ranch of California and the McCormick Ranch—no other company had built several such communities in multiple locations. Arvida had the properties; selecting among these, I began to consider appropriate locations for Arvida's first large-scale community development.

WHY BOCA RATON?

The clear choice was Boca Raton. Everything was there for a large-scale community: the expanding population base of southern Florida; a major transportation network—I-95—about to be opened; and a young university. Furthermore, while the area was at that time without an industrial base, it had the available land to accommodate one. All in all, Boca Raton seemed to have the potential to be in the same league as the Irvine Ranch, the Ranch of California, the McCormick Ranch, and Columbia, Maryland. It was where I wanted to locate the flagship of the new Arvida Corporation.

Zoning for the site had been granted, but it was important to me that the citizens of Boca Raton know that this proposed development was to be an important and high-quality addition to the community. Accordingly, Arvida spent several months preparing and revising its plan and working with public officials. As a result, the officials supported the new plan.

Unfortunately, a citizens' group, alarmed at the picture of a major new development in its midst, began a countereffort. Of course, their reasons for concern were understandable. The proposed development included several features of questionable value or appeal to the current retiree and tourist population, such as industrial facilities and moderate-cost housing. While anticipating this negative reaction, I also hoped that the merits of the plan, when properly communicated, would turn the reaction around. Instead, the issue became larger than one simply of merit or quality. It became an issue of growth or no-growth in the city of Boca Raton.

THE LAWSUITS

The citizens' group met in their own homes and prepared, without research, a five-page report recommending a 40,000-unit growth cap for Boca Raton. In response to the city council's refusal to consider what was, in effect, a population cap, the group gathered signed petitions and put their proposal up for a referendum. This was ultimately voted upon and approved.

We at Arvida firmly believed the cap to be unconstitutional. Therefore, we took legal action against the city. After five years of litigation, the courts found the proposed development to be an appropriate one. Arvida had challenged and proven the unconstitutionality of the new ordinance in every court up to the U.S. Supreme Court—spending in the process several million dollars in legal fees. Similarly, the city spent nearly $2 million.

THE EFFECTS

Meanwhile, for five years, nothing happened on my plan for a new community. With my initial enthusiasm severely dampened, I gave in and built what Boca Raton was programmed for, namely, an exclusionary community of high-priced homes. The effects of this strategy, depending upon your perspective, have been good and bad. We probably ended up with more money: millions could have been lost if delays caused by the lawsuit had not happened to coincide with the building recession of 1973 through 1975. Furthermore, the upscale image of the community as we built it has reaped tremendous financial reward.

On the other hand, almost none of our 2,000 employees at the Boca Raton Hotel and Club can afford to live in Boca Raton, and only about 20 percent of the over 10,000 employees in Arvida's Park of Commerce have chosen to work and live in the same community. It is simply more economically feasible for most of these people to live in the surrounding towns.

THE TRADE-OFF AND ITS IMPLICATIONS FOR REGIONAL PLANNING

Antigrowth attitudes in Boca Raton have turned real profits for Arvida. But have they served the interests of the region's citizens? Probably not. Boca Raton has simply pushed its housing needs onto the surrounding communities. Regional planning is sorely needed.

While the growth cap issue was still pending, the governor came forward with a framework for regional planning through the Developments of Regional Impact (DRI) law. Florida has been one of the few states to introduce this landmark legislation, which requires the application of a regional perspective to issues of land use planning. Ironically, my experience in Boca Raton had made me possibly the only developer to support DRI. Local opposition had made it impossible for my company to create an industrial base, however, and neither could we offer moderate-cost housing opportunities, to a region very much in need of both.

Unfortunately, DRI has not yet fulfilled the expectations of its supporters. Instead, it has functioned as another layer in the bureaucracy for turning down projects already approved by communities. But the theory of DRI is excellent, and it's a step in the right direction, toward the real regional planning process that's urgently needed for future growth management efforts.

Charles E. Cobb, Jr., is president and chief executive officer of Arvida Disney Corporation in Miami, Florida. His contribution to this book is drawn from an address he made at the ULI/Lincoln Institute seminar on growth management issues.

GROWTH MANAGEMENT STUDY OF BOCA RATON

ECO NORTHWEST, INC.

B oca Raton, located in Palm Beach County, Florida, occupies a 10-by-110-mile urbanized coastal strip between the Atlantic Ocean and the Florida Everglades. Situated 20 miles south of West Palm Beach and 20 miles north of Fort Lauderdale, Boca Raton was originally a town of single-family houses developed around the exclusive Boca Raton Country Club. An estimated population of 53,728 lived in the city's 31-square-mile area in 1977. (Of that population, one person in every 43 was reputed to have been a millionaire.) The 1970-estimated median age in the city was 42.6 years (as compared with 32.3 for Florida and 28.1 for the nation), with 23.4 percent of the population 65 years old or older (as compared with 16 percent for Florida and 9.7 percent for the nation.) Boca Raton's subtropical climate attracts retirees, tourists (especially those drawn to the five-star Boca Raton Hotel), and amenity-oriented light industry (notably, an IBM plant with 2,700 employees). The trades and the service, construction, financial, and real estate industries are directed to these groups. In-migration is the overwhelming cause of the county's increase in population from 228,106 in 1960 to 348,993 in 1970.

The population of Boca Raton increased at an annual rate of 15.2 percent between 1960 and 1970, and 12.1 percent between 1970 and 1975. (Nineteen seventy, however, was the year of a major annexation.) The city's booming construction industry built about four multifamily units for each single-family house from 1970 through 1973.

THE CONTROL MEASURES

In 1972, citizens concerned with the rapid growth and the quickly changing character of the city formed a group committed to controlling population, in order to prevent "the destruction of our way of life in this lovely city." The group initiated a charter referendum limiting total housing units to 40,000. This limitation on housing units, together with an average household size of 2.6 for Boca Raton, would allow an approximate total of 105,000 city residents. The proposed referendum passed in 1972.

An interim technique was implemented to allow sufficient time to develop lower-density zoning categories. A 45-day moratorium on building permits and subdivision plats was instituted and later extended for a total of 17 months. The moratorium required all housing proposals, except those for single-family and duplex units, to be reviewed by a special moratorium-variance advisory board (MVAB) before permits or plat approvals could be obtained from the city council. The review was to determine if the proposed project conformed with the interim rules established by the city council. During the moratorium, the city planning staff developed lower-density zoning categories consistent with the mandate of the charter referendum, and submitted them to the planning board. Then, following its procedural requirements, the planning board approved these "remedial rezonings" or "cap implementations," and recommended that the city council approve them. These rezonings became the interim rules and served to guide the MVAB's reviews.

The city council adopted final zoning revisions in 1974. Although some densities remained unchanged, others (for instance, the multifamily density) dropped by 50 percent; several areas zoned for residential use were rezoned for commercial or industrial use. A new zoning district was created—the recreational district—which allowed 0.5 dwelling units per acre for land currently in golf courses though previously zoned for higher densities. Before this rezoning, the city had passed an ordinance providing periodic review of the cap, and resubmission of it to the electorate every two years. A subsequent proposal to increase the total number of building permits by 4,000 failed to receive voter approval.

Boca Raton also followed an open-space procurement policy, in order to enhance and implement its population cap policy. The city purchased outright 74 acres of beachfront property, through a $20 million bond issue. The zoning in these areas would otherwise have allowed the building of an additional 1,300 housing units. These areas are now used as public beaches and are among the few beach areas north or south of Boca Raton's original city limits *not* given up to intense development.

According to a city estimate made in June 1979, the zoning allows for an eventual 38,400 to 40,000 dwelling units, depending upon the specific zoning districts and densities that will eventuate in vacant areas. A goal of the 1979 comprehensive plan is to maintain an overall low-density residential character. (The city zoning currently allows an average of 3.1 dwelling units per acre.)

THE RESERVE AREA

To the west and northwest of Boca Raton are unincorporated areas, designated as reserve areas, that are likely candidates for annexation to Boca Raton. The total reserve area now has 1,500 dwelling units built on it. The city recently attempted rezoning the reserve area in a manner similar to and compatible with the city's zoning. The county zoning allowed higher-density development, and the county was issuing large numbers of building permits. In the subsequent court action, brought by the county to avoid complying with the city's rezoning and comprehensive plan, the court upheld the county's right to zone the area as it wished, even if its wishes were incompatible with the city's zoning. This ruling suggests that cooperation is strictly voluntary between the jurisdictions, although the city will have to contend with the consequences of development upon annexation. Ths reserve area has a potential for 37,045 dwelling units at buildout, assuming its current zoning designation and an average density of 5.5 dwelling units per acre.

In 1977, the average price of a single-family, three-bedroom house in the city was $62,000 and in the reserve area, $67,000; condominiums were $60,000 in the city and $50,000 in the reserve area. The 2,905 rental units in the city (with only a 2 to 5 percent vacancy rate) had average monthly rents of $220 for one-bedroom units and $305 for three-bedroom units.

Tremendous growth has occurred in this entire southern portion of Palm Beach County, as in the northern section of Broward County, immediately adjacent to and south of Boca Raton. This has been especially true since the completion of I-95. The highway reduced commuting time from the unincorporated Boca Raton reserve area to Deerfield Beach (in northern Broward County), when compared with the commuting time to Deerfield Beach from unincorporated areas west of it. (Deerfield Beach is presently the second fastest-growing community in Broward County.) This circumstance has generated growth pressures on Boca Raton's reserve area.

THE RESULTS OF THE MEASURES

Howard Head of the Florida Atlantic Builders Association feels that the growth management policies have 1) driven the price of land "sky-high" in Boca Raton and surrounding areas; 2) slowed growth in the city proper; 3) pushed development into the reserve area, where the city has no jurisdiction; and 4) threatened to force a probable increase in Boca Raton's tax rate—although the building permit fees have subsequently been raised to offset this probable increase. Harry Posin, a housing-market research consultant for Goodkin Research in Fort Lauderdale, stresses the importance of the completion of I-95, and of the extreme price sensitivity of the second-home and retirement housing markets, as influences on the growth in Palm Beach and Broward Counties. He believes that, because of the general attractiveness of many locations in the region for retirement or second homes, a $2,000 difference in price between two locations will shift demand for these types of housing to the less expensive location.

Areas near Boca Raton, particularly Del Ray Beach and Boynton to the north, are now attractively priced, relative to Boca Raton and its reserve area. As a result, Del Ray Beach has had an increase in population from 19,915 in 1970 to 36,242 in 1977 (an 8.9 percent annual compound growth rate). Housing demand's sensitivity to price is demonstrated in part by the number of building permits for single-family and multifamily dwellings issued in various areas, as shown in Figure 1.

FIGURE 1
RESIDENTIAL BUILDING PERMITS IN THE BOCA RATON AREA

	Del Ray Beach		Deerfield Beach		Boca Raton		Palm Beach County	
Year	Single-Family Dwellings	Multi-family Dwellings	Single-Family Dwellings	Multi-family Dwellings	Single-Family Dwellings	Multi-family Dwellings	Single-Family Dwellings	Multi-family Dwellings
1975	45	27	44	105	206	247	1,985	2,253
1976	133	290	46	1,094	216	285	3,597	3,250
1977	565	1,456	150	2,500	332	123	6,766	7,383
1978	548	1,711	353	1,160	685	469	9,506	11,235

Source: State of Florida, *Building Construction Annual* (Tallahassee: State of Florida).

LITIGATION

The population cap was contested in state and federal courts by a development corporation owning undeveloped property where the allowed density had been halved by rezoning. A Florida circuit court ruled in 1975 that:
- The charter amendment of 1972 violated state and federal constitutional guarantees of due process;
- The city ordinances implementing the population cap were invalid;
- The small-town character the cap was intended to preserve no longer existed in 1972;
- The cap was arbitrary, and passed without the benefit of support from professional or scientific studies;
- The 50 percent reductions in density approved in 1974 were exclusionary and placed a burden on surrounding communities to provide amounts of low- and moderate-income housing that they could not accommodate.

The city appealed the decision, but the lower court's opinion was upheld by the district court of appeals (1977). The city again appealed, and a decision has yet to be reached by a higher court. Meanwhile, the revised zoning densities that were passed in 1974 remain, and the cap survives. According to Mark David, senior planner for Boca Raton, the city fully intends to pursue appeals in federal courts, if the current appeal fails. Howard Head estimates that Boca Raton has spent approximately $500,000 in legal fees, including $80,000 in expert witness fees to the Home Builders Association, which testified for the plaintiffs in the original court suit to overturn the reduced-density zoning. (Mark David adds that it is interesting to see the plaintiff—Arvida Corporation—advertising residences in "wonderful, low-density Boca Raton".)

ECO Northwest, Inc., prepared this report in 1980 for the planning department of the city of Eugene, Oregon.

PART II.

GROWTH MANAGEMENT TIED TO INFRASTRUCTURE SUPPORT

One of the most celebrated cases in the growth management literature involved the town of Ramapo, New York. In 1969, after seeing a virtual doubling of its population in 10 years, Ramapo adopted a new ordinance requiring a special permit for residential development. Each permit called for the residential site to be located in an area served by a specified level of community facilities: sewerage, drainage, parks, roads, recreational amenities, and fire stations. In addition, the community formulated an 18-year capital improvements program to install these facilities in the 60 square miles of developable land contained in the unincorporated part of the township. Through this time-phased system of controlled development keyed to the provision of public facilities, the town hoped to avoid rampant, random development. In 1972, in *Golden* v. *Planning Board of Town of Ramapo*, the court of appeals, the highest court in New York, upheld the action of the town.

By an ironic twist of fate, Ramapo jettisoned its own system in 1983 to stimulate a new interest in growth. Its capital improvements program had fallen prey, first, to the costs of repairing the damages suffered in several severe storms, and, second, to a lack of intergovernmental cooperation. Nonetheless, the Ramapo case had set the stage for many communities' decisions to tie growth into their available infrastructure capacities. Among those local governments having the most extensive experience in the uses of this technique are San Diego, California, and Montgomery County, Maryland. Both jurisdictions have formulated comprehensive and complex plans for growth. Both have adopted a panoply of special zoning, subdivision, and other regulations to implement those plans. And both are still experiencing continuing political tensions over growth and its impacts.

In this section of the book, five papers and articles discuss the experiences of these two communities through the years. With regard to San Diego, Michael Stepner describes the framework of planning that discouraged development outside the city's urban service limit, and George Colburn discusses the issues connected with this and other planning initiatives. Then, concerning Montgomery County, Maryland, Norman Christeller charts the ways in which the county requires infrastructure as a precondition to development. Joseph Clancy offers a developer's viewpoint on how that system works. And finally, an excerpt from a citizens' task force report reveals how the county's growth management process still creates controversies.

Douglas R. Porter

SAN DIEGO'S SYSTEM: IS IT WORKING?

MICHAEL STEPNER

S an Diego—with a population of 1 million and an area of over 350 square miles—is the eighth largest city in the United States. Located in the south-western corner of the nation, San Diego is bordered to the east by mountains and desert, to the west by the Pacific Ocean, to the north by Camp Pendleton Marine Base in Orange County, and to the south by Mexico. San Diego is a city of contrasts: it is not as densely built up as many other large cities, but its nodes of high intensity are separated from each other by many square miles of suburban development. Yet the city still has 20 percent of its area in undeveloped lands.

The community's residential growth management plan became official with the adoption of the San Diego Progress Guide and General Plan on February 26, 1979. Before that, the program had consisted of a collection of policies, studies, and discussion documents that had each resulted from an attempt to deal with an immediate problem of rapid growth and development. Not until the 1970s did "growth management" become, in my opinion, a euphemism for planning.

BACKGROUND

Early Days

In 1967, after years of study, citizens' referendums, and efforts toward adoption, the city's first general plan in 40 years was approved by the city council. The plan, although very general by today's standards, did attempt to focus on San Diego's future growth. It was not followed up.

But the growth itself continued. And in pursuing my own history of that growth, and of the measures taken in the 1970s to rein it in, I have drawn upon the outline given in Bill Rick's 1978 article in *Urban Land*. Because of the usefulness of that summary, I have followed it pretty closely.[1]

---

[1]William B. Rick, "Growth Management in San Diego," *Urban Land*, April 1978, pp. 3ff.

In 1970 and 1971, San Diego grew rapidly by means of a number of new suburbs along its fringes. The suburb of Rancho Bernardo attracted both national attention and an Economic Development Administration grant for industrial development. (Also in this northern section of San Diego are Rancho Penasquitos, in which the Teamsters' Pension Fund invested heavily, and the upper-income community of Scripps-Miramar Ranch.) Nineteen seventy saw more than 5,000 housing starts, and 1971, 10,000.

Part of San Diego's housing boom included the subdivision of Mira Mesa. Started in the early 1960s, Mira Mesa had floundered through bankruptcy and lack of buyer interest; had graded its streets; and had laid its sewer and water lines. But no houses were built until the late 1960s. As close-in sites became exhausted, Mira Mesa became the one place in San Diego with houses below $20,000.

Unfortunately, not all facilities and services were available. No parks existed within the whole area; elementary schools and fire stations were converted homes; the high school was 10 miles to the south and becoming overcrowded by any standard; and the main connection to San Diego—U.S. 395—was congested during the morning and evening hours.

As this pressure on facilities and politicians began to build, the city council continued to approve plans for additional new communities in that part of the city— Lago Dorado, 3,500 homes (1970); Chicarita Creek, 4,000 homes (1970); Carmel Mountain East, 6,000 homes (1971); and Carmel Valley, 6,250 homes (1970). Applications had also been made for others.

Planning Efforts of the Early and Mid-1970s

In 1971, the planning department began an update of the general plan, in accordance with the city council's policy, which requires such review in five-year increments. The plan was to be updated and strengthened, in order to meet the growing concerns over the form that San Diego's development was taking.

In December of 1972, Pete Wilson took office as mayor. In his first state-of-the-city message, one month later, he summarized his program:

> What will be the shape of San Diego tomorrow? This one question raises a host of others. [For instance,] the exciting and challenging requirement that we revise and update our general plan . . .
>
> But also involved will be the continuing necessity to seek, in the courts and in the legislature, the clear authority and tools needed to permit the *city, rather than the developer, to determine the timing and location of new development.*[2]
>
> The need to impose controls upon development is imposed upon us by two related but distinct problem situations.
>
> First is the ill of existing residential developments (sic) that were permitted to proceed, even though they had outpaced the abilities of the city and its school districts to provide adequate essential services. . . .
>
> The second problem . . . involves . . . development in areas within our city limits, but so far out on the fringes that if services can in fact be provided, it will only be at a cost to the city that far outweighs any increase it adds to the tax base.

Wilson's first major battle was over an effort to place a building moratorium on Mira Mesa. The effort was met by massed "hard hats," picketing the council chambers. The overt effort failed, but the council did enact policies that required public facilities as prerequisites to development approvals.

At this same time, the planning department held a series of town meetings throughout the city, to find out what the citizens wanted, and thus to help deter-

---

[2]Stepner's italics.

mine the direction the general plan should take. Few of the meetings were well attended, and if there was any consensus, it was that the city had grown enough—the status quo should be retained.

These moves paralleled an effort by the Sierra Club to have a proposition put on the ballot that would limit growth to the national average. No new permits were even to be issued until the rest of the country caught up with us. But the proposition failed to get signatures because the formula it used to calculate growth was too complicated.

With the results of the community meetings and with the mayor's policy stated, the city staff embarked on a program to revise the general plan within a growth management framework. To assist them in this effort, the staff retained Robert Freilich—attorney and professor at the University of Missouri, Kansas City—who had been involved in the Ramapo, New York, plan of limiting development according to a plan of limiting capital facilities. His philosophy and successful record had caught Wilson's attention. With the city council's support, the mayor engaged Freilich in June 1975.

Within my space allotment here, I can only take note of Freilich's assistance to San Diego. But the fact is, he became increasingly influential—even controversially so. Bill Rick's interesting coverage of the local dramas of the 1970s, however, gives some details of Freilich's involvement and viewpoint.[3]

With a consultant's aid, then, the city hoped, neither to limit growth nor to allow it to proceed unimpeded under a different mantle, but to *accommodate* it in a manner sensitive to the particular needs of San Diego—with special reference to matters of timing and phasing.

A Temporary Paradise?

The city's goals received reinforcement in 1974 and 1975 from the release of a report entitled *Temporary Paradise?: A Look at the Special Landscape of the San Diego Region.* This report—prepared by noted city planners Kevin Lynch and Donald Appleyard, through a grant from San Diego's Marston family—was a regional reconnaissance of the San Diego area. It was not a plan but a sketchbook of ideas and issue-identifications. Topics covered included the valleys and the canyons; the sea coast; the existing communities; the major centers; the question of "Growth where?" and "What kind of growth?"; the methods of "getting about town"; and the "Mexican Connection."

Temporary Paradise? was built on people's perceptions of their community, as well as on an analysis of the factors that have made San Diego what it is. Although the report was not adopted by the city council, it was widely distributed (30,000 copies) and became the structural framework for the general plan, and the basis for subsequent policy and ordinance development.

The growth management battle came to a head in late 1976, with the presentation of an interim growth management ordinance, which would have limited building to the older sections and to selected suburbs. It would also have designated environmentally sensitive areas as not-to-be-developed.

The business community demanded to know the economic and social costs of growth management. With the council's concurrence, and with funding from the construction industry, the chamber of commerce appointed an oversight committee in January 1976. At the same time, the city council contracted with several consultants—besides Freilich—for economic, social, and environmental studies of the growth management program.

---

[3]William B. Rick, op. cit.

In a series of meetings and at various forums, the proponents and opponents became more polarized. Gradually, it became clear that the major issue was the interim "Tier III" map, which would have divided suburban areas into two zones: one that might be developed, and another that could not be developed for 18 years.

Mayor Wilson's decision was to split the policy question from that of the map, and on July 20, 1977, the city council adopted a residential growth strategy for San Diego. In August 1977, the planning commission assigned the interim ordinance and its maps to oblivion.

RECENT HISTORY

Between August 1978 and August 1979, the general plan was readied for public hearings. Hearings commenced before the planning commission in September 1979, and the city council adopted the plan on February 26, 1980.

The land use element of the new general plan divides the city into four distinct categories:

- *Urbanized Communities.* Those older sections of the city (by California standards)—namely, those built before 1965. The objectives for these communities stress the conservation of the social/environmental characteristics, and the rehabilitation of deteriorating neighborhoods.
- *Planned Urbanizing Communities.* The areas where development has begun but has not yet reached the buildout point. The objectives for these sections mainly involve supporting the additional public investment necessary 1) to complete their development, and 2) to allow the growth of those subareas within them that are already served by capital facilities. Land is opened for urbanization in contiguous stages, through the orderly extension of public facilities, and the provision of housing for a variety of income levels.
- *Future Urbanizing Area.* Land that is now vacant and, for the most part, zoned for agriculture. This land is to be held as an "urban reserve" and released for development as the planned communities are built out, or as chances to further the city's land use goals arise.

Many sections of the city might be characterized as "anywhere, USA," or at least as "anywhere, Southern California." (In fact, rumor has it that the TV series "Simon and Simon" was forced to leave San Diego because the city made too boring a backdrop.) But this impression is relieved to some extent by the ocean and by the open spaces. The latter are the components of a popular municipal conservation system, which constitutes the fourth category of San Diego land:

- *Open Space.* The canyons, hillsides, and mesas that San Diego is blessed with, throughout its confines. These landscape features are preserved through purchase, dedication, and control.

The city is further subdivided into more than 40 individual and distinct communities. These range in size from 50 acres to 15 square miles; they are defined, not only by natural and manmade features, but also—perhaps most importantly—by emotions and perceptions. Each of these areas has a council-recognized planning group.

The city is further diversified by nature, in that it spans some 26 climate zones. This results in some widely differing weather patterns throughout the city.

PRESENT CONDITIONS

Currently, San Diego has a population of 1 million. The county population is some 2 million, and the nearest neighbor to the south, Tijuana, may have a population as large as 1 million.

San Diego now has a growth rate of 2.25 percent per year. At this rate, the county will have a population of 2.7 million by the year 2000, and the city will have 1,250,000 million. Tijuana, which has 1 million residents now—most of whom are approaching childbearing age—should have 2 to 3 million by the year 2000.

Major variables other than city policies do bring about this kind of growth in San Diego. These include:

Inflation, Interest Rates, and the Economy. Even minor changes in interest rates dramatically affect both the availability of mortgage money, and a household's ability to undertake a mortgage or other such obligation. Furthermore, interest rates on construction loans significantly affect housing costs.

During the early 1970s, the country experienced a severe recession. By 1980, it was apparent that the recovery had resulted in far greater growth than anticipated by San Diego's 1976 projections.

Housing Costs: Rising Faster than the Cost of Living. In recent decades, the costs of building materials—particularly those of lumber and cement, labor and land—taken together with the costs of construction loans, have made the cost of housing rise faster than the cost of living. This means that people's ranges of choice of housing have significantly narrowed, particularly in Southern California, where the average cost of a new home runs about twice the national average.

Population Shifts to the Sunbelt. Since the 1960s, a major shift in population has occurred from the northeastern to the southern and southwestern states. Although this trend was most marked in the early 1970s, it continues today.

Population Shifts within the Sunbelt. Shifts are occurring within the Sunbelt, too—in response to local conditions. The I-15 corridor in San Diego, for example, is attracting high-tech industries from other locales in California because of its pleasant environment and competitive rents. Another such shift involves the growing number of employees in Orange County who can no longer afford to live there, and who are seeking housing in San Diego, as in other cities outside Orange County.

Changing Household Sizes and Lifestyles. Nationally, as well as in San Diego as a whole, average household size continues to decline, and two-income households to increase. Such changes influence the sizes, types, and locations of homes sought.

In some communities within San Diego, the opposite trend in household sizes has occurred because of increases in the immigrant population.

Immigration (Legal and Illegal). Because of its location on the United States/Mexico border, and because of its nearness to the port of Los Angeles, San Diego is particularly attractive to immigrants to the country. These households differ widely in size, in number of school-aged children, and in other characteristics, from other local households.

Ownership Patterns of Undeveloped Land in San Diego. As of 1983, 68 percent of the vacant developable land in the city's Planned Urbanizing Communities was owned by only 12 developer/landowners. Among the largest of these 12 landowners are two major Canadian corporations, and several corporations that have operations extending throughout California and other portions of the United States. The decisions of such landowners as to when and how to develop their landholdings are determined at least as much by corporate considerations in other parts of the country or the world, as by growth incentives or disincentives established by the city of San Diego.

Proposition 13. "Proposition 13" serves here as an umbrella term for several amendments to the state constitution and to local laws that have acted, starting with Proposition 13 itself in 1978, to limit city revenues and to control growth in such revenues over time. If it were not for Proposition 13—and for the city's Proposition J, and the state's Gann Initiative—greater capital and operating funds would be available for community facilities and services.

As a result, the city's ability to carry out its goal of raising the levels of its facilities and urban services has been severely curtailed.

SOME ASSESSMENTS AND STATISTICS

The growth management program has worked with some degree of success in accommodating growth, while still maintaining the "quality of life when."

When the growth management plan was formulated, the overall city growth rate for 1980 through 1985 was predicted to be 9 percent. The actual growth rate for the same period is now estimated at 11 percent.

Growth for this period largely took place in the Urbanized Area—an eventuality running counter to expectations. It had been anticipated that the population of the Urbanized Area would rise by a mere 7,800 (or 1 percent) for the years 1980 through 1985. In fact, however, the increase will probably have approximated 63,900 (9 percent). In contrast, the Planned Urbanizing Area's population had been projected to grow during the same period by 65,000 (43 percent); its actual growth, however, should only have amounted to the considerably lower figure of 32,700 (25 percent).

DISCREPANCIES

Population growth had been due both to new housing development and to socio-economic changes that have altered family sizes. In the Urbanized Communities, for instance, new housing was responsible for about 57 percent of the population growth between 1980 and 1984, with increased family size accounting for the other 43 percent. In the Planned Urbanizing Area, on the other hand, new housing development caused almost 90 percent of population growth, while changes in family size only added a little more than 10 percent.

Both the slowdown in the development of the Planned Urbanizing Areas, and the simultaneous, faster-than-expected growth of the older Urbanized Communities, partly ensued from national economic trends and from the differing characteristics of the housing projects in the two areas. The major recession in 1980 and 1981 badly hurt the abilities of large-scale suburban builders to satisfy market demand. Smaller-scale infill development was less affected and, in fact, was accelerated to meet the pent-up demand for housing. As the national economy recovered, the local development pattern appears to have moved back toward that of previous years, with growth in the Planned Urbanizing Area predominating.

Recently, concerns about growth in the older neighborhoods, about the quality of growth in the newer ones, and about the pressures to allow growth in the Future Urbanizing Area—again made the city's growth management program a topic of heated discussion—in limited circles, of course. And, as usual, the concerns conflicted.

THE TASK FORCE

Because of these divergent preoccupations, the mayor set up a "blue ribbon" growth management review task force in January 1984. The task force consisted of 12 members who together represented a broad cross-section of the community. Their charge was to review the general plan and to determine how well it had been working. (The Lincoln Institute was called upon to assist in these efforts.)

Findings: Infrastructure

Important questions to be considered were, "How well have facilities and services been phased and provided for?" and "How have they been funded?"

The task force concluded that facilities and services had indeed been adequately phased and provided for within the Planned Urbanizing Area. Specifically, this conclusion followed from the responses to a survey questionnaire prepared by a consultant and distributed to a random 5 percent of residents within the Planned Urbanizing Communities of Rancho Bernardo and Mira Mesa. (The consultant felt that these two communities were reasonably representative of those within the Planned Urbanizing Area.) With only one exception, all of the eight community services tested—schools, parks, libraries, police protection, fire protection, public transit, freeways and highways, and local streets—were rated "good" or "very good" by most respondents in both communities. The sole exception was "public transit" in Mira Mesa.

On the other hand, public facilities and services within the Urbanized Communities are and will continue to be underfunded because of existing and projected revenue shortfalls.

The capital costs of facilities and services supplied by the city have traditionally been funded from a variety of sources. Within the Urbanized Area, the city's capital improvement program has always given the funds for parks, libraries, transportation, drainage, recreation facilities, and fire stations (new construction and remodeling). In addition, some park fees, as well as federal and state grants, have gone toward infrastructure improvements.

Within the Planned Urbanizing Area, on the other hand, capital funds for public facilities and infrastructure have been derived through use of special fees and park fees; cost recovery districts; state and federal grants; special assessment districts; development impact fees; facilities-benefit assessment districts; and the provisions of the Subdivision Map Act.

Although within the Urbanized Area, the funding of school capital facilities has fallen to the school districts themselves, in the Planned Urbanizing Area, school facilities are funded both by the school districts and by developer fees, in those sections where the city requires letters of school availability. The funding of freeways and of other state highways has continued to be the responsibility of Caltrans in all districts.

Findings: Forms of New Housing

The form of development—single-family versus multiple-family—has differed materially between the Urbanized and Planned Urbanizing Areas in recent years. From 1980 through 1984, single-family dwellings constituted 20 percent of all units completed within the Urbanized Area. For the same time period, singles accounted for 36 percent of all completions within the Planned Urbanizing Area.

REPORT OF THE
GROWTH MANAGEMENT REVIEW TASK FORCE
SAN DIEGO, CALIFORNIA
(Summarized Excerpt)

VI. Other Significant Related Issues, Problems, and Proposals

During the task force's deliberations, a number of issues, problems, and proposals surfaced that, while not squarely within the scope of the mayor's charge, were nonetheless felt to warrant greater public exposure. Typically, these were not matters of original discovery on the part of the task force; however, the latter did feel an obligation to underscore their importance and thereby to promote public discussion and, ultimately, corrective action. Their presentation below is in no particular order of priority:

1) *Preemption of designated industrial lands by commercial and other non-industrial uses.* The task force affirmed the findings of previous studies as to the detrimental effects of the usurpation of planned industrial areas by nonindustrial uses. Further, the task force considered that remedial measures must probably include the application of more exclusive industrial zones; and that the city "should continue being an active participant in the industrial development business," because "public agencies may be the only participants with sufficient holding power to carry the burdens of major new industrial development."

2) *Need for large (minimum, 20 acres) industrial parcels.* The task force decried "the consistent lack of [industrial] site opportunities for large-acre users." It concluded that such lack would "continue to force local industry, as well as anticipated new companies, to look toward other competing regions of the country"; and recommended that newly zoned industrial property be required "to provide a 20 percent reservation for large-parcel users over a 10-year time frame."

3) *Need for the city to be a direct participant in the industrialization of Otay Mesa.* The task force concluded that "current land use strategies . . . may economically preclude the ability of [Otay Mesa] to generate sigificant employment opportunities for the South Bay labor market." Consequently, it recommended that the city should work with property owners/developers of the Otay Mesa industrial area, to the end that land costs may be establishable at levels comparable with those of competing industrial areas.

4) *A plan for North City.* The task force found that North City, including the city's sphere of influence, represents "the most significant demand for high-end use in the industrial market for office, R&D space, and technology-based industry." In view of this strong industrial interest attaching to North City, it was felt desirable that certain basic planning determinations be made. Therefore, the task force recommended that a generalized land use and phasing plan be prepared for the entire North City area.

The reasons for this recommendation include the realizations that: a) pressures for urbanization within the Future Urbanizing Area are great and can be expected to increase; b) there may be a need to increase industrial land availability; and c) historically, the land planning process for major new areas has been in a broad range, but on the order of 10 years, more or less. The generalized land use and phasing plan would also allow the study of land use interrelationships and help to avoid what might otherwise later be seen as planning mistakes. Such a plan would also tend to shorten the lead time necessary to bring developable land to market, once it had been determined that such land should be shifted out of the Future Urbanizing Area.

5) *"Pay-as-you-grow" versus increased housing costs.* The task force recognized the inherent dilemma in pursuing a "pay-as-you-grow" financing policy in the Planned Urbanizing Area: namely, that the imposition of assessments and exactions on new development inevitably translates into higher housing costs and prices. Nevertheless, it felt that continuation of this financing policy was mandatory for the foreseeable future.

6) *Desirability of differing public facility standards for the Urbanized and Planned Urbanizing Areas.* The task force concluded that, "Due to financial and physical limitations and other factors, public facility standards applicable to suburban Planned Urbanizing Area communities cannot feasibly be applied to Urbanized Area communities." Consequently, it recommended that city staff undertake a thorough study of public facility standards to determine the differentials between the Planned Urbanizing and Urbanized Areas that might reasonably be established. Such a study could be undertaken in conjunction with the upcoming comprehensive review of the city's general plan.

7) *Requirement for phasing and facility financing plans.* In view of the city's overriding responsibility to assure an adequate level of public services and facilities as growth occurs, the task force recommended that realistic phasing and facility financing plans be required components of all Urbanized Area community plans, as well as of all Planned Urbanizing Area community plans.

8) *Need for regional planning cooperation and coordination.* The task force clearly recognized that the city's growth management plan operated within the context of the San Diego region; and that it both impacted upon, and was impacted by, adjacent jurisdictions. In fact, unless fairly high degrees of interagency cooperation and coordinated planning were achieved and maintained, the city's growth management efforts could well be substantially negated.

9) *Increased attention to natural resource preservation.* As urbanization proceeds, lands containing natural resources of special value will come under increased urbanization pressures. Yet, as the city grows, retention of these values takes on greater importance. The task force recommended that special attention be given to floodplains, canyons, and other steep slopes; special vegetation and wildlife; and all other natural resources of unique value to San Diego.

10) *A higher priority for urban design.* The task force believed that the potential of urban design to affect positively the quality of life for all San Diegans must be more generally acknowledged and effectively realized. To further these ends, the task force recommended that the city's urban design program be adequately funded, and that urban design staff be enabled to participate at an early stage in the planning and design of all public projects.

11) *Need for an expanded mass transit system.* The task force fully supported the related propositions that: a) a balanced transportation system is critical to enhancing the quality of life for San Diegans by "avoiding future congestion, providing all options of travel, and

minimizing air pollution"; and b) an expanded mass transit system is essential to San Diego's achievement of a balanced transportation system. Consequently, the task force recommended strong, continuing efforts to develop local funding sources and implementation mechanisms that will hasten the realization of an appropriately expanded system. The mass transit plan should be implemented sufficiently in advance a) to allow various planning projects and community plans to be modified to accommodate proposed transit facilities, and b) to assure that transit facilities are operational in time to meet (rather than to lag behind) the transportation needs that will accompany population growth.

12) *Need to facilitate private development approvals when proposed development is consistent with relevant plans.* As an important means of fostering plan implementation, the task force recommended that city staff be directed to facilitate the processing of private development proposals that are clearly consistent with approved community or other relevant plans.

13) *Need to provide balanced land use mixes.* Continuation of the significant increases in housing costs that have occurred in the recent past will hurt the city's ability to maintain a balanced industrial base. This base affords a wide range of job opportunities. Accordingly, the city should have a continuing program to provide a cross-section of housing opportunities throughout the city. Housing should be conveniently located near the employment base, taking into account physical constraints upon development.

14) *Need for community plans to assure implementation of the growth management plan.* The task force recognized that the individual community plans are the principal planning documents for implementing the general plan and, hence, the growth management plan. Accordingly, the task force recommended that each community plan

Findings: General Success of Growth Management Measures

The main question of growth accommodation has continually arisen—namely, "Does the plan sensitively limit future growth, rather than artificially constrain the land available?"

To this general question, the task force's answer was a qualified "yes." In terms of the raw numbers for projected population growth, market demand, and land inventory, there is more than sufficient capacity in the community plans in both the Planned Urbanizing and Urbanized Areas to accommodate population growth and its attendant needs for additional housing through the year 2000.

As noted, the "yes" answer was qualified, however. Although sufficient capacity exists to accommodate future residential growth, the realization of that capacity appears likely to effect marked changes in the types and locations of future housing development.

Historically, residential development in San Diego has occurred predominately on vacant, relatively level land. As the supply of such land has diminished, many new projects have required revitalization activities and raised densities on previously developed sites.

The task force recommended that future housing development remain within the capacities of the adopted community plans. If necessary, housing capacity should

should include a growth management element, so as to assist community residents in developing an improved understanding of what growth management means to their community, and of the community's relationship to the citywide growth management plan.

15) *Need for improved plan implementation and monitoring.* The task force was strongly aware of the need to maintain plans in as updated a status as practicable, in order that they may serve more effectively. Consequently, it recommended that the city's plan-monitoring capabilities be significantly advanced, and that necessary plan adjustments be promptly identified and processed.

16) *Need to monitor public perceptions.* The task force further recommended that surveys of the public's perceptions of levels of community services and of the quality of life be regularly undertaken, and that the results be incorporated within the city's development monitoring system. Also, the city should survey residents of the five monitored communities to find out their suggested reasons for the perceived decreases in quality of life in their own communities.

17) *Need for ongoing monitoring and evaluation of the growth management plan.* The task force recognized that the various forces to which the growth management plan responds are dynamic. As these forces continue to evolve, the growth management plan should be monitored, both to assure its implementation and to evaluate its effectiveness. To these ends, the task force recommended, first, that in 1989, the growth management plan undergo a second comprehensive examination modeled after the current task force review; and, second, that the planning commission retain an independent consultant to conduct an annual audit of the city's planning activities to determine their conformance with the growth management plan—with a report of that audit to be returned to the planning commission for public discussion.

be increased in the Planned Urbanizing Area, or lands should be shifted from the Future Urbanizing Area. Some communities in the Urbanized Area are among those most in need of economic revitalization, of upgraded facilities, and of better services, but not necessarily of additional housing and population growth. Great care must be taken to assure that efforts toward accomplishment of the city's goals of preserving natural canyons, hillsides, and manmade amenities do not founder—especially in the Urbanized Area.

Data and Recommendations: Land Availability

To the question, "How much vacant, developable land remains in the older Urbanized Communities?," the task force responded with the following data:

As of November 1983, about 11,800 gross acres of vacant land zoned for residential use existed in San Diego. However, of these acres, only 3,101 were relatively level, and less than half of them (1,349 acres) were in the Urbanized Area.

Projections indicate that by the year 2000, San Diego will need 100,000 more dwelling units to accommodate its population growth.

Even though the inventory of vacant lands might suggest where some of the additional units could be built, it does not paint a complete picture. Some existing residential neighborhoods are underdeveloped, compared with their planned and zoned density designations. Redevelopment of these neighborhoods to higher densities could accommodate some of the future growth. In addition, rezonings are anticipated, in places where community plans call for residential use but where current zoning is for nonresidential use. Both redevelopment programs and rezonings, therefore, could add to the pool of land available for new construction.

The Report's Projections

A comparison of projected housing needs for the year 2000 with the current levels of residential use reveals that only 60 percent of the total citywide capacity has been built. That is, 363,500 units exist today, although the capacity is 535,300 units. This leaves an unused potential of some 172,000 units, which will be more than enough to provide for the year 2000's demand for 100,000 homes. No encroachment upon designated open spaces will be called for.

Unsurprisingly, the data confirm that major changes will occur in future housing development patterns. Whereas more than 60 percent of new housing during the last five years has been built in the Urbanized Area, an analysis of community plans suggests that only about 26 percent of the total of future development will occur there, through the year 2000. The Planned Urbanizing Area will, therefore, assume a much greater role.

In addition, it should be noted that, though the Planned Urbanizing Area is only 35 percent built out, the Urbanized Area is about 81 percent built out. The remaining 19 percent of capacity in the Urbanized Area is projected to absorb more than 26,000 additional housing units by the year 2000. The city's goals for additional housing and for environmental preservation may well begin to conflict, as efforts are made throughout the city to accommodate this growth. So these goals must be carefully balanced.

The task force concluded its work with 91 recommendations for future actions. Happily, these fall into only four major categories: 1) infrastructure financing; 2) quality of life; 3) community development capacity; and 4) industrial development. (A summarized excerpt from the report accompanies this article.)

UPDATE

The growth management program has set criteria for opening up the Future Urbanizing Area on the bases of need, or of overriding benefit to the city. In July 1984, these criteria were put to a test. The city council gave the developers of a 4,000-acre parcel the go-ahead for planning. This decision rested heavily on the developers' promises of industrial development and of a "Christian university." But the proposed project split the community. Signatures were gathered for an initiative that appeared on the ballot in November 1985.

In the event of the initiative's success, *all* proposals for development in the Future Urbanizing Area would need voter approval. Proponents of both sides of this issue used the same slogan: "No L.A.! Vote No [or Yes] on 'A'."

As it happened, the initiative passed—by a 2-to-1 margin.

Meanwhile, San Diego's growth management program—with all of this give-and-take, and with all of its citizens' input—is working well. And, judging from the direction in which these activities are heading, the program should continue to work well.

Michael Stepner is assistant planning director for the city of San Diego. His contribution to this book is drawn from an address he made at the ULI/Lincoln Institute seminar on growth management.

SAN DIEGO: BEYOND SPIT AND POLISH

GEORGE A. COLBURN

I n San Diego, everyone in a position of power must cope with the legacy of Pete
Wilson, mayor for 11 years of this sun-drenched city on America's southwestern
tip. The main element of that legacy is a political and governmental policy of
"managed growth" that was supposed to settle for at least a generation the emotional matter of new construction in the city's undeveloped areas.

Thought by some to be a precise roadmap that would validate the city's long-time
boast of being "America's Finest City," the growth policy was seen by others as
merely a set of flexible guidelines that could be changed whenever local governing
bodies recognized new realities.

The battle over these conflicting interpretations of managed growth will come to
a head November 5 [1985], when the city electorate votes on an initiative proposition aimed at stopping encroachment by city council action into the northern part
of the "urban reserve," 20,000 acres that were to remain undeveloped until 1995.
[And, in a late-breaking development, the current mayor has been hanging on to
his job by a thread.]

Another major aspect of Wilson's legacy was his vision of a revitalized downtown,
including a new convention center on San Diego Bay. Wilson set events in motion
that have pushed that vision close to reality, and today all elements of the city seem
to be united on the desirability of changing the downtown landscape dramatically.
In a frenzy of self-congratulation, these elements joined hands in August to open
the Horton Plaza Shopping Center, a bold, $180 million, six-block development that
the architect refers to as nothing less than an attempt "to reinvent the American
city."

All around the shopping center, development abounds—new housing, a historic
district, hotels, office buildings, and the like. Under the smooth and innovative
leadership of Gerald M. Trimble, the Centre City Development Corporation (the
city's redevelopment agency) has invested some $120 million in incentives to stim-
ulate $3.5 billion worth of projects in its 300-acre domain over the past 10 years. As-
sessed valuation has grown from $92 million to $559 million, while the tax take has
increased from $1 million to $6 million, and is expected to rise another 30 to 40
percent by 1990.

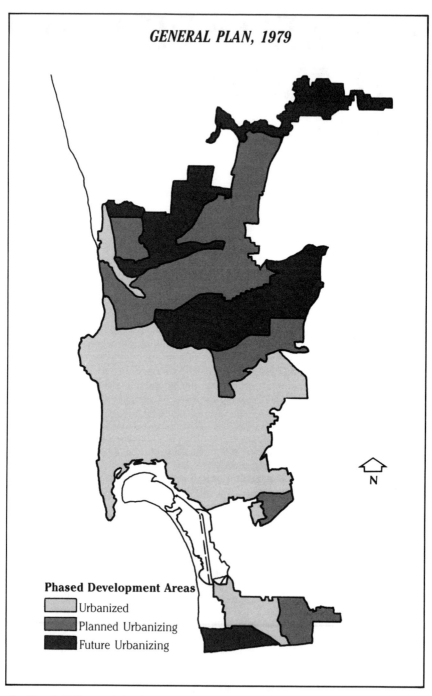

GENERAL PLAN, 1979

Phased Development Areas

Urbanized
Planned Urbanizing
Future Urbanizing

N

San Diego's 1979 general plan indicates the urban reserve (shown as "future urbanization") that has generated so much controversy.

Trimble, who says he thinks of himself as a developer rather than as a bureaucrat, refers with pride to the business deals he has made for CCDC with developers who have taken advantage of the city incentives. For example, as part of the deal on Horton Plaza—where the city invested some $40 million—the developer is giving the city 10 percent of the average rent for the 170 shops, 25 percent of the parking revenue, and 10 percent of the net cash flow on office space.

By 1988, the new convention center will be opened. Already dubbed by city boosters in national ads as "The Meeting Place of Your Dreams," the dramatic structure on the bay, by Canadian architect Arthur Erickson, will have more than 340,000 square feet of exhibit space and could draw up to 400,000 conventiongoers into the city annually—spending some $200 million and creating 4,500 new jobs. The new center will allow San Diego to compete with cities like San Francisco and Atlanta, and to go after big events like the national political conventions—finally putting behind the memory of the loss of the 1972 Republican convention even though Richard Nixon considered it his "lucky city." Despite all that, though, city voters had made it clear on several occasions that they didn't want to pay for a convention center. Finally, the cash-rich San Diego Unified Port District came up with a plan to build the center and lease it to the city for $1 a year.

In fact, the entire city is booming, giving the impression to an outsider that San Diego will have to work hard to avoid being overwhelmed by the success of its own publicity campaign to the rest of America. With a population of almost 900,000 and an annual growth rate of about 2.6 percent, it's already the nation's eighth largest city, second in California only to Los Angeles. Unemployment is a respectable 6.2 percent, while employment rose last year by 55,600 jobs—a hefty increase compared with national averages—and a figure of particular interest to the city's 150,000 Hispanics, most of whom live in the southern sections closest to the Mexican border.

- In the northwestern section, a short distance from the Pacific Ocean and just east of Interstate 5, a whole new community for 40,000 residents is being built. Nearby, the presence of the science- and technology-oriented University of California at San Diego, the Salk Institute, and the Scripps Institution of Oceanography has led to an influx of corporations connected with what San Diego calls the "sunrise industries"— e.g., the health-related, biomedical, and computer industries.
- To the east, the "Golden Triangle" of shopping centers, office buildings, and residential communities continues its rapid growth.
- Along Interstate 8, the city's main east/west corridor (and only a few miles from downtown), the Mission Valley area has received city council approval for major new commercial, industrial, and residential development.
- Further east, along the Interstate 15 north/south corridor, major developments are underway that will bring jobs, even more office space, and modestly priced housing into what was once a remote fringe area.

THE POLITICIANS

But dealing with the forces that stimulate growth, while still keeping faith with the managed growth philosophy, has not been easy since Republican Wilson got himself elected to the U.S. Senate in 1982. His successor, Roger Hedgecock, 39, a first-rate politician (also a Republican) and environmental activist, and a supporter of Wilson's policies, was thought by many the perfect man to handle the pressures and demands of the mayor's job in the 1980s.

But, only a few months into his term, the new mayor was accused of taking $350,000 in illegal campaign assistance from a group of friends who were involved in an investment scam that rocked the city last year. Mastermind of the bogus operation that swindled some 1,000 San Diegans of $80 million over a six-year period was J. David Dominelli, already sentenced to 20 years in federal prison.

Although under indictment, the mayor won election to a full term over almost token opposition in 1984. Then, last February [1985], his trial ended with a jury locked, 11 to one, for conviction on charges of conspiracy and perjury. The trial obviously weakened Hedgecock's standing with the voters and led, at least indirectly, to the November 5 ballot issue, which seriously divides city residents.

With almost daily publicity on the charges against him—and the Dominelli scandal fascinating the entire city—Hedgecock could not deliver the votes in the summer of 1984 to stop council approval of a scheme allowing 5,100 acres of the urban reserve to be opened for the construction of a graduate-level Christian university and a linked 750-acre industrial park. The council's five-to-four vote to approve the La Jolla Valley development, in a remote northeastern section of the city, also provided approval for a major residential development on the site—after 1995, the earliest date set for opening the reserve.

The council action—which, in one stroke, allowed development of one-sixth of the total urban reserve—dismayed many residents, including the environmental coalition that proved its clout in the Wilson era and during the Hedgecock campaigns.

As far as the city's planning director, Jack Van Cleave, is concerned, the entire urban reserve should be left alone until at least 1995. Of the city's total 211,000 acres, almost 81,000 are considered "urbanized" for general plan purposes. Another 67,500 are planned for urbanization. The entire urban reserve currently consists of almost 31,00 unplanned acres, plus another 32,000 acres controlled by the military.

Van Cleave, who has been director for the last six years, and with the department for 38 years, says the staff recommended denial of the La Jolla Valley project "because the case boiled down to [the developers'] argument that there was a need for industrial land in the city. Our study indicated that such land was not needed." The proposed university, Van Cleave points out, may be considered by city agencies at any time in any area under a conditional use permit. Van Cleave also notes that the ongoing controversy over La Jolla Valley puts a considerable strain on the already overtaxed resources of the $5 million planning department and its staff of 120, including 45 planners.

While Van Cleave's position puts him in league with environmental groups like the Sierra Club, which led the drive for an initiative, he is bothered by the fact that planning decisions for the urban reserve will be in the hands of the voters, rather than the city council, if voters approve Proposition A on November 5. The mayor, however, had no such qualms. A bad eight-to-one loser in the city council on the issue of approving more development in the already sprawling Mission Valley (which includes the recently enlarged San Diego Stadium, home of the football Chargers and baseball Padres), Hedgecock vehemently endorsed the proposition.

He expressed outrage, for example, at the fact that in the six years since the growth management plan was adopted, the council had changed more than one-third of the northern urban reserve to the status of "planned urbanizing" area—thus allowing development to move forward there.

Like Mayor Wilson before him, Hedgecock couched his position in economic terms, so as not to unduly alarm Republican backers. He claimed, as Wilson did, that the city's budget could not handle the strain of providing services in outlying areas without damaging services in built-up areas. He and his citizen allies, who gathered more than 75,000 signatures in a few weeks to force the November 5 ballot issue (which would reverse the city council approval of La Jolla Valley), said there was plenty of room in the city's designated "urbanized" and "planned urbanizing" areas to accommodate steady growth over the next decade.

If votes didn't take a hand in the planning process, the mayor said, the council would continue its "slaughter of the urban reserve," making it likely that San Diego would become "just a slightly smaller version of Los Angeles." Indeed, that thought became the slogan of the proponents of the November 5 initiative vote: "No L.A.! Yes on 'A'."

Then, on October 9, initiative backers almost lost their main supporter. The mayor's second trial ended in a conviction on 13 counts, several of them felonies. California law ordinarily would have forced him to resign his office. Soon after the conviction, however, allegations of jury tampering became public, and the mayor said he would stay in office until the issue was resolved.

Still, most political observers believe the initiative proposition will pass, despite a well-financed "education campaign" organized by building industry leaders. Before Hedgecock's conviction, a private poll showed Proposition A leading by three to one. With the most visible backer of the proposition now preoccupied with the effort to overturn his conviction, and the "anti-A" forces readying a counterattack, the final vote could be close. No one expects the initiative to lose, however.

THE DEVELOPMENT GANG

Hedgecock had claimed openly that the campaign to defeat the initiative proposition was being financed "by the usual gang of developers who had so successfully controlled city council decisions" and didn't want to lose that control to the voters.

A key player has been Louis Wolfsheimer, Peter Wilson's planning commission chairman and a leading architect of the growth management concept and plan. A lawyer for the church group seeking to build the university in La Jolla Valley, and a member of the San Diego Unified Port District Commission (which is building the long-awaited convention center), Wolfsheimer believes that Wilson's concept of "infilling" the city's developed areas "has worked too well." In his view, the intensity of development (fueled by city incentives) has led to a breakdown of public services in the older parts of the city. He also notes that land is so scarce in these older areas that many of the canyons that give San Diego a special topographical beauty are being destroyed by new construction.

Wolfsheimer argues that the mayor and his allies see the growth management plan as something "set in concrete." Yet, he says, when the plan was developed in the mid-1970s and finally incorporated into the general plan in 1979, it was intended to be flexible. "Now we are short of industrial land, and if we cannot accommodate those who want to build here, we will have missed the boat," and the tax base and jobs that could be provided by such industrial development will merely "leapfrog" into the unincorporated areas.

Wolfsheimer, who came to San Diego from Baltimore 22 years ago, says he perceives an "elitist mentality" among the anti–La Jolla Valley forces now working to keep out newcomers. "And some politicians pander to this attitude," he claims.

In the wheeling and dealing that led to council approval for La Jolla Valley after the planning staff and commission turned it down, Wolfsheimer and his client— Campus Crusade for Christ—agreed to postpone the residential element in the plan until 1995. Still, he thinks it makes no sense for the city to stop residential growth while housing is being built all around it in the unincorporated areas of San Diego County. "North County residents come into San Diego, where the jobs are, but the city gets no tax money from this growing commuter population, which clogs our main highways every day."

Allied with Wolfsheimer on the La Jolla Valley project is another city resident with clout. William Rick is chairman of the port commission and head of Rick Engineering, the company begun by his late father, long-time planning director for the city until the mid-1950s. Rick's firm directed a study for Campus Crusade that claimed there was a pressing need in the northern part of the city for industrial land such as that proposed by his clients. Rick contends that, had it not been for the distraction of the area's previous owners, the Teamsters' Pension Fund, when the city revised the general plan in 1979, the La Jolla Valley would not have been part of the urban reserve at all.

Another advocate of La Jolla Valley is Mike Madigan, the senior vice president of the Pardee Construction company, a division of Weyerhaeuser Real Estate and a major builder of residences in San Diego. Madigan, a former aide to Mayor Pete Wilson, helped cut the deals that led to Wilson's solution of the growth issue that divided the city in the 1970s. But today, he says, "Growth is no longer the issue. The issue is *how* the city will grow." Madigan claims that the city's plans for its developed areas are no longer valid. "Unless you build on steep hills, in the canyons, and tear down a lot of older structures, the development potential in the urban areas is now severely limited," he says.

And, according to Madigan, the city has failed badly in the urban reserve because it has not figured out what to do there despite the passage of six years since growth management became official city policy. The general plan, he notes, is a compilation of 30 or so community plans that represent the thinking of small subareas, all with their own limited views of what the city should do. Thus, it represents "macrothinking" and is outdated. Instead of allowing itself to get in the position of reacting to someone else's plan for the La Jolla Valley, he adds, the city should be considering how the area fits into the broader picture. Madigan suggests that the general plan should be updated every five years, if San Diego is to cope coherently with the reality of ongoing growth.

George A. Colburn is a freelance writer based in New York City. He spent eight years of the Pete Wilson reign as a resident of San Diego.

This article is excerpted from the November 1985 issue of *Planning*. Reprinting is by permission.

WRESTLING WITH GROWTH IN MONTGOMERY COUNTY, MARYLAND

NORMAN L. CHRISTELLER

Just to say a little about the setting of Montgomery County: it lies to the north and northwest of Washington, D.C. The county extends to about 500 square miles, with environments ranging from highly urbanized employment centers to rural farmland. The population in 1984 was 610,000, distributed among some 228,000 households.

Before World War II, Montgomery County was very little developed. There were a number of railroad commuter villages and rural communities, and some suburbs near the District of Columbia. The first major spurt of development in the county occurred, as it did in so many places in the country, after World War II, when a very fast growth rate quickly made the county one of the principal bedroom communities surrounding Washington.

In our more recent experience, our growth has included considerable amounts of economic development, and we have, in fact, become an employment center in ourselves. Instead of being a bedroom community, we now have a significant share of the employment of the region. Of our 331,000 employed residents, for example, some 60 percent now work within the county—a far cry from the days when all of them commuted into Washington.

And, in fact, the number of people commuting into the county daily exceeds the number commuting out of it.

LAND USE HISTORY

Montgomery County boasts a long history of land use planning. In 1927, the Maryland-National Capital Park and Planning Commission was established to serve both Montgomery County and its neighboring county, Prince Georges, which lies to the east and south of Washington, and borders on some of the Virginia suburbs.

This commission has had two double-barreled functions: 1) to develop and operate a park system for each county; and 2) to adopt and maintain a plan for the physical development of each county.

The planning boards from the two counties make up the commission itself. The board members each serve in the dual capacity of member of the bicounty commission and member of the planning board for his or her own county.

Our own present general plan was written more than 20 years ago and derived from studies for a year-2000 plan for the region. Recognizing the important role of the radial transportation corridors serving Washington and the region as access routes to the central city, the general plan prescribes that development outside the urban ring around Washington be directed into the I-270 corridor in the western part of the county, and into our (U.S 29) portion of the I-95 corridor in the eastern part of the county.

The general plan has been called a "wedges and corridors plan" because one of its main aims was to preserve the wedges between the corridors—to preserve them in agriculture and in open space, with some low-density residential use.

In the jargon of the planners and civic activists of that day, one of the purposes of the general plan was to prevent or at least to manage suburban sprawl. Until then, most of the county had been zoned for half-acre residential uses, interspersed with retail and service/commercial islands. The general plan, as updated in 1969, remains the foundation of the county's policies for managing growth and development today.

Now, this was necessarily a generalized set of land use policies—a strategic plan, if you will, for housing and jobs, communities, transportation, and environmental preservation. To convert it into an effective guide for the county's development, it was necessary to add much more detailed comprehensive plans for the various geographic subareas.

Besides these revised comprehensive plans, over the years, we have refined a rather complex and sophisticated system of planning and zoning tools. In particular, we have developed more flexible zoning tools than before: a highly successful set of performance zones for central business districts; an effective form of inclusive zoning that is producing a good amount of moderately priced housing; and an agricultural and open-space preservation program that uses transferable development rights to preserve indefinitely the agricultural sections of the wedges.

Now, concurrent with the fashioning and application of these new regulatory tools came changes in the form and content of the county government. In 1948, we had become a chartered county under Maryland law; this redefinition gave us a high degree of home rule. And this, our first charter, provided governance by a county council and an appointed county manager.

In 1970, a fundamentally overhauled charter went into effect, providing for an elected county executive and a separation of powers between the executive and legislative powers of the council. One of the important features of this change was the continuation of the past stipulation that the county council have the final responsibility for land use planning, as well as for zoning and subdivision regulations.

But perhaps, for the purposes of this seminar's present concern—infrastructure mechanisms—the most significant aspect of that new charter was the requirement of a six-year capital improvements program and a six-year public services program, in addition to a comprehensive annual operating budget. Thus it was that, in the early 1970s, the planning board set out to research and implement a growth policy for Montgomery County.

THE FIRST GROWTH POLICY STUDIES

As board members, we had come to recognize that the comprehensive planning program we were just putting in place was intended to *accommodate* growth, and

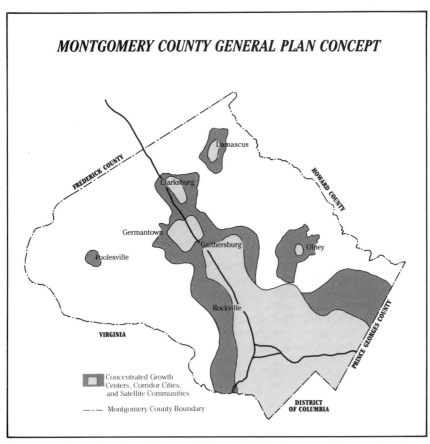

MONTGOMERY COUNTY GENERAL PLAN CONCEPT

Damascus

FREDERICK COUNTY

HOWARD COUNTY

Clarksburg

Germantown

Gaithersburg

Olney

Poolesville

Rockville

VIRGINIA

PRINCE GEORGES COUNTY

Concentrated Growth
Centers, Corridor Cities,
and Satellite Communities

——— Montgomery County Boundary

DISTRICT
OF COLUMBIA

Montgomery County has planned to concentrate growth in the lower part of the county, where it can also concentrate its investment in infrastructure.

to manage it only to the extent needed to moderate its ill effects. But the new growth policy studies were an attempt to go beyond that and introduce a new element into the system. For want of a better term, we refer to it as "staging."

Until then, our principal efforts had been quantitative, qualitative, and geographic. That is, we had addressed the location of development, the quantity of development, and the quality of development. But we had not addressed the timing of development, nor had we adequately addressed its public costs.

I should note that these policies were coming into being at a time when we had a fair number of citizens saying we had a choice, and that we could and should close down the borders of the county to any further growth overspill from Washington or even Baltimore. There was a mentality that we have sometimes called the "gangplank mentality": "I'm on board; pull up the gangplank."

The planning board and the county council at the time insisted that we were a part of the metropolitan region, and that its growth pressures, which were natural ones for the nation's capital, must be shared by the entire region. The only responsible policy was to control and manage that growth, and neither to attempt to prohibit it nor to allow it to proceed without direction or moderation.

Meanwhile, these no-growth pressures were rising in a great many communities across the nation. In many ways, these pressures had valid bases on the part of the people who were expressing concern about the effects of development on their own communities: on their quality of life, and on their environments. They hoped to preserve their quality of life by restricting the community benefits to residents who were already there. In fact, I had several exchanges with these advocates at the time, in which I asked, "Where would you expect your children to live?" One of my respondents was frank enough to say that if the policies that I was espousing were to continue, she wouldn't want her children to live in Montgomery County, and I was quick to point out that if her policies were espoused, they wouldn't be able to live in Montgomery County.

FACILITIES PROVISION AND TIMING

We felt, however, that there must be a middle ground that would allow the county to accept its share of regional growth while still protecting its quality of life. And this is really what we were seeking in the growth policy studies that extended over a period of some seven years.

For instance, there was the new element of staging. At the time of these new policy studies, in the early 1970s, the county also received an important new tool from the state. This was a new state law requiring each county to develop and maintain its own 10-year water and sewerage system plan. This law gave the local officials more effective control over the location and timing of extensions of water and sewer lines. It became an important element in our comprehensive master plans because we were able to rely on this functional plan to establish some control over the timing of development.

Early during our studies of growth management, the planning board proposed, and the county council enacted, an important amendment to the subdivision regulations, known as the "adequate public facilities ordinance." This was to be the principal mechanism by which we would coordinate the timing of private development with the timing of the public provision of the infrastructure needed to support it. In its simplest form, the adequate public facilities ordinance directed the planning board to reject a requested subdivision of land unless the board could find that the public facilities would be adequate to serve it.

The ordinance directed the planning board to examine eight specific public facilities and services, in order to determine their adequacy to serve proposed development. These facilities were water supply, sewage disposal, roads, transit, schools, police protection, fire protection, and health clinics. And we were to address these questions at the time we were reviewing preliminary subdivision plans—fairly early in the development review process, perhaps two to five years before development was likely even to begin.

The planning board was also directed by the ordinance to take into account the facilities that had been included in the approved six-year capital improvements program and, of course, the demand from all previously approved developments, as well as from the proposed subdivision. So, when considering transportation facilities, for instance, the planning board must compare future traffic against future transportation capacity.

Earlier, I touched briefly upon the fact that the 10-year plan for the water and sewerage system was a useful staging device at the "macro" level for controlling the buildout of comprehensive master plans. These plans are end-state plans, and obviously, they cannot all be built out immediately. The 10-year water and sewerage plan also serves at the "micro" level: we have established that, under the adequate public facilities review, if the land area has not yet been designated as appropriate for extension of sewer and water lines within the next few years, the subdivision is ineligible for approval anyway. The exceptions, of course, are those subdivisions to be developed on wells and septic systems; these call for separate measures of approval.

A CASE IN POINT: ROADS, HIGHWAYS, AND TRANSIT

The major focus for the past decade has been on the transportation element of the plan. It must come as no surprise to anyone that this has been the major concern. (Although, recently, the growth pressures in some of the newer nodes in the county have begun to divert our attention to questions of the adequacy of school facilities.)

But, with regard to transportation, the planning board originally looked to the nearby intersections and did a form of site impact analysis. The board used published trip-generation rates for each type of development and for all other approved developments; made estimates of trip distribution; then assigned the traffic to the local streets near the proposed subdivision. If there was a problem with one of these intersections, the facilities would be found to be inadequate.

And the planners used, as their standards for measuring, the "D" level of service in the urban sections, and the "C" level of service in the rural ones. Well, it soon became evident that neither the measurement technology nor the systems analysis was adequate. There were a number of problems.

Four New Problems in the Last Ten Years

One problem arose out of the fact that the pattern of development involves points of concentration surrounded by expanses of lesser concentration. Now, if a level-of-service traffic standard is used that requires the same rate of flow for every major intersection, this practice implies that the highway engineering will be such that there is a significant increase in the highways' capacities near every point of concentration. The level will be kept the same everywhere.

And it is possible to do just this in many cases. But then the question arises: "Can we really pave over all of the surroundings of a concentrated development?" Actually, from a cost standpoint, if from no other, we will have to accept somewhat greater congestion near a development concentration than would be desirable elsewhere.

A second problem we have become aware of is that we cannot achieve perfect equilibrium between public and private developments for extended periods of time.

Basically, we have recognized that private development occurs in relatively small increments, while new or expanded public facilities entail relatively large increments. We cannot maintain the two in perfect equilibrium all the time. The only way to do that would involve citizens willing to have the county build the facilities well in advance of the need. And I might add that the willingness would even have to evolve in advance of the *perceived* need: in general, the voters oppose public expenditures until they perceive the need for them.

So, we in Montgomery County have concluded that we had to build into the system a range of tolerance whereby these counterweights could be held within reasonable balance, without their having to achieve absolute balance all of the time. And we felt that attaining this balance would help us respond to some of the measurement shortcomings we had identified. Imbalance accounted for our inability to measure accurately and to predict traffic down to every intersection. And it accounted for the variability in the traffic. One of the other things we felt we had to build into the system; then, was some consideration of this tolerance range.

Yet a third problem we were encountering was that the system we were using did not allow for the "downstream effect"—the way in which development outside an immediate locale we were looking at was going to be sending some traffic through that locale. We had to find some method of taking this into account. We could not do that under the system whereby we were just looking at the nearby approved development and at the proposed subdivision, and then trying to measure only their own traffic effects.

Fourth, we recognized we were probably being too lax in the way we were counting the program's public facilities. At the outset, we had said that anything—any expenditures for a road in the capital improvements program—would mean we could count that road. We soon came to realize that we had to shorten the cycle on that, and say that we could only count it if 50 percent of the construction funds would be spent during the first six-year period. After all, we knew that that would mean the road would usually be completed within seven years, sometimes eight.

Subsequently, we have decided that even this cycle needs to be tightened, and now we will only count a project in the capital improvements program if it is 80 percent funded. Essentially, this puts us in the position of saying, "There's traffic on the road within the six-year period," because by "80 percent," we mean 80 percent expenditure during six years, and there is usually at least 20 percent expenditure after the traffic is actually on the road.

Two New Levels of Evaluation

Having identified these problems, the planning staff put in many long hours restudying how to deal with them. My own standard comment about this is, if you don't like the system, blame the planning board, and if you do like it, give the credit to the planning staff. They're the ones who really did the job of developing a workable system.

Policy Areas. The basic system we use now involves two levels of examination for any given subdivision. The first level is a policy area or "traffic shed," for which we determine the total amount of new development that could be accepted. If the subdivision clears this obstacle, it may then be tested for its more localized impacts on intersections or road lengths.

The policy areas were established with reference to transit availability. We took a hard look at where transit lines would run in the county. (Remember that at this time, Metrorail was in the process of building its subway system for the region, and, fortunately for Montgomery County, the major line on our western side is now complete. We are still awaiting completion of the line on the eastern side, but we took that into account in establishing the levels of transit availability.) We recognized that the Metrorail lines were fed by a system of feeder buses, and also by some additional regional buses, in corridors where Metrorail would not be provided.

But the point here was to see that, where there was greater transit availability— that is, more available alternatives to auto travel—then in those places, we should be able to tolerate greater congestion than in places with lesser amounts of transit service. Thus, we set policy areas and established what the areas would be set up for, in terms of the kinds of congestion we could permit.

Now, to deal with that, we had to develop a statistical method for determining average levels of service in a given subarea. In each case, we were dealing with what we call a "traffic shed," which is a policy area served by a network of roads among which traffic flow shifts. As congestion occurs in one point, the traffic tends to shift to other points. As stated earlier, we were concerned that we could not maintain identical levels of service at all intersections; therefore, we felt we had to go to some kind of an average system. So, we established for each of the policy areas an acceptable average level of service for the road system that was a counterpart to the transit. In short, we permitted more congestion where more transit was available.

Thus, the policy areas were set up in order to aid in measuring the traffic.

Measurement of Actual Traffic Amounts. In dealing with measurement, we take all of the existing traffic, plus all of the traffic that would come from all approved developments, and compare this sum, first, to the existing traffic capacity and, second, to the capacity as increased by the roads within the six-year capital improvements program. If we find that there is more capacity than will be used by all of the existing approved developments, then we can set a threshold amount of additional traffic that can be accommodated. That extra capacity is a number that has come out of a rerun of the statistical model. This process of determination also entails a judgment factor: we consult the zoning recommendations of the master plans to see how much of the new development can be residential, and how much can be employment development.

The first aspect of a master plan we consult is its zoning ceiling. This is the amount of development that could occur within the zoning recommended by the master plan. Second is the so-called "threshold," which is the total amount of development that can be handled by the capital improvements program. And third is the "pipeline," and that, of course, is all of the development that has been approved but has not yet been built. And we put these against our current forecasts, using both a high and a low forecast of future development—our present projections of the amounts of household development and of employment development that will occur during the coming years.

The thresholds in particular have become integral parts of the regulatory process, in that they are the first considerations that the subdivision must look to. If, in fact, some capacity still remains, then either the subdivision is approved, or it goes on to the second level of review. But if no capacity remains in the vicinity, then the board is charged with denying the subdivision at that time.

I will come back in a moment to some alternatives to denial. But if a subdivision does pass the large-scale screen of the threshold analysis, then it faces a smaller-scale screen to determine whether it must be examined at the local level. Basically, this step involves questioning whether the development is a significantly sized one, that is, 1) whether it will generate enough trips for us to measure their impact on a given intersection; 2) whether there is a nearby critical intersection or roadway operating at the "D" level of service or worse; and 3) whether the planned development would bring the level of approved development in that area to within 5 percent of the threshold.

At this point, further study might be called for. The county might have to analyze the impacts of the existing development, of the proposed subdivision, and of all the other approved developments, on the most critical intersections.

In effect, this system has us looking, first, at the large scale and, second, at the smaller scale. Now, what happens if a developer fails to pass this local review? Frankly, the planning board's first posture is that we are required by law to disapprove the subdivision. In most cases, the developer, when faced with this outcome, has asked, "What can I do to avoid this delay?" Normally, we have had to say, "You have to wait until the county or the state can provide the road improvement." In most cases, the developers have found that the cost of holding the land indefinitely while awaiting that public action is probably greater than proceeding to help, or, in fact, to build the improvement themselves.

We have had several cases of intersection improvements' being provided by developers, in order to avoid denials based on failing intersections near their proposed projects.

Now, what happens if a developer does not even get this far? What happens if there is no threshold? For instance, we have had a few cases in which the master plan for one of our corridor cities has said that the threshold is clearly going to be a problem for some years.

The Road Clubs

In these cases, we have allowed the developers to join in consortiums to build major roads that the state would have been unable to get to for a number of years. We have come to call these arrangements "road clubs." By means of a road club, we once approved a huge number of residential units and a large amount of commercial development, contingent upon the applicant participating on a pro rata basis in the construction of Maryland Route 118 from the I-270 interchange for a mile and a half into the communities—which entailed an improvement of a two-lane road into a six-lane road. So, we expect major improvements from a road club. But these clubs do make a big difference in the county's ability to handle a new development.

The road club idea has been used in many parts of the county. The example just described was the largest one by far. But there have been a number of cases of three or four developers' joining together to prepare major intersection improvements, or to accelerate a road that was not going to be in either the county's plans or the state's plans.

Recently, we have also recognized that we cannot solve these problems forever with new roads or wider roads. We are going to have to have other methods of reducing the commuting traffic. In one case, in one of our corridor cities, a proposal came in to build an apartment complex. We had to say that there was no threshold there, and that there was an intersection problem. That developer is now dealing with the threshold problem by devising a program that will take at least the number of cars *off* the road that his development will be generating. He is soliciting, encouraging, and maintaining a ridesharing program. And it is so calculated that, within two years of the opening of the apartment complex, 100 cars will be taken off the road during the peak hour and in the peak direction. And the developer will maintain that program over a 10-year period.

To the best of my recollection, to do that, he will have to deal with the residents of some 7,500 dwelling units, in order to guarantee achieving that minimum result of at least 200 people joining car pools—or more than 200, if there will be more than two people to a car.

The county is also using residentially based van pooling, commercially based van pooling, and a number of other familiar techniques for solving the traffic problem when it cannot be solved with physical improvements to the road system. These are among the alternatives now being used by the development community in the county to respond to the problems it faces if the county's capital improvements program is not moving fast enough to meet its needs.

Transportation Results

Now, how is the system working? Well, it depends on one's point of view. From the standpoint of the development industry, it is primarily working a hardship because the program is forcing greater costs on developers to avoid the delays that might otherwise occur. On the other hand, many people in the civic community would say, "It's not working well enough because we still have congestion." I will return to these problems shortly.

One of the other indications of the system's success or failure is, however, that it is making the capital improvements program much more credible on paper and much more responsive in practice. In the early years of this system—we now know by hindsight—the capital improvements program was really just a wish list, and nobody was really planning to build all the roads they were saying they were going to build. Until just a few years ago, the county government was spending only about 50 percent of what it had claimed it would spend.

What has happened lately is that the county now has two groups of watchdogs on this matter. The planning board regularly reminds the county government that it (the board) has been relying on these roads in approving new subdivisions, and that failures to build the roads are causing the increased congestion. In addition, the development industry reminds the county that it (the industry) needs more roads within the capital improvements program, to prevent the developers' facing a moratorium.

Because of the two watchdogs, I think we have a much more answerable capital improvements program. We are putting a large quantity of money into roads. The latest capital improvements program had, I believe, some $250 million to build roads over a six-year period. Partly, this big allocation resulted from our remarkably high growth rate.

This takes me back to my remarks about the civic community. During the 1970s, when we had yet to assemble this system, we were faced with the problem that many roads were being counted on by the planning board in approving subdivisions but were not being built. Partly, this was just because the system was unsophisticated, and partly, it was because the state was quite simply running out of money for roads. During the period of highest inflation, of course, the state highway programs throughout the county were having great difficulty in keeping up with both road maintenance and road construction costs. The state road program fell about 10 years behind, relative to our needs.

Fortunately, a few years ago, the legislature did take steps to increase the gasoline tax and to make it a little more inflation-sensitive. This move helped the state to come back into the roadbuilding business that it had almost entirely left. But at this moment, we are still catching up. We have many approved developments coming onstream, and the roads are now being designed and built, but they are not there yet. So, we hear a lot of complaints from residents who are battling congestion while commuting.

I might add, people go out to buy a house, look at the houses on Saturday and Sunday, and never go visit them during the peak traffic hours during the week. Therefore, it comes as a great shock to them when they move in and, the next week, discover how long it is going to take them to get to work.

Right now, the county council has before it proposals to clamp down more severely on near-term development through limitations on the numbers of building permits to be issued. The planning board has real problems with some of the probable side effects of this kind of proposal, but at least, the proposals are attempts to deal seriously with an existing problem—namely, that until the roads are more in balance with the development that has already occurred, unrest will continue within the civic community.

THE SCHOOLS

As mentioned earlier, another planning dilemma is the schools. For many years, the school system indicated to us, mostly by saying nothing, that it had no problem with handling the effects of new development. To some degree, it was enabled to react so naively by Maryland's state school construction program, which has implied a promise that the state will build almost all of the new schools. Last year, however, the state's school construction program would have proved insufficient to cover more than one-fourth to one-third of the school construction needs in Montgomery County alone—to say nothing of those in the other 23 counties in Maryland.

So, obviously, the state school construction program really cannot be relied upon, and the county will have to face the cost of new schools itself—as it has, in fact, done for some time.

Although we have developed a highly sophisticated means of measuring traffic and of relating it to projections of future road capacities, the board still suffers over school capacities. These are different. As we keep trying to explain to the county council, when we do a traffic study, we do not have to know the ages of the drivers. But when we do a school study, we have to worry about the ages of the school-children because we are looking at elementary schools, middle schools, and senior high schools. And each component changes every year. Somehow or other, those kids get a year older every year.

If someone moves out of a given subdivision, and someone else buys the house and moves in, the traffic will probably not change. The new occupants of that house are probably going to have about the same impact on the traffic as the old ones did. But, quite possibly, the new residents are bringing in elementary-school kids, while the old residents are removing high-school kids from the system. Household changes, then, do affect the schools more than they do the transport picture.

For some months, the board has been struggling with a method of dealing with this school issue—an agreement with the school board by which the latter accepts a certain amount of flexibility in its system. The school board would agree to estimate whether a given subdivision would adversely affect a given elementary school, whether that school would become overcrowded, and whether nearby elementary schools could handle the overflow.

Another kind of responsibility that we have been urging upon the schools is that of noticing the results when they change their policies on what they call the "articulation" between elementary school, junior high school, and high school. The grade-level organization changes when a school district goes from a junior high school to a middle school. These changes can influence a district's ability to handle new development. So, articulations are no longer moves that the districts can make without considering the impacts on development.

I cannot give you the final answers on the school system, other than to say that we have a highly complex and difficult situation there. It is clear that we are going to be under heavy pressure to find a way to deal with it.

CLOSING THOUGHTS

In closing, then, it should be said that Montgomery County has devised a method that tries to keep public facilities and private development in balance. The planning board believes that this method is both appropriate and successful, at least for the water and sewerage systems, and for the transportation systems.

Furthermore, having studied them thoroughly, the planning board is staunchly opposed to the proposals that would tie development down to the fourth decimal place. A system must have a certain amount of slack built into it, and the county's planners are convinced that it is very difficult to try to put this kind of control mechanism in so close to the development stage.

Some people have said, "You ought to do the controlling at the building-permit stage." But can one really expect a developer to get all the way up through grading for roads, and putting in sewer and water lines and other utilities, only to discover at the building-permit stage that the other facilities will be inadequate? It is our belief that developers deserve an earlier finding, and that the public must learn to accept the slack that will arise from our approving some development *in anticipation* of its occurring in phase with facilities provision.

In short, our present job is to persuade the county's policy makers that we can achieve a balance as we look ahead into the future—when, actually, we achieve a balance every week. One can and must accept some imbalance as time goes by, as long as one can know that, within a reasonable time, things will go back into balance again.

Norman L. Christeller chairs the planning board of Montgomery County, Maryland. His contribution to this book is drawn from an address he made at the ULI/Lincoln Institute seminar on growth management.

After Norman Christeller's seminar presentation on Montgomery County's program of growth management through infrastructure mechanisms, the question-and-answer session began and—with some omissions—proceeded as follows:

Niebanck *[as moderator]: "It's as though we're having a planner's fantasy fulfilled in [Norman's telling of] this experiment. The sound general plan leads the transportation plan, leads the capital improvements plan, leads the soft services and the minor infrastructure, and leads the development pattern—with the public and private sectors interacting on small-scale problems with relative ease and conviviality.*

"That overstates it a little, but to some degree, that's the way it comes across. And I'm wondering whether there are normative issues we want to get into that can exhibit the sorts of choices we all recognize need to be made from time to time. Paul? Michael?"

Danish: *"Well . . . Boulder has been coordinating its capital improvements plan with its comprehensive plan for a long time now. In fact, the comprehensive plan is structured so as to divide the approximately 60 square miles of the Boulder Valley into several areas: Area 1, which is the annexed area of the city; Area 2-A, which is an area scheduled for annexation and development within the next, say, three years; Area 2-B, which is scheduled for development at some point during the life of the present comprehensive plan; and Area 3, which is not scheduled for immediate development.*

"By making these distinctions, you can then start budgeting your capital improvements, in such a way that they will be serving the areas where growth can be expected to occur. And the city has been fairly successful in providing these services and—since it started doing this in the early 1970s—has never really gotten into a crunch on services provision.

"One reason for this success is that there has been a willingness to abide by that plan, and not to depart from it everytime somebody comes in with a project that is essentially in violation and says, 'Oh, please build this one. It's a very special case.' Generally speaking, what I've seen happen in nearby municipalities in those cases is that, if it's a small special case, it gets turned down. If it's a big special case, they say, "Let's go for the gold." And the municipality usually gets screwed rather badly in the end because of that. . . .

"On the general problems of traffic and providing for it: perhaps it's the area I live in—the Denver metropolitan area has the highest number of automobile regis-

trations per capita in the United States. It has the second worst air pollution problem in the United States. I got off the plane last night and was astonished by how clean the air was in National Airport's parking lot, compared with Denver's. This, in a western state that originally earned its reputation as a tourist spot because people used to go out there to get well from tuberculosis. Now, they go out there to get lung cancer.

"At present, the Denver metropolitan area, in order to get into clean air compliance and to keep from losing its highway money, has instituted a system of voluntary no-drive days. The first year's experience with this has led to a claimed reduction in vehicle use of 5 percent. I think that's a damn lie. I think it's utter garbage, in fact; the numbers are cooked, but at least, that's what the claim is.

"But, even if you assume that that number is correct, that gain will be wiped out in the space of 12 to 18 months, simply by the normal rate of expansion. And the thing that the citizenry is being told regularly is that, if you don't voluntarily have no-drive days, there will be a legislative mandate of no-drive days. I'd like to see them try it. I think I could guarantee that any public official who tried to do that would be out of office so fast his head would spin. He would, in effect, be subsidizing further growth and development through restrictions on the freedom of movement of people who are already there. And that is not going to wash in the United States.

"I question whether, in any long-term way, you can control growth through roads. I think, ultimately, you're going to have to control growth by deciding whether or not you want to have residential or commercial development built. I think it's very important to have a coordination between comprehensive planning and infrastructure building. But I don't think that that in itself is enough. I think, in the end, if you're going to manage growth, you're going to have to say how much you want, say why you want that much, and then directly control whether or not that growth occurs."

Neibanck: *"Mike?"*

Stepner: *"Thank you. I just have a couple of comments. Something that really struck me personally, and that I must comment on, is the remark by Norm that he likes to pass the word along that, if something works, we praise the planning staff, and if it doesn't work, we give the heat to the planning board. I've always been taught it's the other way around—that the elected official gets the credit, and we take all the heat. But I like his attitude.*

"It's interesting, in listening to these comments on Montgomery County, to see how similar the concerns are across the country. They're the same concerns that we had in Southern California—in San Diego, where I'm from.

"In California, the link between planning and CIP [capital improvements programs] has been in existence for a long time, although we weren't always able to deal with it. And I think that's what gave rise to [the voters' strong interest in] growth management in San Diego. . . .

"It sounds like, in Montgomery County, the way it's staged is that, if the developer's willing to wait, the county will eventually pay for the public facilities, and if he wants to go ahead, he will have to pay for them upfront. It's a luxury that we have not been able to have in California, as a result of a couple of recent ballot propositions. In the last five years, we have had both Proposition 13 and Proposition 4, both of which, essentially, limit the local jurisdiction's and the state's abilities to collect taxes. Today, this means that, in all our newly developing areas—or, as we call them, Planned Urbanizing Areas—the developer must pay as he goes. That is part of the comprehensive plan for his particular area of that town: the capital improvements program is worked out, and so is his share of the capital improvements—and that's everything, from sewers, water, schools, parks, and roads, to public transit. His share is prorated, based either on number of residential build-

ing permits or on equivalent numbers of dwelling units. And he pays into the fund, so that those facilities are in place as his development occurs.

"And one of the things that has happened in the last 20 or 25 years in this country is that people have become unwilling to wait to have a community built up after they've arrived there. They want those facilities in place when they move in.

"We pass all these costs on to the developer, who, in turn, of course, passes them on to the homebuyer. This raises the cost of housing in San Diego, and in California generally, to the extent that it becomes very exclusionary in some places. But it's the people's choice. That's the way the election went, and that's what we ended up doing. The public can or will no longer pay for the facilities that they used to pay for as a matter of routine.

"I will point out a couple of things that we have found. In areas that are 'hot,' the developers are more than willing to pay for public facilities. We are building a transit system in San Diego. The first link has been open for a couple of years, paying its own way. The second link is about to open. We have an area called Mission Valley, where the developers have been brought into a system of density bonuses based on the transit being in place, and it looks like we're going to have the transit running in this 10-mile stretch of the valley long before it's able to connect with anything else in the city. This is because it's a hot area, and developers are willing to put up with that kind of exaction, in order to get their feet on the ground—or get their development on the ground—in order to capture that market."

[Later] **[Audience member]:** *"Mr Christeller, what are your enforcement tools against the developer?"*

Christeller: *"On the road projects, the developers enter into public improvements agreements with the county that are enforceable. In the case of the non-road alternatives, they enter into joint agreements with the county and the planning board that contain in them default clauses so that if, in fact, they're not doing what they've agreed to do, the county will take over each program. The defaulting parties pay specified amounts to the county for the remainder of the time period in question, in order to finance the county's costs in shouldering the management of the program."*

[Later] **Niebanck:** *"But can the public really provide some participation—at least, a responsible level of participation? And are they willing to put up with an exclusionary policy? Norman?"*

Christeller: *"Let me just say that there's no question that the exclusionary issue is going to be one for the public to address. . . . But our policies have not been of such magnitude as to have a major impact on the cost of housing and, therefore, have not been, I think, in that sense, exclusionary. In fact, we have an inclusionary provision in our residential zoning that will assure that at least 12.5 percent of every subdivision over 50 units will consist of moderately priced houses."*

[Audience]: *"Do you see any long-term liability, if you cannot deliver your capital improvements program over a seven- or eight-year period?"*

Christeller: *"Yeah, I'd say there could be some real problems. I didn't have time to discuss what we like to describe as the police power/purse power dichotomy. It's the police power that we're using to regulate the development—to regulate the private sector. And it's the purse power that enables the public to provide the facilities. There's clearly a different set of controlling circumstances. The willingness of the taxpayers to pay for the public facilities is the ultimate controlling factor on the purse side, on the facilities side.*

"The constitutional protections do limit what we can do on the regulatory side. And there's no question that we cannot defer a development indefinitely. We would have to demonstrate to a court that the amount of delay was a reasonable amount, in terms of the public purposes being served. And I spend a great deal of my time

warning the county council and the county executive that we must have a continuing program of facilities provision. Otherwise, we're going to be in trouble—even if we have been delaying the projects, rather than allowing them to be built."

Niebanck: *"Thank you so much, Paul and Michael. And especially, Norman. Norman, my last thought is: Robert Moses had nothing on you."—Editor*

MONTGOMERY COUNTY'S DEVELOPMENT HURDLES

JOSEPH CLANCY

A t the outset, I must say that I agree with just about everything that Norman Christeller said. Unfortunately, my firm, unlike the Arvida Corporation in its experience with Boca Raton, does not seem to have time on its side.

THE PROPOSAL

The Washingtonian Center—the project that I am working on in Montgomery County—stands at the northwest corner of the intersection of I-270—the major north/south artery in the county—with Shady Grove Road. Over 20 years ago, the site was developed with a motel, a golf course, and a high-rise condominium that was to have been one of several. No additional units were built, however. The golf course will operate for awhile longer, but the motel has been closed for several months.

The I-270 corridor is unusual in that it surrounds the county's only north/south interstate highway, which has relatively few interchanges. In addition, the Metrorail system's Red Line has only four stations north of the Capital Beltway (I-495), and one of these four stations is its terminus at Shady Grove, just east of the I-270 interchange with Shady Grove Road. This corridor has seen explosive growth, especially in housing but also in employment. The most prestigious housing in the county lies just south of this area, and more affordable housing has been developed to the north. And commuters in Montgomery County must reach I-270 (or its Metro stations) via arterial roadways such as Shady Grove Road.

The Washingtonian Center proposes to take advantage of the site's 5,000 linear feet of frontage on I-270 and on a new arterial highway, I-370. This new highway is now being built between the Metro station and a new I-270 interchange. It will be extended by my firm, to the west, to a new county arterial road called the Great Seneca Highway. This will place the project between two I-270 interchanges and the new arterials to the north and west of the site. Because of the local traffic problems—both existing and future—my company has proposed to withhold development until the new interchange is underway.

The development planned for the site includes 4.5 million square feet of commercial space, of which 3.3 million is expected to be office space. In addition, approximately 1,500 housing units—primarily condominiums and garden apartments—are planned. The first phase of development, for which approval is being sought, comprises 1.825 million square feet of commercial space and 784 dwelling units; in other words, about half of the total space is in residential units, and 40 percent of the total is in commercial uses.

The application for rezoning was enthusiastically endorsed by the planning board in January 1985. The hearing before the county's hearing examiner concluded with a positive recommendation in September of that year. Now, the county council must approve the application.

THE OBSTACLES

In July 1985, two council members introduced legislation to put a cap on building permits, primarily because of mounting traffic congestion in the county. If that proposed legislation is read in its most restrictive sense, it would require the planning board to allocate permits, in a planning area such as this one, according to some unknown criteria to be set by the planning board at a future date. The legislation was specific neither on the nature of the criteria, nor on when they would be made known.

The legislation would all but eliminate our ability to proceed with this project. With this proposed legislation, we might not receive a permit, even after we had already gone ahead and spent a significant amount of money for on-site and off-site work.

The planning board has recommended against adoption of the legislation. Currently, the county council is trying to determine whether it ought to adopt this legislation or do something else. Therefore, we are in the unenviable position of being considered for zoning when zoning really means nothing.

THE PART PLAYED BY FACILITIES PROVISION

This situation has arisen in a county that administers one of the most stringent growth management programs in the Washington area, and possibly on the East Coast. When we bought the site in early 1983, it was clear that road capacity, and the adequacy of other public facilities in this rapidly developing section, would be the keys to moving ahead. (An earlier developer who had taken an option on the property walked away from development, rather than face the delays caused by road capacity's unavailability).

In 1982, Montgomery County adopted its "adequate public facilities ordinance." Later, it tightened this ordinance by requiring that a proposed roadway could not be considered as offering traffic capacity for new development unless 80 percent of its costs were authorized, either in the county's capital improvements program or in the state's consolidated road construction program. Fortunately, this requirement was entirely in line with this developer's intentions, because we did not intend to break ground until site accessibility was guaranteed to be available when it was needed. After all, no marketing campaign for the Center could really have succeeded unless we could show that new road capacity was planned and programmed.

Into these controls over the pace of development, the planning board introduced a new wrinkle in late 1984. At that time, it approved a master plan for this sector of the county that included a staging element: the plan specified certain road im-

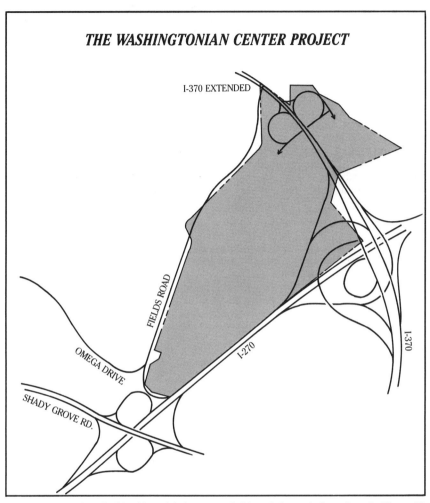

THE WASHINGTONIAN CENTER PROJECT

I-370 EXTENDED

FIELDS ROAD

OMEGA DRIVE

SHADY GROVE RD.

I-270

I-370

The project site described in this article is surrounded by existing and planned roads. These will provide critical links to I-270 from development west of the site.

provements as "triggers" for development on certain parcels. For the Washingtonian Center, the triggers were the road improvements already described, which already had to be 80 percent funded, as I stated earlier. With the new staging element, these same roads now have to be contracted for, with their construction all but underway.

So far, the regulatory process has been strict but reasonable—and a known quantity. But now, the newest legislation—as proposed with building permit caps, and as some observers understand it—would base issuance of building permits on traffic analyses and on projections that would demonstrate available capacities.

It will be impossible to proceed with financing and development if the year-to-year pace of development depends upon a traffic analysis, to be made before a permit can be obtained. On the one hand, that procedure would put too much faith in intersection analysis, trip generation, and other kinds of traffic studies. Some public officials believe that this type of analysis has been developed into a science that can project what will happen with specific parcels and specific buildings at any moment in time. But land planners and transportation planners realize that a traffic analysis provides only one part of the picture of whether a development is desirable or not.

On the other hand, and more importantly, the proposed new procedure would place an unpredictable limit on development that would raise the financial risk to unacceptable levels.

It is imperative for elected officials to listen to the planning board and the planning staff regarding growth management techniques. In Montgomery County, the board and its staff deal with traffic, schools, and other growth issues daily. But the adequate public facilities ordinance has slowed development, or even stopped it in certain congested areas. Such mechanisms provide enough control without these alarming new proposals that will truly stifle development.

Joseph Clancy is senior vice president for Ackerman & Company of Gaithersburg, Maryland. His contribution to this book is drawn from an address he made at the ULI/Lincoln Institute seminar on growth management.

THE MONTGOMERY COUNTY BLUE RIBBON COMMITTEE ON THE PLANNING PROCESS, 1985[1]

Volume 1—Report
(Excerpt)

CHAPTER III

PROBLEMS WITH PLANNING AND DEVELOPMENT IN MONTGOMERY COUNTY

T he link between private development and public facilities and services is meant to be addressed by the Montgomery County Adequate Public Facilities Ordinance. However, in some instances, it appears that approvals of private development have occurred disproportionately to the existing and planned public facilities and services. In other areas, the provision of public facilities and services has not kept pace with planned development. Consequently, the committee has found the process of private development approval in need of repair and, further, believes there is a need for more coherent plans to guide development.

---

[1]At the time of the seminar, when Norman Christeller presented his discussion of the county's growth management system (see article appearing earlier in this part of the book), a major political battle was shaping up in the county, with growth management as its focus. After the county executive (effectively, an elected mayor) announced his interest in reshaping the planning process in the county, the executive formed a citizens' committee to study it and to arrive at recommendations. To no one's surprise, the committee's findings echoed his own intentions, which sought to gain more executive control over the planning commission's activities.

The battle over whether the county council will continue to control commission appointments, and over other aspects of the planning process, continues unabated as of this writing. This excerpt from the citizens' committee report summarizes some of the growth management problems, as seen by at least one faction of the community.—Editor

I. TRANSPORTATION INFRASTRUCTURE AND SERVICES

The committee examined the planning process for transportation facilities to determine the major obstacles to timely and efficient transportation planning and implementation. The following section presents the findings of the committee on the county's transportation problems, and the committee's conclusions on the causes of those problems.

Considerable growth in the number of county residents over the past five years (31,000 people), and major increases in traffic passing through the county, have added significant burdens to the county's highways. According to the county government's transportation planners, the average daily traffic on major thoroughfares in the county increased dramatically between 1975 and 1983. On I-270 between Md. 28 and Montrose Road, traffic has increased by 60 percent—from 66,800 to 105,000 trips per day. On Md. 355 at Shady Grove Road, average daily traffic has more than doubled—from 26,300 to 54,400 trips per day.

In many areas of the county, there is a transportation facility gap. In some cases, such as the Bethesda central business district, private development has been approved that will overburden the anticipated transportation system. In other areas, necessary improvements in transportation facilities and services have not kept pace with commercial and residential development. These circumstances have resulted in a moratorium on approvals of new residential subdivisions and of new industrial and commercial development in a large part of the county. New residential and/or commercial development cannot be approved in the following planning areas, as a result of administering the adequate public facilities ordinance: Germantown West, Germantown East, Clovery, Fairland/White Oak, Gaithersburg, and the Bethesda central business district. However, the committee has been informed that approximately 46,000 housing units were approved by the planning board before the shutdown and, therefore, can proceed despite the moratorium.

The six-year capital improvements program for the fiscal years between 1986 and 1991 includes $365 million for transportation—an amount that helps the county catch up with current development but that does little to accommodate future development. Additional resources will be required to pay for the roads needed to support the housing units already approved by the planning board but not yet built.

The committee found that no *one* person, agency, department, commission, or legislative body has been solely responsible for the current transportation facilities gap. Delays in the construction of transportation facilities have been caused by:

- County council–initiated slippage in the capital improvements program (CIP);
- County executive–initiated slippage in the CIP;
- A reluctance to build facilities during periods of high interest rates on general obligation bonds;
- A self-imposed county cap on bonded indebtedness (to preserve the county's AAA bond rating);
- An underfunded Maryland State Highway Administration (SHA) budget, which has been due to the gasoline tax's basis in the wholesale price of gasoline; and
- The fact that no one organization coordinates the entire process, despite staff liaison that is taking place informally between the county department of transportation, the planning board staff, and the state department of transportation. (Effective communication has largely depended on the personalities involved, rather than on formal communication links.)

The committee found that the problems in transportation planning are symptomatic of serious problems in all those areas of the county planning process controlled by multiple entities, with no clear control by a body of elected officials directly responsible to the electorate. Lack of agreement among these multiple entities in establishing priorities for transportation needs adversely affects the ability of the county to obtain sufficient funds from the state to meet these legitimate needs.

Although a case could be made that the county is receiving a proportionate share of transportation funds (including transit support) according to existing allocation formulas, the fact remains that the county is not receiving sufficient funds to meet its real highway needs. In addition, testimony from SHA officials makes it clear that disagreements among county-elected officials, and among civic groups in establishing priorities for these funds, adversely affect the ability of the county to obtain sufficient highway funding in competition with the other counties and municipalities of the state that have argued their own needs more effectively.

Transportation problems are related to the fact that the county does not have a comprehensive transportation plan. There is no single document, available to officials and citizens alike, to allow them an opportunity to address the full range of transportation issues, and better to understand transportation policies and budgets for both capital and operating programs. Although there does exist a master plan of highways that was proposed by the planning board and approved by the county council, the committee found that this is nothing more than a map indicating an alignment of roads and rapid rail transit facilities that has been collected from the various master plans.

When reviewing transportation facilities, as related to master plans specifically, the following issues were identified by the committee:

- Some master plans and their amendments have been based on overly optimistic projections of alternative modes of transportation expected to become available.
- The idealistic plans produced in Montgomery County do not include enough realistic assumptions—especially on the question of ability to implement all the elements in a plan, given fiscal constraints.
- Density of development in comprehensive master plans is tied so closely to specific transportation facilities that changing conditions in the community are difficult to incorporate into transportation implementation decisions.

The committee also found that mandatory referral of all transportation facility plans to the planning board for comment has resulted, in some cases, in significant delays, despite the fact that approximately 75 percent of the projects are reviewed without comment. Although the executive branch may request a specific deadline for comment, and the planning board attempt to respond in a timely fashion, the absence of a mandated time limit may cause additional delay. The planning board does not have the power to reject transportation facility plans on mandatory referral: it does, however, have political leverage because of its influence with the county council, particularly in the budget process. This procedure needs to be modified so that it does not cause delays.

II. PLANNING FOR SCHOOLS AND OTHER INFRASTRUCTURE

In addition to examining the transportation problems of the county, the committee investigated nontransportation infrastructure issues. As with transportation facilities, the committee found that the county is also experiencing problems regarding planning and provision of educational facilities. In its examination of other public facilities, such as water and sewer systems, recreational amenities, fire and police stations, and libraries, the committee found no major issues at the present time. However, as with schools, each of these has a potential to cause serious problems in the future (as they have done in the past). The following section outlines the committee's findings on planning for schools and other infrastructure.

A. Problems with Planning for School Facilities

In the 1950s and 1960s, both the county and the state were constructing schools to accommodate "baby boom" growth. Then, in the 1970s, the county's school-age population started to decline, and the county responded by closing schools. In 1984, as a result of growth in housing, this trend was reversed when the school system experienced its first increase in enrollments in more than a decade. This growth is projected by the planning board and by school planners to continue through 1991.

This growth in school population has had, and will continue to have, a significant impact on the county's six-year capital improvements program. For example, in the approved 1985–1990 CIP, three new elementary schools, at a projected cost of $14.6 million, were included in the six-year program. In contrast, in the 1986–1991 CIP, which was approved one year later, *nine* new elementary and *two* new secondary schools, at a projected cost of $97.3 million, were included in the revised six-year program.

Not only has there been a notably greater need for additional schools, but also the county has had to assume a significantly larger share of the funding for school construction, as resources from the state have decreased. The county council–approved capital improvements program for schools for 1986–1991 is $204 million—with only $21 million, or approximately 10 percent, anticipated from the state. This is a significant change in the source of capital funding: over the past 14 years, the state has provided approximately two-thirds of the funding for school facilities.

Current problems with school facilities' capacities failing to keep pace with development are related to the separation of the responsibility for planning for private development, from the responsibility for the implementation of the capital program. (See III, below.) These problems also relate to the way in which school capacity was considered during zoning reviews in the past. The board of education was asked, during zoning hearings, to comment on the impact of rezonings on school capacity. The committee found that the board of education usually commented that it could make adjustments that would allow additional students from a subdivision to attend a school: it could always use temporary classrooms, change attendance boundaries, or build new schools. Therefore, when tested for school capacity, rezonings were generally approved, even if capacity in a given region was not yet available.

Currently, when tested for school capacity during adequate public facilities review by the planning board, subdivisions still are generally approved. This results from the fact that the planning board feels it does not have a uniform and legally defensible method of denying subdivisions based on inadequate school capacity—so long as excess capacity exists anywhere in the system. Since development rarely is denied because of school capacity, the county executive's role in the school planning process, and in the planning process in general, becomes reactive. The elected executive's capital improvements program must react to growth decisions made by the appointed planning board. Once private development is approved through the subdivision process, school capacity must be provided to accommodate the approved growth and to prevent problems.

The committee also found that problems exist with the consistency of demographic assumptions and projections, and with the maintenance of data records used for projections in planning school facilities. The planning board's projections are not available in the format, or at the level of detail, necessary for individual school planning. Therefore, the board of education prepares separate projections. The dual projections appear to create confusion as to which projections to use. It also appears that not all the data necessary to make accurate projections exist.

Therefore, the commitee recommends that the problem of demographic projections be studied in detail.

B. Problems with Planning for Other Infrastructure

As mentioned above, the committee found no major issues at the present time with the planning efforts related to water, sewer, recreational, fire-protection, police, or library facilities. However, the same fragmentation and lack of coordination that has caused problems with planning for school and transportation facilities and services could affect other facilities in the future, if development gets ahead of the facilities to serve it.

Water and sewerage services to most of the county are provided by the Washington Suburban Sanitary Commission, a bicounty agency. The executive is charged under state law with the planning of water and sewerage services. The committee notes that, under such management, the executive has taken a leadership role, and major regional agreements have been reached for both water-supply and sewerage services that provide adequate services, at less cost, for the county and region beyond the year 2000.

The libraries, recreation, and fire departments either have prepared, or are in the process of preparing, long-range facilities plans. These agencies' plans will be based on demographic assumptions from the planning board. These departments' plans for long-range facilities will be incorporated into the executive's recommended capital improvements program. Executive agencies involved with the planning for these facilities did not identify any significant planning problems. Problems related to the failure of these facilities to keep pace with development are more difficult to identify than are problems with roads, sewers, and schools.

III. CONNECTION BETWEEN PRIVATE DEVELOPMENT AND PUBLIC FACILITIES

The adequate public facilities ordinance (APFO) is designed to be the link between planning and implementation. The APFO requires that subdivision approvals be based on public facilities' being either a) adequate to support and service the area of the proposed subdivision, or b) scheduled in the adopted CIP. The planning board is responsible for APFO administration, and the county executive is responsible for public facilities implementation.

This separation of responsibilities appears to have caused problems in synchronizing the provision of public facilities with subdivision approvals. Once subdivisions are approved by the planning board, it is difficult to project exactly when the development will be built, or, in any given year, what needs the buildout will yield. To compound the problem further, priorities in the CIP may change by the time the development actually occurs. The CIP is revised annually to reflect changing priorities and changing construction schedules. Priorities may change as more urgent needs are identified, or as levels of funding decrease. Therefore—since there is no legal connection between changing priorities in the CIP, and subdivisions that have been approved—planning and implementation problems occur.

IV. FRAGMENTATION, RESPONSIBILITY, AND ACCOUNTABILITY

The committee finds that fragmentation of responsibility for private development approvals, and for the development of public facilities and services, is the root cause of our problems. Under the present legal structure of the county government, the seven members of the county council alone have the final responsibility and accountability for the problems we face. Because of the statutory fragmentation of responsibilities, the executive cannot be held accountable for synchronizing public facilities development with land use decisions, just as the planning board cannot be held accountable for synchronizing decisions on land use with public facilities development.

The current planning system, though legally consistent with the county charter and with state law, is basically inconsistent with the intent of the charter, as amended in 1968. At that time, the charter's drafters envisioned the office of the chief elected official as providing policy leadership across the range of government concerns. The council was seen as being relieved of its executive and administrative functions, to allow it more time for broad policy considerations. Although the reasons then appeared valid, however, this basic premise has not been followed on land use planning. Even though the charter clearly mandates a two-part government, a de facto tripartite structure has developed.

There are no effective checks and balances between the legislative branch and the executive branch because—although the Regional District Act allows the council full decision-making powers in land use planning—the county charter precludes an executive veto on planning decisions. Even the potential balance that would follow from executive appointment of planning board members was removed in 1972, when the Regional District Act was amended to give appointment powers to the county council.

In practice, then, the council appoints its own staff (the planning board) to draw up master plans. Then, it approves those plans without fear of authoritative contradiction (i.e., veto) from the other elected county official, the executive. Rather than functioning, in itself, as a policy maker and a legislative overseer, the council uses the planning board and planning staff to perform work that would normally be done by the executive branch.

The Montgomery County Blue Ribbon Committee was appointed by the county executive in 1985. Later in the same year, the committee made public the report of which this is an excerpt.

PART III.

TWO COMMUNITIES SEARCHING FOR ANSWERS

A ustin, Texas, and Hilton Head, South Carolina, are two very different places attempting distinctly different kinds of growth management. Austin, a city attracting an influx of high-tech industries, is not finding the rapid growth associated with such development desirable. Over the past few years, the city has enacted one ordinance after another to regulate development; the resulting policies and requirements do not add up to a cohesive system of development management. As the two articles by Norman Standerfer and Kaye Northcott demonstrate, the citizens and public officials of Austin are having a tough time reaching a consensus on how to control future development.

On the other hand, Hilton Head, which represents a group of resort developments that recently incorporated as a municipality, is trying to agree on its first comprehensive plan. Establishing a limit to the amount of growth to be allowed on the barrier island (really a peninsula) is one major concern of the planners, but assuring environmental preservation in general and providing for infrastructure also receive high priorities. John Rahenkamp describes the citizen-based process by which Hilton Head is attempting to reach consensus; and a summary of the current comprehensive plan, taken verbatim from its own text, illustrates the results of those efforts.

Douglas R. Porter

GETTING IT TOGETHER IN AUSTIN, TEXAS

NORMAN R. STANDERFER

A ustin is going through a considerable amount of turmoil now, in trying to decide if and how to manage its growth. Austin began growing rapidly in the 1970s, and that growth has accelerated in the 1980s. Officially, in the 1980 census, Austin had a population of 340,000 persons. By the last count, in December 1984, the population had grown to about 450,000 —a 33 percent increase within four years.

Austin is the high-tech darling of America, another Silicon Valley—known locally as "Silicon Gulf"—growing up in Texas. It is the most dynamic city in the state, with possibly the wealthiest university in the United States acting as the engine for its economy.

LOCAL GOVERNMENTS' POWERLESSNESS

This kind of growth calls for a lot of guidance, but in Texas, the local governments are given little power to control their futures. Much of the growth is taking place outside Austin's city limits —for example, in the county. Of the 400,000 persons or so who are expected to come into Austin within the next 35 years, 85 percent will live outside the present city limits. But the county has little power to plan or regulate its own land use and development. And at the same time, Austin cannot easily annex this land because the law requires the city to deliver police and fire protection within 60 days, and to begin affording infrastructure services within two and one-half years. The city would take a risk that annexation would be followed up with insufficient bond issues to pay for the new infrastructure.

What the city can do is plan for the area within five miles of the city limits. And Austin has special authority for the state to annex for planning and zoning purposes. But delivery of services to this area presents a real problem. Interestingly, it is not a problem for developers because in Texas, developers can choose among several special districts they can set up to provide roads, water supply, and sewage treatment—all at the expense of future residents.

THE POLITICAL ENVIRONMENT

All of the above are institutional obstacles to good planning and growth management, but there is another kind of obstacle that probably poses a more serious threat: the diffuse political setting that cannot reach a consensus on growth issues. Austin has a lot of educated people, and these people want to keep their quality of life, in what is widely regarded as the most livable city in Texas. They organize an action group for every issue they can think of, and they constantly come before the city council with ideas on how to handle each issue. And they fight and bicker among themselves all the time. The standard way to approach a problem in Austin is to have a group identify the problem and then appoint a task force to study it. At any one time, it seems as if there are 100 task forces operating in Austin on various growth and development issues—this, in a state where planning is an alien concept. Then, someone writes new regulations, and if the right group is in power that year, the regulations get passed.

The fact that all of the city council members stand for election every two years — in a sort of biennial coup d'etat—does not help. When the environmentalists are in power, they pass a bunch of ordinances. Then, they are kicked out of office, and the progrowth folks come in and pass a different set of ordinances. The resulting pile of development regulations has built up requirements that are at once redundant, divergent, and disorganized, and has hatched a city bureaucracy to match. Everyone has an opportunity to delay development proposals, and that opportunity is exercised with vigor.

How to forge consensus on growth issues in this atmosphere? This atmosphere that is the most intense political environment this speaker has ever seen in his life? Austin is about to embark on a two-year consensus-building program, to begin with the formation of a steering committee balancing all of the interests. Whether this attempt will work or not, only time will tell. But perhaps Austin's citizens can be reached by pointing out the bad economics of the present system. After all, taxes seem to be a big issue in the city, perhaps because the voters just approved a $1.1 billion bond issue, the largest municipal bond program in American history.

The problem will lie in getting the people to the table. Once this feat has been accomplished, this citizen effort will begin to deal with the ways to coordinate provision of services to developing areas—probably the key to managing growth.

GROWTH MANAGEMENT VERSUS PLANNING

Growth management techniques in themselves, however, are not very useful without agreement on a good plan. The city must persuade, not only the general public, but also the development community, of the severe economic consequences that accrue to the public without good planning. Once the planning has been accomplished, and an adequate facilities ordinance with some teeth in it has been enacted, then Austin can begin to concern itself with growth management mechanisms to fine-tune the system. Starting now, Austin is laying a better foundation for revamping its approach to growth management.

Norman Standerfer is director of planning and growth management for the city of Austin. This article is drawn from his presentation at the ULI/Lincoln Institute seminar on growth management.

AUSTIN: THE PERILS OF POPULARITY

KAYE NORTHCOTT

A ustin is Texas's most cerebral and least materialistic city. Where a Houstonian might ask, "If you're so smart, why aren't you rich?," an Austinite asks, "If you're so rich, why aren't you smart?" Virtually everyone who lives here, new-comer or old hand, loves the lakes, the spring-fed swimming pools, the cedar-scented hills, the live oaks, the pale violet sunsets, and the mellow ambiance that once earned Austin the nickname of the "hippie Palm Springs."

The business community believes that Austin can protect its special qualities, even while embracing the current boom, which last year made the three-county Austin area the fastest-growing major metropolitan area in United States, and which increased the metro area population from 537,000 in 1981 to 671,000 today. The boom is sending land values and the once-low cost of living into the stratosphere. Many neighborhood leaders and enviromentalists already see Austin as Paradise Lost. Although Austin is one of the few major cities in this free enterprise state that has seriously attempted to direct growth, instead of simply allowing market forces to determine its destiny, the results have been mixed at best.

BALANCE OF POWER

Austin politics are volatile; the balance of power tilts from neighborhood groups one year to developers the next. Growth pains and uncertainty about the future make city hall a revolving-door type of place. In 1981, Dan Davidson, a planner by training and the strongest city manager in recent history, was eased out by a newly elected, neighborhood-dominated council. Many on the council believed Davidson had been following his own prodeveloper agenda rather than implementing the council's policies. Davidson's supporters countered that Austin wasn't acting as a council/manager form of government should, that the council members were acting like city managers. Given the choice of quitting or being fired, Davidson quit and went to work for the Nash/Phillips-Copus Company, Austin's largest homebuilder.

Where Davidson had been criticized for having too strong a hold over city depart-ments, his successor, Nicholas Meiszer, was fired early this year for lack of initiative and failure to gain the respect of his staff. Meiszer's replacement was the deputy city manager, Jorge Carrasco, who so far has received good reviews.

In addition to Meiszer, Austin so far this year has lost an assistant city manager, human services director, director of water and wastewater, utilities director, parks and recreation director, vehicle and equipment director, finance director, city attorney, police chief, and a covey of planners. Some staffers resigned in Meiszer's wake. Others were fired for personal pecadilloes or incompetence. Many found more lucrative employment with development companies.

This administrative instability may simply reflect the anguish of a city seriously trying to deal with its future. But, nationally, Austin is developing a reputation for making mincemeat of its bureaucrats. When Davidson resigned three and one-half years ago, there were 300 applications for his job; this time around, there were only 60 applications, and those mainly from administrators in smaller cities.

RECONFIGURATION

Planning Director Dick Lillie, who had been with the city for 19 years, left when Carrasco decided to divide the planning department into a 45-position planning and growth management department (for long-range planning) and a 125-position office of land development services (for zoning and permits). Lillie insisted that he had not resigned because of the reorganization but because, "at the age of 53, I had reached that point in a career where you either stay until retirement or you go off and do something else." Shortly after his resignation, Lillie went to work for the former Texas governor and Nixon cabinet official, John Connally, and the former lieutenant governor, Ben Barnes, whose Austin-based partnership is building shopping centers, offices, and housing in various Texas cities.

Two new planners were brought in from Broward County, south Florida's sprawling boom county. James B. Duncan was hired to oversee land development services for Austin, a job similar to the one he held in Florida. There, he was given credit for streamlining permit processing and computerizing the system, thereby reducing development application time from 90 to 30 days. Council members hope that Duncan can loosen the permit logjam in Austin's overworked and underorganized planning department.

Austin's new director of planning and growth management is Norman Standerfer, who had been in charge of Broward County's long-range planning for four years. Standerfer and Duncan have been friends and colleagues since they attended the University of Oklahoma in the early 1960s. Together, they say, they hope to use their experience to help Austin avoid some of the mistakes made by Broward County. Standerfer told the *Austin American-Statesman*, "There's an opportunity to sit down with the population of Austin and say, 'Austin is about to explode. If growth is going to happen, just don't shut your eyes and let it happen. If there is no plan, you're going to end up like Broward County, and that's the pits.' "

In Austin, however, the new planning twosome will not have as many growth control tools at hand as it did in Florida, which authorizes local and regional development controls. Texas does not even give its counties ordinance-making authority. And Austin, for all its good intentions, has never enacted the controls necessary to force compliance with its master plan. In zoning cases, neighborhoods and developers battle to win over the city's planning commissioners, political appointees all. The city council has the final say on zoning, and each week it spends precious hours refereeing disputes.

RECENT HISTORY

Austin's master plan is based on goals enunciated in the "Austin Tomorrow" goals program, which retiring Planning Director Lillie counts as one of his major

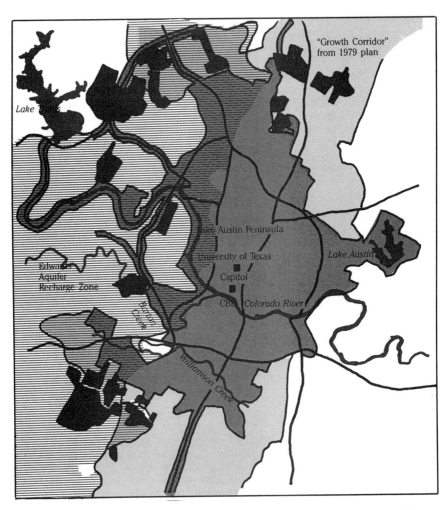

Although the 1979 master plan encouraged growth along a narrow north/south corridor (light gray), much of today's development is occurring in the hills to the west, over the sensitive aquifer recharge zone. In many cases, infrastructure was financed through the municipal utility districts (MUDs) (black) that now ring the city.

accomplishments. Between 1973 and 1975, the planning department brought 3,500 residents together to think about the future of Austin. (These planning sessions stimulated the growth of neighborhood groups, which today number close to 200.)

The plan adopted by the council in 1979, on the heels of the goals program, was the city's first substantial revision of its 1961 master plan. It called for commercial and industrial projects to be located on a north/south axis defined by Interstate 35, which cuts through the center of the city. The hills, the lake shores, and the Edwards Aquifer recharge zone, all to the west, were flagged as the least desirable for growth. The reasons were the high cost of extending services, and the danger of polluting the water supply and scarring the natural beauty of the hills.

Although the plan's intentions were good, neither it nor the 1961 plan, for that matter, has had much effect on the form of the city. Many would agree with the assessment of Robert Cullick, who reports on growth for the *American-Statesman* and who says, "The Austin master plan has been effectively shelved." The western hills, for example, where intense growth was proscribed by the 1979 plan, are the latest target for heavy development.

As part of the Austin Tomorrow effort, an "ongoing committee" was appointed to "help guide city government in the direction of citizens' goals." But the plan has not been implemented through growth control or through zoning ordinances. The nine-member planning commission recently sent the refined master plan to the city council for adoption, but attorney Jim Butler, a member of the commission, says, "I don't think the master plan is being looked at very seriously. I think our recommendations are fairly useless."

John P. Watson, a prominent developer, who, in a recent, much-publicized move, helped bring the Microelectronics & Computer Technology Corporation and the 3M Company to Austin, speaks for the business community when he says, "You can't absolutely draw a line in the dirt and say, no, this is nondevelopable." Indeed, 3M has announced it will build a research campus in the northwest hills, near Lakes Travis and Austin, the sources of the city's water supply.

The council seems to have given up on growth prohibitions, but it may choose to offer economic incentives—lower water connection fees, for example—to encourage north/south corridor growth.

CATACLYSMIC GROWTH

For most of its recent history, Austin grew at a heady, but potentially manageable, 3 to 3.5 percent a year. Last year, its growth rate shot up to 9.6 percent, according to the Austin-based Population Research Service. At least a dozen new hotels are planned. Thousands of apartments are going up, as is a new generation of downtown office high-rises. Speculators are making quick millions by flipping both raw and developed land. Where traditional Austinites built modest houses that hugged the contours of the land or renovated old houses in the inner city, developers are now building pretentious $500,000, even million-dollar, speculative houses on the tops of the western hills and over the Edwards Aquifer recharge zone. "No city can sustain this growth rate and not have problems," says Sally Shipman, a council member and planner who also serves on the American Planning Association's board of directors.

Dowell Myers, who teaches community and regional planning at the University of Texas, recently issued a disturbing report on Austin. Myers noted that rapidly rising housing costs are putting a strain on all sectors of the community, that crime has doubled since 1970, and that the quality of the water supply has deteriorated significantly. He also observed that, while Austin has the lowest unemployment rate in Texas (3.6 percent in August), real income has risen far less for minorities than for the general population. In 1970, for instance, the per capita income for Austin blacks (12 percent of the population) was 52.3 percent of the average; for Hispanics (18 percent of the population), it was 59.3 percent.

A sad sidenote of Myers's report is that, while Austinites have better restaurants and more varied entertainment than in 1970, the city's fabled music scene is in decline, reflecting both the high cost of club space and the aging of the audience.

SCHISMS

Up until the mid-1970s, the Austin city council, which is elected at large, was populated by owners of small local businesses. They were not particularly interested in attracting new industry to the city, or in opening up the governing process. Being the capital city and the premier campus of the University of Texas also has created problems. It's hard for a city to gain control of its own destiny when two of its major components remove land from the tax rolls and carry out independent building programs. Revenue from the university's $2 billion endowment is used primarily for extravagant construction, which is not subject to city ordinances.

During the 1970s, UT began increasing its enrollment (today the Austin campus has 47,500 students), but failed to build new dormitories. Thousands of politically active students were cast out into the community. In 1975, a coalition of students, white-collar liberals, and minorities gained control of the city council. City boards and commissions began reflecting the true diversity of the city and people began talking about growth control.

Simultaneously, the Austin Tomorrow goals program was helping to nurture the fledgling neighborhood movement. By the time the activist students had graduated, the environmentalists and the neighborhood groups were ready to take their places as the standard bearers for growth control.

Since then, the city council majority has seesawed between the business establishment and the neighborhoods. The black and Hispanic council members sometimes vote with the chamber of commerce, sometimes with the neighborhoods. Even before the current growth crunch, it was hard to set long-term goals for the city because of the shifting consensus.

In 1981–1982, the council tilted toward the neighborhoods. With two exceptions—planning-trained Sally Shipman and environmentally oriented Roger Duncan—the current council is largely developer-oriented. (However, a quirk in Texas zoning law allows Shipman and Duncan to block some upzoning proposals: it takes a six-to-one majority to approve a zoning change when the owners of 20 percent of the property surrounding the site in question oppose the change.)

Next year, it's possible that the neighborhoods will regain control of the council, when districts are instituted, as the result of a lawsuit filed by the NAACP. Only the mayor will be elected at large, and the council will be expanded from seven to nine members.

NUCLEAR POWER POLITICS

Austin's attitude toward nuclear power illustrates the schism that characterizes the city's politics. In 1972, in a very close referendum, voters declined to join Houston, San Antonio, and Corpus Christi in building the South Texas Nuclear Plant in Bay City. Two years later, voters reversed themselves, and the city bought 16 percent of the power plant. But the project was plagued by bad engineering and escalating costs, and every time the city council asked voters for additional bond money, the slow-growthers and environmentalists raised a ruckus.

Finally, in 1981, voters authorized Austin to bail out of the STNP, whose cost had risen from the original billion-dollar estimate to $4.5 billion. But the city can't find a buyer for its share of the plant, and the city council recently passed a resolution favoring cancellation of the project.

Meanwhile, the city council, in May [1984], on a five-to-two vote (Duncan and Shipman against)—without sending the question to the voters—took the unprecedented step of issuing $605 million in revenue bonds to pay the nuclear plant's ever-increasing construction costs. (Austin's city charter requires referendums to vali-

WINS AND LOSSES

Over the past decade, Austin's planning victories have included:
- A revised zoning ordinance. When the new ordinance goes into effect in January [1985], it will end cumulative zoning and establish both new design compatibility standards and neighborhood conservation districts. The most controversial sections have been written by an ad hoc group of developers and neighborhood leaders, with city planners refereeing the "match." The ordinance grandfathers in all existing zoned property.
- A revised subdivision ordinance that upgrades the quality of new construction, sets new standards for infrastructure, and recognizes the differences between construction on flat terrain and on hills.
- A tougher floodplain ordinance. Enacted in response to a 1981 flood that killed 13 people, the ordinance prohibits construction in the 25- and 100-year floodplains, but has a lot of loopholes, including the exemption of the central business district.
- Various watershed ordinances designed to protect the area's lakes, creeks, and aquifers from pollution, but under attack by environmentalists, who believe the ordinances are too little, too late.
- An ordinance offering some protection to trees with a circumference of 60 inches or more.
- An ordinance requiring special permits for building anything other than single-family housing in some inner-city neighborhoods now besieged by condominium and office projects.
- Revocation of the old practice of reimbursing developers for laying utilities. Builders of both residential and commercial projects now must pick up the tab for some of the infrastructure.
- Ambitious energy conservation programs.
- Development of hike-and-bike trails along Town Lake and elsewhere.
- A capitol views ordinance to protect those remaining scenic views of the pink granite state capitol that are not yet blocked by downtown office towers. In 1973, 1979, and 1981, the city council passed resolutions favoring preservation of capitol views, but it was not until August of this year [1984] that an ordinance, drafted by Sally Shipman and requiring review of new construction in view corridors, was approved.

Major planning failures in recent years include:
- Failure to enact a toxic substances ordinance, despite the rush of new technology firms into the area.
- Failure of the infrastructure to keep pace with growth.
- Failure to preserve moderate and low-income housing.
- Failure to set aside sufficient land for new parks.
- Failure to enforce city regulations. For example, the city has only one arborist, and he doesn't have time to ensure that the tree ordinance is enforced. Builders who destroy trees are rarely fined or required to plant replacements.
- Approval of inappropriate construction in the floodplain, failure to replace undersized bridges and culverts, and failure to maintain the city's 167 miles of dedicated creeks and drainage ways.

This feature box accompanied the *Planning* article of which this is a reprint.

date the sale of revenue bonds, but state law does not, and it probably takes precedence.) The action was so controversial that a petition campaign, so far unsuccessful, was launched to remove from office the council members who voted yes. Meanwhile, Austin continues to pay $9 million per month for a project it voted to kill.

Mayor Ron Mullen has since proposed a change in the city charter to allow bonds to be issued without voter approval—a step strongly opposed by neighborhood and environmental groups. The mayor blames the bond referendum law, and the uncertainty it creates, for the decision last August by Moody's Investors Service to lower the city's bond rating from A1 to A.

In September [1984], however, Austin and Travis County voters passed a $955 million bond package to build new water and wastewater treatment plants, a coal-fired generating plant, and new roads. Included in the bond package were funds to provide infrastructure in the northwestern hills, an area the master plan designates as unsuitable for intense development. The announcement of the new 3M research campus there has set off a frenzy of land speculation. The city council and city planners have yet to decide exactly how much development to allow.

SEWAGE ON WHEELS

"The thing that has troubled us the most," says former Planning Director Dick Lillie, "is not keeping up with the utility needs of the city." Although Austin has abundant water, the delivery system is inadequate. Last summer, a strict water rationing program was imposed temporarily. Meanwhile, the state of Texas, a coalition of neighborhood groups, as well as the city of Bastrop and Bastrop County (downstream from Austin), are suing the city for polluting the Colorado River with insufficiently treated sewage from three overburdened plants.

When a state judge called a halt to new sewer taps in the fast-growing southern suburbs, developers came forth with a scheme for trucking sewage from the Williamson plant to another, slightly less burdened city plant. "Sewage on wheels," a local magazine calls this stopgap measure. The judge is now parceling out new sewer taps whenever the storage pond levels drop.

Mayor Mullen blames the sewage crisis on the idealists who voted against bonds in the 1970s. However, Sally Shipman, who is on a committee studying where Austin's sewer planning went wrong, says voters should not be blamed for the current mess: "It's true," she says, "some bond issues failed, but we later passed an $84 million bond for a new Onion Creek sewage plant. The city management never moved forward to build it."

Shipman and other members of the investigating committee say they were amazed to hear that for years, the city's water and wastewater department had approved wastewater hookups for Austin with no clear notion of the system's capacity. Austin and several adjacent communities are now studying the feasibility of a regional sewage system.

"MUD" MANIA

Austin's early efforts in the direction of growth control fall into the category of benign neglect. In the 1970s, the city refused to annex new land and declined to provide the infrastructure needed for new suburbs. This strategy backfired when developers turned instead to a form of state-authorized special district known as a "municipal utility district" (MUD), which has the power to issue bonds and levy taxes to pay for services. (Under state law, if a city turns down a developer's request for services, the state water resources board can authorize a MUD—and usually does.)

Twenty-three MUDs have been created so far within Austin's five-mile extraterritorial jurisdiction. (Texas gives cities subdivision approval, but not zoning, powers within their ETJs—the sizes of which vary in population.)

Although MUDs, by their nature, are outside direct city control, negotiations usually bring them into general compliance with city policy, and in many cases, they agree to future annexation. Annexation gives Austin influence over a MUD, but it also means that the city eventually absorbs the MUD's debt for building in an area the city was reluctant to serve in the first place.

[The pros and cons of MUDs are covered fully in an article by Kent Butler and Dowell Myers in the Autumn 1984 *APA Journal*. The authors conclude that MUD-type negotiated development agreements may be the only viable way of directing growth in a boom economy. But they also point out that their creation may result in a proliferation of satellite cities with bond costs borne by future residents.]

This summer, Austin imposed limited-purpose annexation on 10,000 acres northwest of town. Limited-purpose annexation allows the city to implement zoning controls without providing city services and without levying taxes. The city has never used limited annexation on so large an area, and the legal staff anticipates a court challenge.

Mark Rose, the council member who sponsored the annexation, wants the city to prepare a comprehensive land use plan for the area, specifying densities and types of allowable uses. That's expected to provoke heated debate between environmentalists and builders. The former say that density limitations are the way to prevent pollution of the lakes and the aquifer; the latter insist that the filtration systems provide adequate protection.

Sally Shipman expresses doubt that the city has the clout to protect the area. She says she fears that most of the land use planning will be done by developers and rubberstamped by the majority of the council.

Another sensitive question is how much of the infrastructure costs the developers will bear. Although Austin has adopted a capital recovery fee that requires builders to finance some of the costs of city services, growth is by no means paying for itself. City Manager Carrasco is negotiating with Nash Phillips-Copus and 3M on how much of the $15 million bill for laying sewer lines through the western hills the developers would be willing to pay.

WHO PAYS?

Meanwhile, city taxes are increasing steadily. Between 1983 and 1984, the total appraised value of real estate in Austin increased by 52.8 percent. Almost 94 percent of the increase was due to revaluations, rather than to growth. Last year, the average home was valued at $60,000; this year [1984], it will be valued at $92,000 —increasing the homeowner's bill by $51.

In addition, Austin will be imposing double-digit increases in utility bills. (The city owns its electric utility, and Austin residents bear the highest debt per capita in the state. But proponents of the recent bond package argued that the debt is not out of line, when you understand that 68 percent of the debt is for the city-owned electric utility.)

Despite its staggering size, this September's bond package will not come near to providing the new infrastructure the city needs, including new sewage treatment plants, water lines, roads and bridges, a new city hall, and a bigger airport. The chamber of commerce is also pushing for a new convention center.

SUSTAINABLE AUSTIN

Under the "Austin Tomorrow" goals program, Austin is to fine-tune the growth control section of its master plan every six years. The late Robert Mather, an architect and University of Texas professor, was acting chairman of the Austin Tomorrow "ongoing committee" 's first six-year rewrite of the growth control plan. His vision of Austin's future, known as the "Sustainable Austin" scenario, was endorsed by neighborhood groups, environmentalists, and other advocates of slow growth.

Looking 30 years into the future, Mather saw a city that would grow compactly on a north/south axis. Mather did not want Interstate 35, the north/south freeway, to become, in his words, "an urban corridor that smears itself all the way to Waco and San Antonio." Instead, Austin would grow in the shape of a barbell, with dense nodules of population at the city's north and south boundaries. Only a small percentage of the population would live in the hill country to the west of the city, or on the shifting clay soils to the east.

Austin would grow to a reasonable size and then level off. Mather's ideal number was 800,000, but 1 million residents within Austin's metropolitan area by the year 2000 is the more common prediction.

He wanted the chamber of commerce to recruit companies to Austin that would hire the people already here, rather than import Yankee technocrats to fill jobs that the local populace was not trained to fill. The chamber was to shun hit-and-run developers who rode in on the crest of the boom and then skipped town—leaving the city to cope with poorly planned, shoddily built projects, once the boom tide receded.

Inner-city neighborhoods would be allowed to mature gracefully, rather than to be cannibalized for condominiums and offices. The creeks and lakes would be pristine. Because the city would grow densely (but not too densely), Austin would enjoy the first good public transportation system in Texas. Such was Mather's popular vision.

Shortly before he died, however, Mather completed a blistering speech in which he claimed that Austin is "on a debt-doubling, energy-gulping, quality-of-life–eroding, mindlessly negotiated, directionless growth pattern."—K.N.

This feature box accompanied the *Planning* article of which this is a reprint.

The test of a city plan is whether it passes from the book to the earth. Many here believe that standard planning processes are simply too slow to cope with the traumatizing rate of development confronting Austin's neighborhoods and natural environment. Sally Shipman is optimistic: "The people who live here are here by choice," she says, "and they will demand the preservation of Austin's assets."

Kaye Northcott writes on urban issues for *Third Coast* magazine in Austin. She is a former editor of the *Texas Observer.*

This article is reprinted from the November 1984 issue of *Planning.* Reprinting is by permission.

COMING TO GRIPS WITH GROWTH IN HILTON HEAD, SOUTH CAROLINA

JOHN RAHENKAMP

H ilton Head is a vacation and resort area of extraordinary reputation. It connects to I-95 and Charleston to the north, and Savannah to the south. Development in Hilton Head began in the 1950s, when Charles Frazier and the
Hack family, among others, built several major planned resort developments, using
the best planning and environmental concepts of the day. They were highly successful, to the extent that there are now 18,000 to 20,000 full-time residents on the
island, overall. Hilton Head is a barrier island, the second largest on the East
Coast, and subject to the ecological and growth stresses of all such islands. These
stresses are compounded by its success.

When development began, the county held land use regulatory powers but did
little besides accommodate the developers' plans, which, indeed, exceeded any
standards the county would have imposed. In 1983, the island residents decided to
incorporate as a town, primarily in order to deal with the emerging growth issues
with the legal power of an elected council and town manager. Following the town's
incorporation, an immediate need arose for a comprehensive plan and for various
land use controls—for which purpose the firm of John Rahenkamp and Associates
was employed.

THE BODY POLITIC AND ITS PART IN PLANNING

The town is still in metamorphosis from a collection of development projects
into a unified entity. In this process, partly because of Hilton Head's short political
history, an open question still remains as to just who composes the body politic.
But there seem to be four interest groups that affect political and planning decisions. One is that of the native islanders, who have lived on Hilton Head since
colonial times, and some of whom still speak a unique dialect—Gullah. Some of
the native islanders are enjoying the appreciation of land values, while others, not
owning lands, are severely threatened by rising costs for land and housing.

The second interest group is made up of the retirees who have moved to Hilton
Head for year-round living. This group represents a significant and growing voice

on the island. Although it is not yet large enough to control the town, it probably will be within three to five years.

Working people—the members of the third group—include among their number all of the service workers employed to keep the resort economy running. Many must be brought in by bus to the island daily from their off-island homes, with some individuals traveling up to one and one-half hours per day. Their importance to the regional economy is immense, and, as residents of the town/or county, they constitute a significant bloc of voters.

The fourth group comprises the developers, who still own a considerable amount of property and are interested in developing yet more of it. They are finding increasing difficulties in financing the infrastructure needed for new development, and are looking to the town for help. Typically, these developments are heavily leveraged on the front end, to furnish the major infrastructure required for a successful resort, such as golf courses, clubhouses, and the usual roads and water and sewer lines. These front-end costs put great pressure on developers to move forward quickly in a predictable way, in order to sell their lots and houses.

Finally, outside these four basic groups, a fifth group makes its weight felt in indirect ways. Tourists are the driving forces behind both the local economy and its land values. In the special context of Hilton Head, many "tourists" are people who return year after year for extended stays. Generally, these people are deeply committed to "their" island, even though they don't exercise a vote.

In order to pull together these divergent interests during the planning process, the comprehensive plan advisory committee (CPAC) was formed. The committee was designed to serve three purposes: 1) it was meant to provide feedback on planning proposals, and to ensure the accuracy of the public data base; 2) its process was intended to enable the making of public policy within an open forum—a forum that would educate the participants about the concepts of planning, the limits of the law, the growth issues, and the ways in which political choices are made; and finally, 3) its structure was meant to place its members in leadership roles in the newly organizing interest groups. CPAC members became both the voices of their constituencies, and their organizing centers.

THE NEW PLAN AND WHAT IT FACES

Because of the history of high-quality products from the development community, a major emphasis of the new plan is on setting performance criteria that relate to the impacts of development, rather than on writing a rigid zoning code. An example of a criterion is that for impervious coverage, as an environmental barometer. One single-family detached house on an acre lot, for instance, covers as much ground as three townhouses, six garden apartments, or 7,500 square feet of industrial or commercial space—making fixed zoning irrelevant and indefensible. The surface coverage by any one of these units of land use will produce relatively similar effects on the environment. Other types of effects can be measured in similar ways, and all elements verify that there is no defensible fixed number, assuming that the capacity exists within the public infrastructure systems.

The plan also stresses dispensing with absolute predictions of which land uses should go where. Instead, it concentrates on providing general directions, and then options, perhaps with incentives. Those involved in drawing up the plan believe that positive encouragement is better than negative restrictions, except in areas of vital public concern. In principle, a development firm could have maximum on-site flexibility, but, in return, it must bear greater responsibility for off-site impacts.

The plan has, as its third emphasis, protecting the environment from the people, and the people from the environment. As a barrier island, Hilton Head is subject to seasonal and annual shifts and changes in its beaches and estuaries. The island forms a long extension from the mainland, which poses a concern for hurricane evacuation. A major storm may inundate large parts of the island, and at the maximum population level of 70,000 during the peak tourist season, not all people could evacuate within the desired 12 hours. Review of hurricane evacuation plans, then, is a needed protection on a barrier island.

One roadblock to growth management resides within the present comprehensive plan. Hilton Head's existing plan, inherited from the county as a result of the town's incorporation, allows up to 100,000 housing units and as many as 11 million square feet of commercial and office space. That compares with the existing 20,000 housing units and 2.5 million square feet of nonresidential space. Although the planned amounts look wildly excessive, permits have already been issued for close to 60,000 housing units. But it was not politically feasible to downzone, or to reduce the impact of commercial and office space. Too much of the financial foundation of the development community rests on the prospect of that intensity. Furthermore, the degree of stringent and ever-present environmental limits that has played such an important role in the case of Sanibel Island is fortunately missing at Hilton Head. Hurricane evacuation limits can be overcome with improvements to the off-island road networks, and water supply is practically limitless, if surface sources and conservation measures are used. The costs of such infrastructure may slow development for a time, but even this obstacle can be overcome with time and money.

The new comprehensive plan, however, does provide timed capacity criteria and performance standards that will begin to monitor and manage the growth rate. Also, absorption in the marketplace will discipline the pace. Despite the high level of approvals, only 2,000 units per year are actually being completed. In addition, the plan will be due for reevaluation in five years. By that time, the organizing activities arising from the original CPAC, and the several-year history of both a working impact-zoning framework, and an expanding body of public knowledge, will have led to an intelligently evolving plan.

UPDATE

In December 1985, the town held its annual election. The more conservative contending group—the retirees and environmentalists—was successful. Also in December 1985, the comprehensive plan was approved—less than 12 months after its inception. Major additions to conventional planning tools included overlay view corridors following major roads and the waterfront; an airport overlay district; and noncontiguous PUDs to encourage clustering. Timed capacities were introduced, as the critical, pressing public concern. In February 1986, a new code was introduced, emphasizing capacity designation of land, as opposed to fixed zoning or, if you will, capacity zoning districts.

In retrospect, the work of CPAC, and the active participation by the planning consultant in the planning dialogue—as opposed to the more traditional passive/neutral planner's role—played crucial parts in forming an intelligent body politic.

John Rahenkamp is president of John Rahenkamp and Associates, Inc., of Philadelphia. Rahenkamp's contribution to this part of the book is drawn from an address he made at the ULI/Lincoln Institute seminar on growth management.

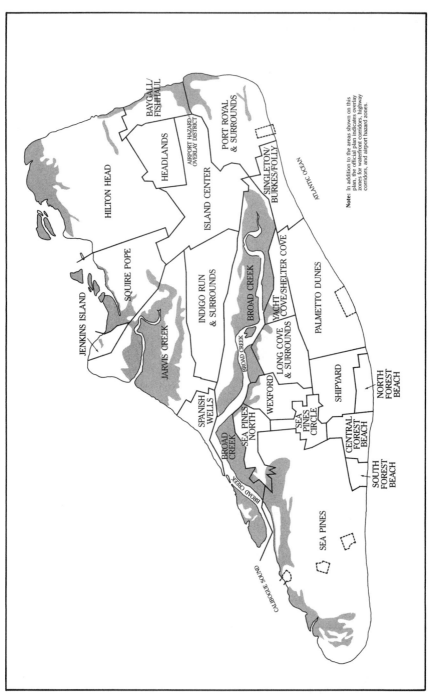

The map contains the following labels:

BAYGALL/FISHHAUL

HEADLANDS

HILTON HEAD

AIRPORT HAZARD OVERLAY DISTRICT

PORT ROYAL & SURROUNDS

ISLAND CENTER

SINGLETON/BURKES/FOLLY

ATLANTIC OCEAN

SQUIRE POPE

JENKINS ISLAND

JARVIS CREEK

INDIGO RUN & SURROUNDS

BROAD CREEK

YACHT COVE/SHELTER COVE

PALMETTO DUNES

BROAD CREEK

LONG COVE & SURROUNDS

SPANISH WELLS

WEXFORD

SHIPYARD

NORTH FOREST BEACH

SEA PINES NORTH

SEA PINES CIRCLE

CENTRAL FOREST BEACH

BROAD CREEK

SOUTH FOREST BEACH

BROAD CREEK

CALIBOGUE SOUND

SEA PINES

Note: In addition to the areas shown on this plan, the official plan indicates overlay zones for waterfront corridors, highway corridors, and airport hazard zones.

The new plan for Hilton Head, adopted in 1985, allocates growth to some parts of the island, while retaining other sections in their natural states.

EXECUTIVE SUMMARY:
Comprehensive Plan For the Town of Hilton Head Island

OVERVIEW OF THE PLAN

T his executive summary provides a synopsis of the major findings and recommendations contained in the comprehensive plan for the town of Hilton Head Island, adopted on November 27, 1985. Since the plan comprises a 158-page report, as well as 38 maps, this summary can only highlight its content and must necessarily omit many of its details. Therefore, it does not represent the town's official, adopted comprehensive plan.

The plan is organized into 10 sections, including: I. Hilton Head Island History; II. The Comprehensive Planning Process; III. Socioeconomic Systems; IV. Environmental Resources; V. Physical Systems; VI. Cultural Systems; VII. Public Services; VIII. The Land Use Plan; IX. Implementation; and X. Appendix.

Section I discusses the history of Hilton Head Island from its first settlements in the 17th century to its incorporation as a municipality in 1983, and to recent experience with self-government. Section II provides a general introduction to planning and impact management, and discusses the planning process by which the comprehensive plan was created, including community participation. This section concludes with a listing of 10 general goals that emerged from the planning process and helped shape the plan.

Sections III through VII present a comprehensive analysis of demographic, economic, and developmental trends; environmental, physical, and cultural conditions or resources; and governmental services on the island. Section VIII presents the land use plan, a broad set of recommendations for the future use and development of the island. Typically, in each of these sections, are found detailed policy statements, or recommendations pertaining to the particular topic. The report contains a total of 84 distinct policy recommendations, which alone constitute a comprehensive and ambitious public agenda.

In general, these policy recommendations will be implemented in one of three distinct ways: either as specific standards in the town's new land use regulations;

as new town policies that go beyond land use regulations; or as new policy initiatives by public or private decision makers outside the town.

The comprehensive plan seeks to respond to a context in which recent demographic, economic, and developmental growth on Hilton Head Island has been rapid and considerable. The island's permanent population has grown from 6,511 in 1975, to 11,344 in 1980, to an estimated population of 17,000 by mid-1985. Employment on the island has increased from 7,540 jobs in 1978 to 14,218 jobs by 1984. As of May 1985, the town of Hilton Head Island contained a total of 18,404 residential dwelling units, as well as hotel and motel accommodations providing 2,200 rooms. Already-built nonresidential space totaled nearly 1.75 million square feet in commercial use, slightly over 0.5 million square feet in office use, and 0.25 million square feet in warehouse and light industrial use.

These numbers are small when compared with projected future development, if all projects that have received either master plan approval or preliminary or final approval, as of May 1985, were built, and if all remaining lands without active development proposals were developed, up to the town's current zoning limits. Projected future development, based upon the above two assumptions, would result in 38,500 additional dwelling units, 4,100 additional hotel rooms, 7.5 million square feet of additional commercial floor space, 1.75 million square feet of additional office space, and nearly 3 million square feet of additional warehouse and light industrial floor space.

The comprehensive plan seeks to set in place sufficient information regarding the town's overall ability to develop further without surpassing the capacities of critical public services, particularly roads and sewers; or damaging irreplaceable natural features, such as dunes, aquifer recharge areas, and wetlands. The land use plan identifies distinct neighborhoods within the town that, given their locations and existing character, require differentiation in their future development intensities and usage patterns. As well, the plan identifies several corridors or critical overlay districts of public concern, particularly along the town's major highways and waterfront, where special policies are recommended to protect and enhance the attractiveness and vitality of the island. These features of the land use plan are summarized below, and also identified on the comprehensive plan of neighborhoods.

MASTER-PLANNED NEIGHBORHOODS

Because of the unique nature of Hilton Head Island's development history, there are already large, established, and relatively fixed master-planned areas, known as the "plantations." These include the following land areas: Hilton Head; Port Royal and Surrounds; Palmetto Dunes (including Shelter Cove); Shipyard; Sea Pines; Wexford; Long Cove; Indigo Run; Spanish Wells; Palmetto Headlands; and Skull Creek Point. These areas have typically been approved through traditional planned unit development processes that included locating a mix of specific uses, such as single-family detached, multifamily, and commercial/office, in specific mapped locations as part of a master-planned community. Also, with the location of uses, each plantation was planned for a total number of units that could be built and for a general understanding of how these units would be distributed over the landscape.

In principle, the plan does not disturb the intended land use systems and related covenants as they are currently planned. These neighborhoods will have densities at the levels indicated in their current master plans and covenants. However, as new sections are brought forward for final approval (or as current development permits lapse), they will be subjected to site plan regulations arising from site-specific environmental and capacity conditions, and from location within or without the critical overlay districts, as described in the plan.

EXISTING RESIDENTIAL NEIGHBORHOODS

South Forest Beach, North Forest Beach, Palmetto Bay

Three neighborhoods on the southern end of the island have an existing character, established by early subdivisions and smaller-scale master plans, and dominated by single-family housing. These communities—South Forest Beach, North Forest Beach, and Palmetto Bay—have been under increasing pressure from resort development. The plan recommends that the town of Hilton Head work in conjunction with current residents to ensure the stability and predominantly residential character of these neighborhoods. Commercial uses will be limited to neighborhood facilities, and will only be approved in conjunction with a planned unit development. The town will assist the area residents to create more detailed neighborhood plans. In the interim, these neighborhoods will be allowed to be developed, consistent with their current low-intensity use of single-family housing.

OTHER RESIDENTIAL NEIGHBORHOODS

Baygall/Fish Haul, Squire Pope, Burkes/Folly

The pattern of large-scale, master-planned neighborhoods in the northern end of the island fragments the area into three residual residential neighborhoods. Baygall/Fish Haul consists of a large contiguous area on Port Royal Sound. Squire Pope is bounded by Hilton Head Plantation, Skull Creek, and U.S. Route 278 (William Hilton Parkway). Burkes/Folly consists of a large parcel bounded by Route 278, the Singleton and Port Royal neighborhoods, and the Atlantic Ocean. These three neighborhoods include most of the remaining heirs' lands. Again, in these neighborhoods, area residents will be encouraged to collaborate with the town to create more detailed neighborhood plans. In the interim, these neighborhoods will be allowed to be developed at moderate intensity.

HIGH-ACTIVITY NEIGHBORHOODS

Island Center, Sea Pines Circle, Central Forest Beach, Singleton Beach

Four neighborhoods are logically identified as centers of commercial, resort, or public activities. Each of these neighborhoods will have a different primary focus. The Island Center neighborhood is encouraged to function as a regional hub, with concomitant commercial, office, governmental, and cultural facilities, with residential as an additional permitted use. The Sea Pines Circle neighborhood is the commercial center of the southern end of the island; Central Forest Beach and Singleton Beach are the primary off-plantation resort neighborhoods.

A central feature of these high-activity neighborhoods will be the inclusion of density and site design incentives offered to developments that address and solve local drainage, parking, beach access, and traffic problems. Special attention will be paid to the linkages through and between these neighborhoods, including pedestrian, bike, auto, and public systems. It is recommended that a neighborhood plan for Central Forest Beach be undertaken as soon as possible, as a cooperative effort between the town and the landowners.

CONSERVATION-AREA NEIGHBORHOODS

Broad Creek, Jarvis Creek

Two conservation-area neighborhoods are defined by a contiguous area surrounding the landmass of Hilton Head Island, following the mean high-water line established by the South Carolina Coastal Council. The plan recommends the preservation of these areas to the fullest extent of the law, in order to ensure the proper functioning of critical natural systems, enhance water quality, and protect the inherent amenity value.

OVERLAY DISTRICTS

Road Corridor, Waterfront Corridor, Conservation, and Airport Hazard Overlay Districts

The plan establishes a road corridor overlay district that transcends neighborhood boundaries along a linear path parallel to the island's major highways, both existing and proposed. The road corridor extends for a distance of five-hundred (500) feet on each side of the centerline of the following routes: 1) existing portion of Route 278; 2) the proposed Cross-Island Route; 3) Palmetto Bay Road and Pope Avenue; and 4) the proposed Island Center Connector Route.

Future development within the road corridor will be subject to the policies specific to the particular neighborhood in which they lie, as well as to several policies that protect the visual or aesthetic quality, including: possible increased buffering requirements to screen unattractive buildings from view, and special standards for signs and street furniture, covering size, materials, lighting, and the like. Applications for new development in the road corridor will include a visual impact analysis that assesses predevelopment visual conditions and shows how the proposed development will affect them. Applicants for development within the 500-foot corridor who can demonstrate that their projects are beyond the depth of visual penetration from the roadway will receive nonimpact determinations.

The plan also establishes a waterfront corridor overlay district in the area landward of the South Carolina Coastal Council's critical line, for a distance of five-hundred (500) feet. As in the road corridor, future development within the waterfront corridor will be subject to special policies to mitigate against impacts on existing views from the water and shoreline.

The plan establishes an airport hazard overlay district that corresponds to the area where significant safety-hazard or noise-level disturbance is caused by flight activity at the Hilton Head Island Airport. Future development within this district will be restricted to nonresidential uses and also subject to the height limitations necessary for safe functioning of aircraft.

The fourth special district that overlays other neighborhoods—a conservation overlay district—occurs where estuary or ocean has been included within the boundaries of master-planned areas. This district is established seaward of the South Carolina Coastal Council line. Future development will be restricted to those activities expressly permitted in the conservation neighborhood.

DEVELOPMENT FLEXIBILITY

Many of the plantation properties were designed and developed earlier as master-planned areas, which have the flexibility both to distribute projectwide (gross) densities over the entire property, and to yield net design densities in each section or phase so as to encourage better professional design, more diverse product types, and residual open space. The same principle of flexibility is encouraged by the plan for future smaller developments, through three incentive opportunities:

- First, in the resort/commercial high-activity neighborhoods, additional dwelling unit densities may be allowed above the by-right density. A system of incentives, including bonus densities, may be awarded to development proposals that include material contributions to alleviate one of several critical health, safety, and welfare issues in these neighborhoods, including, but not limited to 1) improvement of the neighborhood's stormwater detention system, 2) dune and beach preservation, 3) provision of additional parking, 4) provision of additional beach access, and 5) redevelopment activity that will upgrade the area.

  Developers will be eligible for bonus densities, provided these kinds of improvements go beyond the minimum standards for stormwater detention, dune/beach preservation, parking, and beach access that they normally would be required by the town to provide.
- A second incentive involving bonus densities will operate islandwide, as part of the town's policies for encouraging the production of more low- and moderate-income housing. Proposals for this kind of housing will be eligible to receive an increase in dwelling unit density up to 15 units per acre, in any neighborhood where residential use is permitted.

  Additionally, and in order to make the density increase feasible, compliance with specific area or design standards (such as maximum impervious surface coverage) may be waived by the town, on a case-by-case basis. This will occur if the waiver is needed to make the project economically feasible, and if the overall intent of the standards is still achieved.
- A third incentive involving bonus densities will also operate islandwide, throughout the area that has been identified in the plan as the waterfront corridor overlay district. Within the waterfront corridor, all development must comply with certain minimum standards designed to protect against wind and water erosion and storm damage. A minimum building setback from the mean high-water line or from the primary beach dune will be required, similar to that already required by the town's development standards ordinance. As an incentive to encourage even deeper setbacks, and thereby to enhance both visual and health, safety, and welfare concerns, the town will award new development with a density bonus if it exceeds these minimum setbacks. This incentive should result in greater use of clustered development, and in wider architectural variety along the waterfront.

In several neighborhoods, planned unit development may be permitted for proposals in which the lands are under the control of one owner or entity, but are not necessarily contiguous. This program will provide development opportunities for landowners whose properties otherwise might not be so developable, because of size or location. As well, the program is intended to contribute to the density-bonus incentive programs. In the Central Forest Beach and Sea Pines Circle neighborhoods, noncontiguous lands may be brought forward in one development proposal that provides creative solutions to drainage, parking, or redevelopment problems. Here, the noncontiguous program provides a logical technique for awarding density bonuses in Central Forest Beach and Sea Pines Circle. The noncontiguous program will also operate in the Island Center neighborhood, to enable the use of separate lands to establish those amenities, such as public open spaces, pedestrian paths, and parking, needed to interconnect the disparate activities and uses within the Center.

IMPLEMENTATION

Implementation of many of the plan's land use policies will occur, either through amendments to the town's development standards ordinance (DSO), or through replacement of the DSO with a new land management ordinance that will combine into one ordinance what traditionally are zoning regulations, subdivision regulations, site-plan design performance standards, and impact management standards.

The island will be divided into zoning districts that follow the general prescriptions of the comprehensive plan for land uses and intensities in the neighborhoods. The zoning districts, however, will translate neighborhood policies into greater specificity and detail, including permitted uses and maximum densities. The road corridor, waterfront corridor, conservation, and airport hazard areas will become special overlay districts on the zoning map, allowing the specific performance standards necessary for protection of health, safety, and welfare in these corridors to become parts of the zoning fabric.

The system for impact evaluation, which will deal with the issues of capacities (natural, physical, cultural, and fiscal), will be specified, and management methods will be detailed in the land management ordinance. In general, all new applications for development including more than one residence; planned unit developments; hotel developments; and nonresidential projects above a minimum size will be required to demonstrate, before issuance of a development permit, compliance with the impact management standards stipulated in the ordinance. These will govern:

- traffic generation;
- sewer and water demand;
- impacts upon natural features, including hydrology and drainage;
- municipal fiscal impact;
- school fiscal impact;
- hurricane evacuation impact; and
- visual impact, if located within the road or waterfront corridors.

Applicants will be required to submit sufficient documentation to quantify the impacts of their projects, so as to demonstrate either that standards would not be exceeded, or, if exceeded, how the overload would be mitigated. Where it is found that capacity represents a problem, and thus that overload of either a natural or a physical system would result and damage the public, the developer will be required to show how his proposed development will either eliminate or substantially mitigate the negative impacts. If a remedy is not possible, then the proposal will be disapproved, based on health, safety, and welfare considerations.

An integral part of resolving potential impediments to the approval of additional developments will occur through the town's fuller use of a capital improvements program and budget. This will fund and schedule the construction of critical projects.

The source of this document is the comprehensive plan prepared in 1985 by the department of planning and inspections in the town of Hilton Head Island, South Carolina.

PART IV.

STATE AND REGIONAL MANAGEMENT

One answer to local struggles with growth issues has been to elevate responsibilities for management to regional or even state levels. This approach has particularly succeeded when the issues clearly affected vast acreages, and when those issues were seen as vital to the preservation of important environmental qualities. Thus, development in places such as Martha's Vineyard, Lake Tahoe, the states of Vermont and Florida, the California coast, and Colorado's Front Range have received special treatment from regional and state growth management efforts.

As examples, Terrence Moore describes the success of the Pinelands Commission in New Jersey at preserving over 1 million acres of pinelands from piecemeal development, while Babcock and Siemon discuss the genesis of the plan for the Pinelands, which meshes local, regional, state, and national interests.

In the Adirondack region of New York State, a quite different but similarly successful management process has protected a large forested region from unwanted development. How this was done is described by Thomas Ulasewicz, and how the Adirondack methods measure up to those of other management efforts in similar places is described by Hahn and Dyballa.

John DeGrove concludes the discussion with an overview of state initiatives in growth management, and of the tensions that these actions provoke in local governments.

Douglas R. Porter

SAVING THE PINELANDS

TERRENCE D. MOORE

I have been the executive director of the New Jersey Pinelands Commission for all of its six years of existence. I began with brown hair; now it's all gray; and you might believe me when I tell you that next month, I'll only be 30 years old. That, in brief, is the story of growth management in the Pinelands.

After viewing Tom Ulasewicz's beautiful vistas of the Adirondacks, I would be remiss if I failed to mention one of the major scenic features of the Pinelands: the internationally famous Forked River Mountains. These rise to the majestic height of some 205 feet above sea level. Our Pinelands, of course, are flat. They have what we like to call a subtle beauty, with a mixture of pines and oaks. Beneath them is a 17-trillion-gallon aquifer of exceptionally pure water. Water quality and water planning are important parts of Pinelands protection.

I'll begin with some history, and end with the changing focus of our agency. Apparently, we have survived our first six years, and it seems that we will continue to survive in the future. Perhaps, it's time we started talking a little about the success of the New Jersey Pinelands. It is, beyond any shadow of a doubt, the most successful national reserve in the country. The fact that it's the only one (none have been created since) should not detract from my statement.

THE BEGINNINGS

The reserve was created by the National Parks and Recreation Act of 1978 as an experiment in land use: a federal, state, and local partnership; a marriage, fraught with trials, but a marriage nevertheless; an experiment, too, in alternatives to national park systems. We have the power to regulate, the ability to acquire critical areas, a state presence, and a spirit of cooperation. Although we have state control, the toughest effort has been local implementation.

The National Parks and Recreation Act called upon the state of New Jersey to respond. While awaiting the passage of state legislation, then-Governor Byrne speculated, "Why not have a moratorium?" And so there was a moratorium in the New

Jersey Pinelands, beginning in February 1979. It wasn't so much a real moratorium as a stringent development review procedure.

The Pinelands Protection Act, our very strong state legislation, was passed in June 1979, and a commission was born. The Pinelands Commission has 15 members: one federal representative appointed by the U.S. Secretary of the Interior, seven members appointed by the governor, and seven members appointed by their respective counties. It is truly a federal, state, and local partnership.

It can be safely said that the Pinelands Protection Act shocked the state of New Jersey. It called upon the Pinelands Commission—acting as an independent authority, subject only to a governor's veto of its minutes—to draw up a plan within one year, and to implement it through a process of local conformance. Every municipality and every county must, under the Pinelands Protection Act, revise its master plan and zoning ordinance to reflect the provisions of the New Jersey Pinelands Comprehensive Management Plan (CMP).

These local plans and ordinances are submitted to the commission for certification. When a municipality fails to comply, the commission exercises direct land use jurisdiction within the municipality. Not a soft piece of legislation, but one that exerts great authority and pronounces great power. Necessarily, when you have something like that, you use it as little as you possibly can. You start talking with municipalities and persuading them, rather than saying, "You have to do it."

THE PLAN

The comprehensive management plan is made up of a number of different programs. For instance, the reserve has land management areas, each with a different density of development assigned to it by the commission. To the north is the large preservation area (green on the CMP map). That area is delineated by state legislation. Nothing much can be developed there. Residential uses are prohibited within the preservation area, unless a landowner has a very special exemption: he or she must qualify by a two-generation economic tie to the Pines, before a house may be built.

The other areas represent graduated levels of management, with the most developable sections those shown in orange. These sections are the regional growth areas, where future growth within the region is being directed. The brown areas on the CMP map are agricultural production areas. We have a strong agricultural zoning program. It is not a popular program with the agricultural community, but it is one that continues to survive.

We also have, scattered throughout the preservation area, special agricultural production areas. These cranberry and blueberry farms represent a highest and best use of the land. There is really no doubt, today, that cranberry operations are highly viable from an economic standpoint.

Overlaying all of this is a transfer of development rights (TDR) program. We wouldn't recommend it to everyone, but, as a regional TDR program, it is a distinctive one. Landowners in the preservation area, and those in the agricultural production areas, receive Pinelands development credits. These can be sold to developers in regional growth areas, who then receive density bonuses. The bonuses are included within the local zoning ordinances, once the latter have been certified.

Among 14 environmental management programs is one covering wetlands protection. The commission has a stringent wetlands protection program, including a 300-foot buffer around the wetlands. Development is prohibited on all wetlands within the New Jersey Pinelands.

CONFORMANCE

When the CMP was adopted in 1980, and approved by the Secretary of the Interior on January 16, 1981 (just before he went out the door with the change of administrations in Washington), we began the most difficult process: local conformance. We did have some grants for towns: not a great deal, about $600,000, but we did get some initial take, and this proved important to the direction in which our effort would move during the next few years. Towns actually did start coming in, revising their master plans, and rewriting their zoning ordinances.

We are about to certify our 42nd of 52 jurisdictions. This has been a long process—a learning process for both state and local governments. During this time, we moved our management areas' lines a little, while, for their part, municipalities began implementing, through their local actions, some stringent environmental provisions affecting how development will occur there in the future.

We have a changing role now. This kind of activity does take a somewhat predictable course. You go through the heat and excitement, the speed, of planning. A favorite saying of ours was, "When skating on thin ice, you better skate fast." That's just what we had to do.

NEW ROLES FOR THE AGENCY

After towns became certified, the agency received a little more acceptance, and quiet returned to the woods, and to the state, after the third year or so. Now, there is a new focus for our agency—much more of an orientation of research and of service to the municipalities. For example, through a small EDA grant, we are working with a number of towns on an environmental analysis of their publicly owned industrial parks. In this way, when these towns can attract a developer, we can speed up our development review process for a particular activity—which always helps.

We are even becoming popular in certain parts of the Pinelands by our ability to say no. For the first time, a month ago, I received a standing ovation from some 400 people in the municipal building in Winslow, New Jersey, where I used to stand near the door in case a hasty retreat was necessary. The ovation happened because the Pinelands Commission said no to a regional landfill, an environmental issue of some concern. The commission was really the only agency that was going to say no because it had been likely that other state agencies would approve the project. So, the commission became a little more popular.

Also, the agency is focusing on scientific research, and attempting to become a part of the local process by giving municipalities technical assistance that has not really been available to them before.

Moreover, the Pinelands have been designated an international biosphere reserve by the United Nations. With this distinction, we are able to attract researchers from near and far. They are starting to arrive: recently, we were visited by a group of foresters from around the world.

Both the states and the federal government often come up with masterful legislation without making the necessary follow-through. They don't provide grants to take action, or sewers for development, and often, they don't assist an agency in implementing certain recommendations of a plan.

The legislature of New Jersey—that same legislature that, four years ago, and again three years ago, was considering bills to dilute significantly the Pinelands Protection Act—has recently enacted an in-lieu-of-tax bill to assist municipalities demonstrating fiscal stress because of Pinelands protection. These are preservation-area communities. Now, landowners are being aided through the Pinelands Development Credit Bank Act, which was passed this summer [1985] and which created a bank that will buy and sell Pinelands development credits at a guaranteed amount. It will also guarantee farm loans to farmers within the Pinelands. If all goes well, these bills will provide the necessary follow-through.

More importantly, this November [again, 1985], the legislature placed on the ballot a bond issue question, Question Number Three. It was the Pinelands Infrastructure Trust Bond Act, to provide $30 million in grants and loans to assist in construction, primarily of sewers, within certain regional growth areas.[1]

CONCLUDING OBSERVATIONS

There is a sad part of the Pinelands program, and perhaps it is the part that was the great experiment, the federal/state/local partnership. The federal government has retreated from the partnership—not so much at the regional level, where our federal representative (the regional director of the National Park Service) is very active, but at the national level. No encouragement for other activities of this type across the nation seems to exist, and perhaps, we will have to wait a few more years to see if any activity of this kind occurs again.

The great experiment in New Jersey—it has been that, and a somewhat successful one, too—has elements that could be transferred to other regions. Not the strength of the Pinelands Protection Act, necessarily, because that may not work

---

[1] The bond issue was overwhelmingly approved, and the commission will now undertake a plan to determine where that money will go.

everywhere; nor the authority of the Pinelands Commission because many states wouldn't want that; but the ability of a state government, through an independent citizens' commission (we have no department heads on our commission, they're just unpaid human beings), to work to fill the gap between state control and local implementation. If it is quiet in the pine woods again, it is quiet, most of all, because the process of discussion between the state of New Jersey and its local jurisdictions has worked. The communities are implementing this plan.

Perhaps, it's best to close with one other fact because, in my opinion, it is the most important fact in our efforts in the national reserve. Once a municipality is certified by the Pinelands Commission, it gets back its land use authority and makes decisions under its own local ordinance. But the commission has the authority to call up, review, and deny any local approval given. With all of the municipalities that have been certified by the commission, however, it has only exercised that authority on fewer than 3 percent of the applications that have been processed by municipalities. So, the implementation at the local level, at least statistically, appears to be working.

I just want to give you one last little statistic before I close because I always have to go one better than the Adirondack people—if only because we learned a lot from them not long ago. Tom Ulasewicz mentioned they have 9 million visitors per year. For your information, this year, 9 million vehicles traversed the Atlantic City Expressway, going east to the casinos. And they all passed through the New Jersey Pinelands on their way.

Terrence D. Moore is executive director of the New Jersey Pinelands Commission—a regional initiative embracing land use, agriculture, and resource protection within its wide reach. Formerly, he was executive director of New Jersey's Newark Watershed Conservation and Development Corporation.

Moore's contribution to this book is drawn from an address he made at the ULI/Lincoln Institute seminar on growth management.

THE PINELANDS: A RADICAL EXPERIMENT WORKS[1]

RICHARD F. BABCOCK AND CHARLES L. SIEMON

O
n June 28, 1979, months of litigation, debate, and controversy came to an end when the [New Jersey] Pinelands Protection Act was passed after what the press referred to as "stormy hearings and debate." (Several legislators would later claim that the governor crammed the legislation down "their throats.") The Act, as ultimately enacted, was a crazy-quilt patchwork of compromise and amendment; nevertheless, it created the required regional commission and, importantly, empowered the commission to implement the Act.

COMPREHENSIVE MANAGEMENT PLAN (CMP)

When the dust had settled, Governor Byrne's signature put the finishing touch on an astonishing legislative feat—a regional commission with overriding land use control over 52 municipalities, seven counties, and the state itself. Significantly, the commission was established as an independent state agency, immunizing its tasks from direct political influence. Governor Byrne himself characterized the Act as "the thing they will remember me for 100 years from now." For the conservationists, there was but one small catch: the Act declared that a comprehensive management plan (CMP) was to be completed on or before August 8, 1980. This was 18 months after the protection act was enacted. Critics complained that opponents of the bill, who recognized the strength of the governor's position, had sabotaged the effort by exacting a schedule that was impossible to meet.

In July, the Pinelands Commission selected Terrence D. Moore as executive director of the commission, and wished him well on his "mission impossible." Moore, who was described as a "self-styled flaming liberal" in one paper, and was a veteran of Newark's urban and environmental problems, immediately began to put together a staff. Assembling a team of dedicated planners, lawyers, and scientists (largely expropriated from various New Jersey environmental agencies), he (the "E.D.," as

---

[1] This article is an excerpt from *The Zoning Game Revisited* by Babcock and Siemon. Please see last page of article for further information.

he was to become known) set out to prepare and have adopted a comprehensive plan for 1 million acres of land, in less than 13 months.

The commission's work program called for a team of consultants to prepare background reports on the natural and built environments of the Pinelands, and to analyze the legal framework that would control adoption and implementation of the plan. We were among the consultants (delineated as land management consultants) and were responsible for the preparation of a five-volume survey of the land management tools employed by agencies around the country and the world; this survey was ultimately to be the base for the implementing element of the plan. The comprehensiveness of the survey formed a solid background for the many debates that developed about the form and substance of the draft plan.

The plan, according to the commission's work program, should include a scheme to manage lands that were to be protected, and should also examine an array of less costly and more flexible land management techniques. In addition, the Pinelands Plan should include a natural resource assessment; a detailed boundary map; a land use capability map and a comprehensive statement of land use management policies; a study of appropriate public uses of the land; a financial analysis; a program to ensure local government and public participation in land use decisions; and a program to put the plan into effect.

History has recorded that the comprehensive management plan for the 400,000-acre "preservation area" core of the Pinelands was duly enacted on August 8, 1980, and that the entire plan was adopted on November 21, 1980. The effort was completed largely because of the dedication of the people involved, and their willingness to work together toward a common end. The participants did not necessarily agree with everything they worked on. However, very few participants in the process denied the value of the environmental resource to which the effort was directed.

THE COMMISSIONERS

Perhaps most significant among the many principals responsible for the planning program were the commissioners themselves. Appointed by diverse authorities—seven by the governor, one from each of the counties in the Pinelands area, and one representative of the U.S. Department of the Interior—the commissioners carried out their duties with patience, dedication, and care. That is not to say that they acted as one; but their personal integrity carried them and the commission through what was by any measure a very difficult process.

The chairman, Frank Parker, a successful New York attorney who resided in a northern New Jersey suburb, and a long-time conservationist, distinguished himself with infinite patience and a discreet sense of dignity and control. Candace Ashman, a veteran environmental and planning advocate with hands-on experience as the executive director of the New Jersey Association of Environmental Commissions, provided unswerving support for the staff and the environment. This position was reinforced by Gary Patterson, a professor of environmental sciences in a local college.

Budd Chavooshian, a Rutgers professor and a former director of the state planning agency for New Jersey, brought a wealth of experience and technical skill to the commission. Joan Batory, who was appointed by Camden County and was director of that county's environmental agency, contributed technical and practical skills to the effort. Another important contributor was Robert Shinn, a freeholder of Burlington County whose appointment to the Pinelands Commission brought to the deliberations years of experience in political activism on behalf of the Pines (Shinn's Burlington County had itself initiated a preservation program that involved $1 million in conservation easements—a program that would be modified, after the plan's adoption, to encourage use of the plan's transferable development rights [TDR] element.)

Not every member of the commission represented the environmental movement, however; developers and local government enthusiasts provided the needed balance for a forum for the complex issues the commission faced. The commission, in the 10 months between February and November 1980, held dozens of hearings and listened to hundreds of hours of testimony and workshop discussions. One newspaper suggested in an editorial that "the Pinelands Plan has had more public airings than Bing Crosby's 'White Christmas.'"

THE PLANNING PROCESS

The issues confronting the commission ranged from environmental protection to mandatory low- and moderate-income housing, from the esoteric to the practical. Typical of the complexity of the commission's challenge was the question of how to maintain the ecological integrity of a pine forest that depended on, among other things, periodic wildfire. How do you design with nature, where nature will periodically burn down the design? Difficult to grasp on its own terms, resolution of this issue was made even more difficult when word reached New Lisbon that a "controlled burn" in Michigan had gotten out of control and burned 35,000 acres of land.

The issues engendered protracted debate and discussion, and the commission met at least two days a week every week from March until November during the planning program. The commission's durability surprised even the most seasoned observers of the zoning game: "If the Pinelands Commissioners learned one thing this year, it was that you can't please all of the people all of the time, and you can't please some of the people at all."

In April, the commission proposed land use categories for the approximately 1 million acres covered by the Act. Then, they spent the rest of the year fielding suggestions, proposals, and an occasional legal threat from farmers, environmentalists, builders, government officials, and just plain folks. All wanted modifications in the plan that would alternately allow for more or less development of the Pinelands.

To a large degree, the approach to be employed during the planning effort was prescribed in the Pinelands Protection Act. The commission, according to the Act, was to develop a land capability map that would indicate where projected population growth could be accommodated without adversely affecting the ecological character of the Pinelands. The program focused on how much development environmentally sensitive areas could stand, and where growth should be directed. The answer to the latter question proved to be far more controversial than the former. Indeed, the most vocal opponents to the comprehensive management plan turned out to be local authorities who had their own growth management programs, which permitted only limited development, notwithstanding proximity to job centers or the availability of public services.

DRAFT CMP

The first draft to the comprehensive management plan was made public on June 8, 1980. Given that the entire preservation area was slated for no development at all, and was reserved for forestry and berry agriculture, it was predictable that the same interest groups or individuals would be unhappy. Their concerns were heightened (mostly vocally) by the fact that the draft plan called for only limited development (one dwelling unit per thirty-nine acres) for an additional 400,000 acres of land in the protection area. Public response ranged from irate ("It's obscene.") to highly technical dissertations. Typical of the landowner's view was the following observation:

> What right do the state and federal governments have to tell us that our land, which was purchased for future development, cannot be developed? Who will compensate us for our losses, present and future?
>
> What's even more incredible is, not only are we being told we own a worthless piece of property, but also we must still pay taxes on it. Even communist and dictatorial countries that confiscate private property do not demand yearly taxes.

The comprehensive management plan was quite straightforward in its approach. First, the commission conceded that the plan had to accommodate the shelter needs of the regional population projected for the South Jersey region. Second, they agreed that the core of the forest was very sensitive to growth and development, and that new development should be directed to the periphery of the forest, where public services were more readily available. Third, the commission accepted that the ecological integrity of the Pinelands was directly linked to ground- and surface-water quality in the Pines. Fourth, it recognized a distinction between the shelter needs of employees of Pinelands resource-related industries, and successful physicians and lawyers in Philadelphia who were looking for second homes. Fifth, the Pinelands Commission understood that the implementation of the comprehensive management plan would catch ongoing projects in the middle, and therefore set out to deal affirmatively with the issue of so-called vested rights. Finally, the commission recognized that the growth-pattern shift that would result from implementation of the comprehensive management plan would mean windfalls for some landowners and wipe-outs for others; therefore, a mitigation strategy was needed to equalize the economic impacts of the plan.

The draft plan responded to these issues by planning for the full measure of regional growth, and directing that growth to designated "regional growth areas." One means of achieving this redirection of growth was an ambitious transferable development rights (TDR) program. Pinelands development credits (PDCs) were allocated to lands in the preservation area and to prime agricultural lands. The PDCs were transferable to any of the designated regional growth areas—which unexpectedly was the source of opposition to the plan; local authorities objected to the plan because it provided for more development than their own local plans indicated.

The plan contained a few other notable elements. One element, popularly known as the "piney exemption," provided density relief for long-term residents and employees of local resource-related industries. The theory was that limited development directed to the shelter needs of the endemic population and the employee needs of forestry and berry agriculture could be accommodated, even in the preservation area. Another element directed at the shelter needs of the region stated that all residential developments involving more than 25 dwelling units were required to provide 25 percent of the dwelling units for low-, moderate- and middle-income households (at least 10 percent had to qualify as low income households, and 10 percent had to be moderate).

OPPOSITION TO THE PLAN

The private sector (developers, farmers, and sand and gravel miners, among others) responded predictably and aggressively. The Coalition for Sensible Protection, one of the many euphemistically named groups formed in opposition to the planned effort, presented an extensive counterplan that called for the protection or acquisition of the preservation area, and for suburban development of the balance of the Pines.

Agricultural interests were particularly agitated by the plan. According to their "spokesman" (one of the many Trenton lawyers to cash in on the "Lawyers Welfare Reform Act of 1979"), the plan—which contained a detailed agricultural conservation element—would, in fact, destroy agriculture!

> In summary, we find that the plan's provisions are massively and unnecessarily overrestrictive in reference to the commission's legislative mandate, and to the likely environmental consequences of farming activities and development in both the protection and preservation areas. In particular, the continued viability of farming, a long-term, stable, and valuable activity in the region, is threatened by the environmental quality standards proposed, and by the loss of land value resulting from adoption of the plan.

This was so, the lawyer said, because the diminution of the value of farmlands from the implementation of the plan (by eliminating the future development potential of the land) would destroy the farmers' capability to operate. The only way a farmer could secure operating credit, according to the spokesman, was by pledging the development capacity of his land as collateral. In other words, agricultural interests argued that it was necessary to continue suburban development potential in order to preserve agriculture. Of course, future development potential was valuable as collateral only if development was reasonably imminent—a fact that "foretold" the end of agriculture and its replacement by suburban sprawl.

There were, of course, many other opponents of the plan, including large-scale corporate developers, who stayed carefully out of the spotlight and let individual lot owners and small farmers carry the public torch of opposition. Literally hundreds of people slowly walked to the microphones in hearing rooms all over the Pines to invoke a common message:

> I bought my land. I paid good money for my land, and I have been paying taxes for years. What right do you have to come in here and tell me I can't build on my land? What right do you have to tell me I have to preserve a bunch of trees? I thought communism was in Russia, not in my own backyard.

The commission was not unsympathetic to the plight of the individual landowners, and yet the commission's mandate was to preserve the Pines; that responsibility was expressed by Commissioner Tom Darlington, one of the largest landowners in the Pines, and a major berry farmer:

> I'm a farmer, as I guess you know. I certainly share your sympathies in trying to get a fair share, not only for farmers, but for landowners—the people who have preserved this land. All the same, to preserve this by walking roughshod over them is not the way to go.

The tension, of course, was between property rights and environmental integrity, as presented by Commissioner Patterson:

> The track record of local government land use decisions has been disastrous. Five-year-old homes in my area have their wells polluted by their own septic systems, and the lake they are near to is so polluted that children were getting sore throats and ear infections from swimming there.

In the meantime, political maneuvering in Trenton had produced a change in the schedule. When the draft plan had been published in early June, opponents had realized that the commission was intent on meeting the August 8 deadline, and the 500-page draft plan looked imposing. Their responsive tactic was to try to delay the effort, in the hope of exercising more political pressure on the final plan. Bills were filed in the legislature to postpone the deadline; however, Governor Byrne made it known that he would veto any broad attack on the Pinelands Protection Act. An accommodation was finally reached whereby the plan for the preservation area would be adopted on August 8, with the plan for the protection area's deadline set back to December 31, 1980. The primary concern was that any delay in adopting the CMP might jeopardize federal funding, which was expressly contingent on adopting the plan 18 months after disbursement of initial funds.

Slowly, then almost defiantly, the plan began to take shape. By midsummer, the Pinelands Commission staff began to believe the CMP might actually be adopted. Indeed, if opponents' attempts to extend the moratorium were any indication, the August 8, 1980 deadline for the preservation area had become a reality. What originally had been seen by many as the Achilles' heel of the effort—an impossible deadline—had become an unmistakable mandate for indefatigable work and devotion from staff, commission members, and their consultants. The question of whether anyone would spend the night on the couch at New Lisbon had been disposed of long ago, and the only remaining question was who got the couch. Dinner at the diner at 2:30 a.m. was the rule for both staff and commissioners, as the determination to get the plan adopted became self-sustaining.

AUGUST 8, 1980

Friday morning, August 8, 1980, dawned as every morning seems to dawn across the bogs and forests of the Pines—beautiful and misty. The focus of attention, however, was not the delicate calls of birds, rather, it was the theater of the Burlington County Community College in New Lisbon, where the Pinelands Commission was scheduled to take up the preservation area plan.

Chairman Frank Parker opened the meeting and invited the public to submit comments. The speeches were short, impassioned, and equally divided between proponents and opponents. The commission discussion was slightly less balanced, since the hard work on the plan had made the commissioners tense and edgy; indeed, just before the vote, one of the commissioners attacked the character of another commissioner by accusing him of "profiteering." In what can only be described as a tribute to the integrity of the process and the people, there was unanimous condemnation of this attack, followed by several sincere speeches of support for the incorruptibility of the process—one by a developer openly opposed to the substance of the plan.

When this emotional crisis passed, the roll was called, and the preservation area plan was adopted. The goal of regional management for the Pinelands had become a reality. Tom Darlington, the commissioner, landowner, and berry farmer whose integrity had been attacked, summed up the feeling of the moment:

> I've had a lot of pressure from my friends; they even suggested I resign. We hired a professional staff, and what they have done makes sense. I believe the plan is right, it's what the Pines needs. I went to my children last night and said, "What do you think I should do? The plan will significantly reduce the value of our lands, and if you think I am doing wrong, then I would like to know that is how you feel." They told me, "We're behind you 100 percent. You do what you think is right, and we'll back you up."

OPPOSITION TO THE DESIGNATED GROWTH AREAS

Plan opponents, now certain that the commission would meet its deadlines, shifted their strategy from opposition to compromise and amendment. One major area of debate was the designation of growth areas— communities that were earmarked for growth but that did not want to grow. During the planning process, the staff and its consultants had understood that plan opponents would be dissatisfied with the reduced amount of development allocated to their properties. Consequently, an extensive report had been prepared, delineating the legal principles controlling the anticipated downzoning. What the staff and consultants had not fully foreseen, however, was the inevitable conflict of the management plan with the no-growth attitudes of communities that were in the vicinity of Atlantic City and Camden.

Galloway Township was typical of this kind of plan opponent. (Not coincidentally, the Coalition for Preservation's expert planner was the planner for Galloway Township.) A small, relatively undeveloped community of large suburban lots, the township had previously completed a planning program to protect its rural ambience from the onslaught of the less elegant development spawned by the Atlantic City casinos. The township met all of the CMP criteria for a growth area, as the plan called for the deflection of residential development away from the forest core to areas that were close to job centers and major public-service systems. Galloway Township, a planned community, now found itself replanned as a distinctly different type of community— at least, as its officials saw it.

PINELANDS DEVELOPMENT CREDIT (PDC)

Galloway Township's frustration with the plan was heightened by the CMP's proposed pinelands development credit (PDC) program. PDCs are an economic mitigation strategy developed to compensate for the windfalls and wipe-outs created by the plan. They are a transferable development right that can be freely traded on the private market and used by landowners in designated growth areas to secure density bonuses. To ensure that PDC owners would have a real opportunity to mitigate wipe-outs, and to recapture at least a portion of the windfalls created by the plan, the CMP required that all residentially zoned land in "growth areas" be eligible for PDC bonus densities. Townships saw the PDC program as a direct assault on the integrity of their neighborhoods.

The PDC program attracted much more attention than that of the disgruntled growth-area townships. The allocation methodology—who got how many PDCs— came under attack, not surprisingly, by owners of land slated for PDC allocations. One much-discussed element of the PDC program revolved around the issue of farm credit for row-crop farmers.

The outer edges of the Pines had always been among the state's most productive agricultural lands. However, labor and transportation costs, plus the rewards of selling to developers, had created a serious threat to the continued viability of agriculture in South Jersey. The Pinelands Protection Act clearly stated that agriculture was part of the Pinelands, and that it was to be preserved and enhanced. Of course, the preservation of farmlands involves the deflection of development expectations that make up the bulk of the value of the farmers' lands. Deprived of the speculative value of their land for development purposes, the farmers were faced with a shortage of farm credit, which constituted a serious threat to the viability of farming. But if PDCs were allocated to designated agricultural lands, it would be possible for farmers to sell their credits as a means of raising working capital—that is, as a means of taking advantage of the development value of the lands without destroying their usefulness for farming.

ENVIRONMENTAL OPPOSITION

In late October, the commission was holding almost continuous hearings; the vote of the protection area portion of the plan was scheduled for November 21,

1980. The plan had undergone extensive change during the public hearing process, as the commission sought to strike a balance among the various interests affected by the CMP. Now, the environmentalists, always staunch supporters of the program, began to question whether the CMP had been compromised to satisfy local governments and developer interests. They doubted that the revised CMP could protect the Pinelands.

> The commission has gone overboard in grandfathering-in subdivisions; environmentalists' objections "were given very rude, short shrift"; and the weakened plan "was ramrodded down our throats." . . .
> It was supposed to have been a protection plan, not a development plan.

At one hearing, a representative of one of the national environmental groups went so far as to accuse the Pinelands Commission staff of "carrying water for the developers." Few statements were less well received during the entire public hearing process, and another environmentalist rose to defend the staff that had labored, day and night, to prepare a comprehensive management plan for the 1 million acres, 52 municipalities, and seven counties in less than 10 months. The development community found the environmentalist's remarks to be ironic: "It's one tough cookie of a plan. It's the toughest environmental plan in the United States, and . . . environmentalists are calling it too weak."

ADOPTION OF THE PLAN

Final adoption of the plan was almost anticlimactic. The hearing was unexpectedly brief, and the commission voted 11 to four to adopt the CMP. Congratulations were shared among all attendees, including development interests, who begrudgingly admitted that the program had been carried out professionally, fairly, and openly.

For the staff, the planning effort was not over; it was just beginning. The protection act commanded that local governments be given a full opportunity to participate in the implementation of the plan, and the CMP set forth detailed procedures and standards for the certification of local plans and regulations. Throughout the planning process leading to the adoption of the CMP, much concern had been expressed because other regional programs—a plan for the Adirondacks, Oregon's statewide plan, and Florida's Area of Critical Concern—had experienced very little success in inducing local authorities to submit acceptable programs for certification.

In response, the plan included an incentive for rapid certification. The incentive was the solution to another sticky issue faced by the planners and commission; how to deal with the myriad claims for vested rights to platted lots, second phases, secret plans and dreams, and others. Great pressure was brought to bear to include a grandfather clause that would protect the development rights of all individual lot owners; however, the plan limited grandfather rights to areas with certified local plans.

No, the adoption of the comprehensive plan was not the end of the Pinelands saga. Under the Parks and Recreation Act, the plan had to be approved by the governor and then by the Secretary of the U.S. Department of the Interior. Moreover, the Heritage Conservation and Recreation Service (HCRS) was required to prepare an environmental impact statement (EIS) for the Secretary's action, all against a backdrop of the new, incoming Reagan administration. Once again, the governor was assailed about the plan. ("Under the restrictions of the Pinelands Act, this property is practically useless; there can be no development.") On December 2, 1980, nonetheless, he approved the plan and forwarded it to the Secretary of the Interior.

MORE OPPOSITION

In the meantime, HCRS's draft EIS had been circulated for review and comment, and, to no one's surprise, the opponents kept up their attacks. The Coalition for the Sensible Preservation of the Pinelands, for example, said, "We are profoundly disturbed by several statements and conclusions contained therein." Among the outspoken was Representative William J. Hughes, whose objections were quoted in the EIS:

> The state of New Jersey has created an entirely new bureaucracy to plan for and regulate all activities in the Pinelands. This contravenes the intention of the federal law, which was to emphasize home rule and existing laws and regulations, to help meet regional conservation goals.

Hughes, joined by Representative Edwin Forsyth, even went so far as to advise the Secretary of the Interior that they "would oppose the use of federal funds for the Pinelands Plan, if approved in its present form."

Secretary Cecil Andrus, already a lame duck, approved the plan on January 16, 1981. His action was not just an act of political courage. The plan was widely supported in the EIS. For example, the much-debated impact on agriculture was cogently analyzed by the Farmer's Home Administration in the U.S. Department of Agriculture, which, although it foresaw changes, endorsed the CMP as adopted:

> We have determined, based upon the program review, that . . . the Pinelands Comprehensive Management Plan should not have any adverse effects on the management of our programs. . . .
> Implementation of the plan will have an effect in reducing land values, due to the proposed restriction of land uses. This reduction in land values may affect the borrowing capacities of landowners and farmers. The overall effect of this program, however, is considered to be minimal and should adjust itself with the passing of time.

One agency that did not relent was the Department of the Army. The CMP required that federal actions comply with the plan, unless compliance "would prevent achievement of the installation's national defense mission." The commission had recognized the unique character of federal facilities, and had created the "military and federal installation area" (MAFIA) as a special management area.

The Army was nevertheless confident of its independent integrity and, oblivious to any idea that it "could do wrong," objected to the CMP. The Army was convinced it was able to judge whether its actions were good or bad for the Pinelands, and, by its own definition, whatever it did would be good. Ultimately, the Army and the Pinelands Commission reached an accommodation. However, there were numerous occasions when Pogo's lament was recalled: "We have met the enemy and he is us."

OBSERVATIONS

The CMP has been, by all accounts, a great success. There are, of course, detractors, most of whom reside in Atlantic County. The commission nevertheless endures, and 36 municipalities and four counties have amended their local plans and regulations and been certified as conforming with the plan. Ninety-six percent of all development subsequent to the plan's adoption has been located in areas designated for growth.

One aspect of the planning program that is remarkable is the dearth of litigation. Notwithstanding the virulent threats announced during the public hearing process, there have been very few challenges to this plan. An initial challenge that contested particular procedural aspects of the plan, and the so-called piney exemption, was admirably and successfully defended by Rich Hluchan, a deputy attorney general who had been assigned to the commission throughout the planning process.

Observers suggest that absence of litigation is attributable to several considerations. The first is the Pinelands Commission and its staff. Although the results of their efforts may not always have been satisfying, almost everyone agrees that they were fair and responsive. When someone had a legitimate complaint, he or she got action, and the commission exuded an attitude of service quite distinct from the bureaucratic annoyance that generally tends to characterize resource management efforts.

The second consideration is the state and federal commitment to the Pines. Recognizing the inevitability of the Pinelands Commission as a long-term proposition has encouraged cooperation as the preferred alternative to conflict.

Third, the CMP National Reserve and the CMP contain an acquisition element that calls for purchase of critical areas. Litigation is generally the result of extreme examples and the acquisition of critical areas has eliminated many of the most difficult situations.

Finally, the CMP was done correctly. The research on which it was based was sound, and the public was given a full and unconstrained opportunity to participate in the process. Where there were gaps, the plan called for more research. The plan was forthright: it admitted that there would be differing viewpoints, and it tried to be responsive and flexible. It is human nature to appreciate the "effort," even if the effort does not always succeed. The Pinelands Commission and its staff have made an effort second to none, in the comprehensive management plan for the New Jersey Pinelands.

Richard F. Babcock is professor of law at Duke University in Durham, North Carolina. Charles L. Siemon is a partner in Siemon, Larsen & Purdy, a law firm in Chicago, Illinois.

This paper is excerpted from Babcock's and Siemon's book *The Zoning Game Revisited*, published in 1985 by Oelgeschlager, Gunn & Hain, in association with the Lincoln Institute of Land Policy. Reprinting is by permission.

ADIRONDACK PARK: SUCCESSFUL STATE MANAGEMENT

THOMAS A. ULASEWICZ

W hen the Urban Land Institute requested that I speak before this group, I was a little bewildered. My subject, of course, was to be the Adirondack Park—probably one of the most rural places in the continental United States.

But in thinking about it, and in putting my notes together, I immediately recalled one statistic: the Adirondack Park is within one day's drive of some of the largest urban centers on the East Coast: New York City, Boston, virtually all of the New England cities, Montreal, Toronto, and so forth. The statistic is often thrown out that during the height of the tourist season in the Adirondack Park we get up to 9 million people visiting the region, which has, I believe, a year-round population of about 120,000. So it's a substantial element. And there are certainly definite growth pressures in the park.

But before I begin on the main body of my presentation, please understand, first, that since my first day in this particular position, I've referred to the agency as reaching its adolescent years. It is still going through some awkward growing pains, and I hope that, throughout my commentary, you'll see where the pain has been, and how we've attempted to direct it in less painful ways.

Also, please understand that, despite its adolescence, the Adirondack Park Agency reviews approximately 400 project permits per year, plus requests for variances, map amendments, wetland and rivers permits. Two-thirds of our decisions deal with small-scale development in rural use and resource management areas.

DESCRIPTION AND HISTORY OF THE PARK ITSELF

The Adirondack Park, then, is a natural resource unique within the United States. It has some genuine natural treasures, both in terms of resources and of open-space character. The park is 6 million acres in size and constitutes one-fifth of the land mass of New York State. Approximately the size of the state of Vermont, it is also roughly three times the size of Yellowstone National Park.

The park was created in 1892. Within the park are pristine rivers, lakes, ponds, rugged mountains, and a sea of forest—all within a day's drive of 50 million people, in the cities I listed earlier.

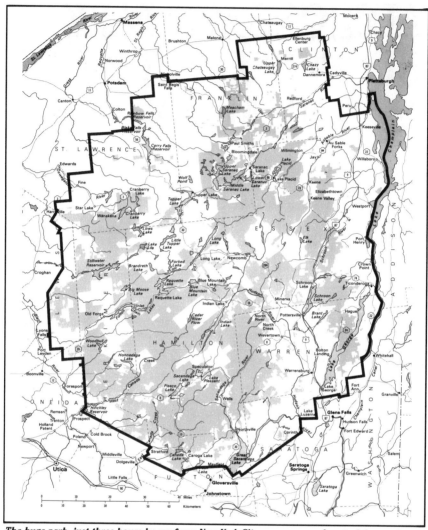

The huge park, just three hours by car from New York City, encompasses forests, lakes, and towns. Planning objectives for these features—natural and manmade—often conflict.

There are more than 40 peaks that rise above 4,000 feet in elevation; of these, 10 have "alpine" summits.

One of the most distinctive features of the park, and one of the reasons why the state of New York decided back in the 1800s to afford it such unusual protection, is that it has 2,800 lakes. This concentration of water is found in no other mountainous region in the United States.

As a park, it's a patchwork of public and private lands. About 40 percent is public (state-owned) land, and the balance is privately owned. Thirty-seven percent of the private land is owned by corporations and out-of-park residents; those corporations—primarily paper companies—own hundreds of thousands of tracts. Paper is an important industry in the Adirondacks.

The public lands are known as the Adirondack State Forest Preserve. The "Forest Preserve in the state of New York" was created in 1885, and New Yorkers are celebrating its 100th anniversary this year. In establishing the forest preserve under Article 14, the state constitution called for the forest preserve lands to be kept forever wild. "Forever wild" means many things: perhaps one of the most controversial mandates is that there will be no cutting or removal of timber on any of these lands. That's a significant prohibition, when 2.5 million acres of the 6-million-acre park is publicly owned forest preserve.

The park's wild character, open space, recreational opportunities, and many hamlets are major draws for it, and tourism and recreation together make for a major source of income to the park's residents. In 1967, Laurance Rockefeller sought a federal proposal to turn the central Adirondacks into a national park. This idea was unanimously opposed by the state's citizens. It was extremely controversial, and, as a result, there's little—some would say no—federal presence in the park to the present day.

THE AGENCY IS BORN

Governor Nelson Rockefeller appointed a temporary study commission on the Adirondacks in 1968. It reported in 1970, calling for an Adirondack Park Agency that would develop a comprehensive land use and development plan for the park. The recommendations of the study commission numbered roughly 150, and this one was among the most significant.

Consequently, in 1971, by an act of the state legislature, the nonpartisan Adirondack Park Agency came into being within the state's executive department. The agency consists of 11 voting members: eight private individuals and three state officials. Those state officials are the commissioner of the department of environmental conservation, the secretary of state, and the commissioner for the department of commerce.

Of the eight private people appointed by the governor and confirmed by the state senate, five are in-park residents, three are out-of-park residents, and no more than five altogether can be from the same political party.

The agency members are aided by a staff of specialists in law, planning, engineering, ecology, and forestry—a total of 45 staff members.

THE PUBLIC LANDS

One of the APA's mandates is to develop and maintain a master plan for the state lands. This was first done in 1972, with the purpose of classifying all of this land, according to its capacity to withstand certain uses. This plan was put together in conjunction with the department of environmental conservation, which is responsible for the day-to-day management of the lands. The APA, on the other hand, is responsible for reviewing any unit management plans, or other management activities, proposed by other state agencies.

State land classifications range from intensive uses like beaches, campsites, and ski slopes, to large wildernesses. Currently, we are revising the state land master plan, which the legislature requires us to do every five years.

The land classifications determine which uses are compatible in different portions of the 2.5 million acres of land. One of the largest controversies over these classifications revolves around the fact that motorized equipment is forbidden in the "wilderness" areas. This represents a problem for our sportsmen, primarily, but the "wild forest" areas, which make up a little in excess of 1 million acres, do allow

Keeping natural areas natural, yet useful, is one of the prime goals of the land management program.

for motorized equipment and for some excellent sports and other recreational activities.

THE PRIVATE LANDS

In addition to the state lands, the agency is responsible for the Adirondack Park Land Use and Development Plan, a plan that regulates development of the private lands—3.5 million acres—and channels growth into established community centers, such as the Hamlet of Old Forge, and into other less restricted growth centers. Its mission here, as elsewhere, is to protect the park's vast open spaces, forest preserves, and other special resources.

The entire plan is classified by an intensity-of-use guideline, as shown by the color-keyed land use classifications on the APA map. These classifications are premised primarily on an average number of allowed principal buildings per square mile.

Our land use planning map is often referred to as the "Fruit Salad Map." The yellow and the green areas on it are the most restricted areas: that is, the resource management, or green areas, and the rural use, or yellow, areas. Resource management, which allows one principal building for every 42 acres, constitutes about 53 percent of the private land. Obviously, this was a highly controversial plan when it was first put into effect, and, in many respects, it remains so.

OTHER PROGRAMS

Local Government Aid

Now, the agency also administers a program of modest assistance for local government land use planning—a subject I'll address more fully when I get into our successes and failures. But we do have about $150,000 in local grants from the legislature annually, to help this process along. The process includes local code administration, zoning, subdivision, and sanitary regulations, plus special projects—for instance, a downtown revitalization scheme for Keeseville.

Other Acts Administered

In addition to the Adirondack Park Agency Act, the agency administers two other important pieces of legislation within the park. One is the New York State Wild, Scenic, and Recreational Rivers Act. This is intended to ensure the continued free flowing of the 1,200 miles of rivers currently in the system.

Also, the agency administers the Freshwater Wetlands Act in the park; the wetlands legislation, passed by the state legislature in 1975, has required an extensive mapping program of most wetlands.

Wetlands Mapping

It has been said that the job in mapping the park's wetlands has been a "monumental task." That's an understatement. Fourteen percent of the park is wetlands. Under our jurisdiction, we map and protect any wetland of one acre or larger. Furthermore, if a smaller wetland connects with an open body of water, any size of activity comes within our regulatory purview.

I have had people in the field morning to night, seven days a week, in the first county that we've mapped, for months. We have been directed by the legislature to map all 12 counties in the Adirondack Park. That mandate came out, as I mentioned, in 1975. We finished our first county about a month ago.

Currently, the agency's newly created resource analysis and scientific services unit (a fancy name for a group of five scientists put together at the agency about a year ago) is involved in wetlands mapping. Their work will result in individual community maps showing wetlands for the entire park. The cartographers look at aerial photos and transfer their information onto maps that we later take to public hearings before the maps become official. At this point, we also notify every affected landowner.

Incidentally, the agency has one of the most sophisticated computerized geographic information systems in the East. This computerized system holds within its memory bank, and shows on its maps, the soil types contained within the acreage of the park, vegetative cover, roads, the park plan maps, and all water bodies. And part of our process in the next 12 months and beyond will be to put mapped wetlands into this geographic information system.

Clearly, this system stores, provides, and coordinates a wealth of information on the park's resources. It has also proved more than helpful in our cooperative agreements with other governmental agencies and with private groups doing research: it has aided in the exchange of data, attracting funding sources and the like.

DIFFICULTIES, SUCCESSES, AND FAILURES

Court Cases

The Taking Controversy. Inevitably, in such a complicated and forward-looking venture, there has been litigation. With regard to the taking issue, in the early years of the agency, we had two primary lawsuits: the first was brought by local landowners who claimed that the Act was far too restrictive and deprived them of reasonable use of their land. The highest court in New York State, the court of appeals, turned down that claim and held that it was a matter of valid police power and public interest that the particular plan, as passed, be implemented by a state agency. So, this one was a success.

The second case of significance was brought by a number of local governments, who made charges of state interference with "home rule." This case, too, was denied by the courts in New York State, which held again that there was a valid public interest that the state should be concerning itself with. On the other hand, there is a means whereby local governments that are so inclined can adopt a program that assumes a lot of the jurisdiction we now exercise at the state level.

Very interesting, although, in our terms, not yet either a success or a failure but a threat, is the federal challenge now being prepared on these same issues. In this matter, the Pacific Legal Foundation was retained by the local government review board, a creation of New York statute set up as a watchdog over the Adirondack Park Agency to look into a federal constitutional challenge. As I understand it, that challenge would focus primarily on the green areas on the map—the 42-acres-per-principal-building areas. It would try to demonstrate that the denial of a principal building, such as a single-family residence, is far too restrictive and infringes upon an individual's constitutional rights. (Indeed, this challenge may be incorporated into a West Coast case now being reviewed by the U.S. Supreme Court on the issue of certiorari: *MacDonald, Sommer, and Frates* v. *County of Yolo* [California Court of Appeals, Third District, January 25, 1985. No. 3 Civ. 22306. Unreported.].)

This lawsuit has been bandied about for a few years; it still has not been formally brought, and even at this time, it is questionable whether it will be brought. The main reason for the doubt is that a number of studies are going on in the Adirondacks now with regard to real property values. The preliminary reports being prepared by New York State's equalization and assessment board have shown that the private land values in the park have increased at an equal or greater rate than have those of comparable lands outside the park. Interesting twist. Maybe this is one of the reasons why the agency is a little better accepted by the public in the 1980s than it was in the 1970s.

A Question of Jurisdiction. One other important matter regarding legal issues and legal challenges. I went to a meeting recently, and a lawyer walked up to me and served me with a summons and a complaint on a decision that we had issued roughly 30 days before. We asserted our wetlands jurisdiction on a portion of a tournament golf course near Lake George. The applicant, a large resort corporation, wanted to use some 22 pesticides—fungicides, herbicides, and insecticides in various combinations—on the course over a three-year period.

Before we did this, we went through a technical assessment that I am honestly proud of. It was as quantitative as it could be. It was a risk assessment, given the lack of information coming out of EPA. We denied use of 19 of the 22 pesticides because of findings of needless risks of contamination to groundwater, streams (potable water supplies), and the lake itself.

We are being sued. The primary allegation there, as far as I'm concerned (although there are about seven counts), is that jurisdiction for the regulation and control of pesticides in New York State rests with the state's department of environmental conservation, and that, thus, we're exceeding our authority under the Freshwater Wetlands Act.

The Towns

On the subject of programs that might be less-than-perfect successes: the APA's local government program covers 107 towns inside the park, 12 counties, and 25 to 30 communities actively seeking money—some of that $150,000. Of these, 16 have agency-approved local plans, and 16 out of 107 is not a success story, in my opinion. About two-thirds of the towns, overall, have availed themselves of local assistance. Among the reasons this program is not successful is the fact that most of the communities are so rural that they're too small to undertake a comprehensive plan: they don't have any staff or money to implement a plan, and there's tremendous political pressure on them. I talk to local officials, and they say, "Why should we do it, when you can take the heat?"

So, the agency is reassessing its local assistance program. It's de-emphasizing the comprehensive plans and trying to deal with the current needs of a community. It's looking at the $150,000 that it distributes annually, and looking at candidates that are interested in hamlet revitalization; interested in riverfront recreational planning; or in need of an ordinance to cover septic system problems, trailer park and mobile home problems, or other problems typical of rural towns.

In the Lake George Park specifically, the agency has six approved towns. A draft study has recently been issued by New York State, revealing that the quality of that lake is declining at a rapid pace; in fact, there is very, very much concern about it.

Local planning within the Lake George Basin is simply not working. Primarily, it is not working for political reasons. There is so much development pressure. There are such large amounts of money in converting motels to condominiums, and in taking lakefront lots and deeding access to non-lakefront townhouses that number 70, 80, 100, or 120 units and that string out for half a mile or so. We're examining the possibility of new legislation that would strengthen local government controls. That way, development below the "regional" permit threshold of the agency would need to get local permit review and to follow sound ecological and planning assessments.

A FEW REASONS FOR CONGRATULATION

In the face of all these difficulties, the agency has still made several great strides.

The APA has survived substantially intact since 1971. Its authority was expanded in 1975, when it got wetlands jurisdiction. Also in 1975, it obtained inclusion of about 1,200 miles of its rivers in a Wild, Scenic, and Recreational Rivers System.

Importantly, the agency has strong nonpartisan support. There's no more talk of abolition, as there was in the 1970s (when I also worked at the agency for two years). "Freedom fighters" for the Adirondack Park are little heard from. We are fully staffed, at 45 individuals, for the first time since the agency's concept was raised in 1970 by the temporary study commission.

All of these facts mean that the APA now has increased budgetary, gubernatorial, and local support for the programs it's undertaking.

Thomas A. Ulasewicz is executive director of the Adirondack Park Agency. Formerly, Ulasewicz was acting general counsel for New York State's department of environmental conservation.

Ulasewicz's contribution to this book is drawn from an address he made at the ULI/Lincoln Institute seminar on growth management.

153

STATE ENVIRONMENTAL PLANNING AND LOCAL INFLUENCE

A Comparison of Three Regional Natural Resource Management Agencies

ALAN J. HAHN AND CYNTHIA D. DYBALLA

N ew York's Adirondack Park Agency (APA) has earned a reputation as a generally successful effort to bring statewide interests to bear on natural resource
management in a particular multicounty region. Despite vigorous local opposition, it has developed plans for both state and private lands within the park,
has been implementing land use regulations since 1973, and has withstood several
serious legislative and judicial challenges.

Environmentalists worry about the agency's capacity to detect violations and enforce compliance, and have occasionally accused it of sacrificing too much environmental protection for the sake of economic development; but for the most
part, advocates of environmental planning seem inclined to accept the APA's status
as a model worth duplicating elsewhere.

There are reasons to question that status, however. Local opposition cannot always be disregarded to the degree that was possible for the APA. This is plainly il-
lustrated by the experiences of two other, less well-known natural resource management agencies in New York. They not only demonstrate the limited transferability of
the APA model, but also suggest some alternative ways of handling conflicts between state policy and local interests.

ANALYTICAL FRAMEWORK

Several rationales exist for intervention at the local level on behalf of extralocal
interests. With respect to land use issues, Healy has summarized them as follows
(1976, p. 6):
- Problems that spill across the boundaries of legal jurisdictions;
- Problems arising when local interests diverge from the interests of a broader
  public;

FIGURE 1
MAP OF NEW YORK, SHOWING THE REGIONS COVERED BY THE CASE-STUDY AGENCIES

Watertown

Adirondack Park

Tug Hill Region

Rochester

Buffalo

Utica

Syracuse

Albany

Catskill Region

Binghamton

Catskill Park

New York City

Three large regions dominate the eastern half of New York State. Each region, however, has approached growth management in a different manner, and with different results.

- Problems arising on lands not subject to effective local control; and
- Problems allied with the implementation of state policies, or the carrying out of state investments.

Each of these factors was involved in the case studies reported in this article, with the second and third having the most direct influence.

Legally, there are few limits on the authority of state governments to intervene in local affairs, regardless of the rationale. New York is not atypical in this respect. Even in its home rule provisions, the state constitution provides local governments with no protection from state intervention by "general laws." Court decisions have given "general laws" a liberal interpretation, and further eroded any legal guarantees of local autonomy (Temporary State Commission on State and Local Finances, 1975).

In short, rationales are readily available for state intervention, and there are virtually no legal obstacles. However, the balance between state and local interests that is actually realized is determined politically—and, in that arena, local people are not powerless. There is already a substantial body of literature demonstrating the absence of any easy or automatic local implementation of state or federal objectives, at least in the case of grant-in-aid programs (Derthick, 1970 and 1972; Jones, 1975; Murphy, 1970; Orfield, 1969; Pressman and Wildavsky, 1979; Van Horn, 1979).

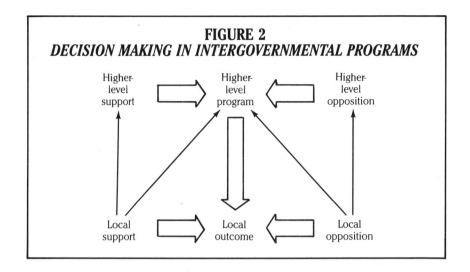

FIGURE 2
DECISION MAKING IN INTERGOVERNMENTAL PROGRAMS

Higher-level support → Higher-level program ← Higher-level opposition

Local support → Local outcome ← Local opposition

This is surely also true of state mandates, and it is the authors' contention that it is true even for direct implementation by state agencies.[1]

Figure 2 provides the authors' interpretation of the literature. State/local conflicts and their outcomes (and federal/local ones as well) can best be understood by knowing the patterns of support and opposition for the programs in question, at both the local and higher levels. Neither level is necessarily monolithic in its interests (Pressman, 1975; Wirt, 1974, Part IV). Both the enactment and the administration of state and federal programs are shaped by competing pressures from supporting and opposing interest groups.

The effectiveness of the programs depends on implementation at the local level, involving decisions by local officials or private sector participants in the case of grants-in-aid or mandates, and by state or federal employees in the case of direct implementation by state or federal agencies. These decisions are also subject to pressures from competing interests at the local level.

Implementation is impeded by the sheer physical difficulty of enforcing compliance in scores or hundreds of localities, by limited higher-level resources, by communication problems, by resistance from opposition groups, etc. (Van Horn and Van Meter, 1976; Van Horn, 1979; Pressman and Wildavsky, 1979). Furthermore, local officials and citizens are often able to evade full compliance by exerting direct influence on state or federal legislative and administrative actions (Grodzins, 1966). Derthick (1970 and 1972) has suggested that the presence of local allies of higher-level objectives may be necessary for successful implementation.

In short, implementation decisions are influenced in part by higher-level programs, but also by an interplay of other, often conflicting, local interests. The combination of these various influences determines the success or failure of the programs, and the balance of local and higher-level interests that is realized.

---

[1] Relevant case studies of direct implementation include Brilliant (1975); Kaufman (1960); Lowi et al. (1976); Lupo, Colcord, and Fowler (1971); and Selznick (1949). There is also a useful body of literature on the local implementation of court decisions—for example, Dolbeare and Hammond (1971) and Milner (1971).

ADIRONDACK PARK AGENCY

The Adirondack Park, presently encompassing 6 million acres, was created by the state legislature in 1892.[2] It includes 107 towns and villages in 12 counties, and consists of a patchwork of private holdings and state forest-preserve lands. The forest preserve was created by the legislature in 1885 and given constitutional protection in 1894. Despite the presence of wealthy landowners and summer residents, and heavy use by recreationists, the park remains sparsely populated and economically depressed.

Creation of the park agency was the culmination of a series of events beginnning in 1967, when a study report recommending an Adirondack national park generated widespread opposition. In September 1968, Governor Nelson Rockefeller appointed the Temporary Study Commission on the Future of the Adirondacks (TSC). Around that time, downstate conservationists and several wealthy Adirondack landowners had grown concerned about potential large-scale second-home development in the mountains. The sense of urgency was further heightened by the increased accessibility of the Adirondacks, resulting from the completion of Interstate 87 between New York City and Montreal in 1968.

The TSC was dominated by people who were not full-time residents of the Adirondacks and were firmly in favor of preservation. Its recommendations, issued in December 1970, included creation of an Adirondacks Park Agency, development and implementation of a comprehensive plan for the park, and regulation of private as well as public land (Temporary Study Commission, 1970). Rockefeller introduced the proposed legislation. While it was predictably opposed by Adirondack area legislators, overwhelming support from the rest of the state resulted in easy passage by both houses of the state legislature. The act was signed by the governor in June 1971.

The APA is governed by an 11-member (originally, nine-member) commission appointed by the governor. At least five members must be park residents; three are ex officio representatives of state agencies (*Laws of New York*, 1971, Chap. 706). Headquarters for the commission and its staff were established at Ray Brook, within the park.

The state land use plan was adopted in June 1972 and generated little controversy. The private land use plan was a different story, however. It was prepared during 1971 and 1972, under considerable time pressure. Hearings were held in each of the 12 Adirondack counties and in Rochester, Buffalo, and New York City. The in-park hearings were characterized by extremely vocal opposition. Numerous adjustments were made (Liroff and Davis, 1981), and the plan was approved by the state legislature and signed by the governor in May 1973.

The plan provides for APA control over projects with substantial regional impacts, and for the assumption of local government control over projects with less regional impact, once local planning programs are approved by the APA and adopted by the local governing body (*Laws of New York*, 1973, Chap. 348; Booth, 1975).

The history of the APA, like its establishment, has been characterized by very strong statewide support, and by widespread and hostile local opposition (Graham, 1978; Sullivan, 1975; Lewis, 1976; Clark, 1976; Anonymous, 1977; Feiss, 1979; and Liroff and Davis, 1981). At the state level, the governor, a majority of the state legislators (especially from downstate), members of the TSC, environmental groups, and

---

[2] The authors' history of the APA relies very heavily on Graham (1978). See also D'Elia (1979) for an account written from the opposition perspective. On the formulation and adoption of the private land use and development plan, Liroff and Davis (1981) is particularly helpful.

most major newspapers have been supportive. State-level opposition has largely been confined to the park area's representatives in the state legislature, notably Assemblyman Glenn Harris and Senator Ronald Stafford.

Within the Adirondacks, the most outspoken opponents have been the Local Government Review Board (LGRB) and such groups as the League for Adirondack Citizens' Rights. The LGRB was established in 1973, when the private land use plan was adopted as part of a compromise with Harris and Stafford (*Laws of New York,* 1973, Chap. 348). Set up to "monitor and assist" the APA, its members—appointed by the park area's county governing boards—have been mostly outspoken opponents of the APA. The LGRB organized a series of emotion-laden, anti-APA, public "speak-outs" in 1975, and has persistently recommended legislative changes to abolish or weaken the APA and to increase local government control (see, for example, Local Government Review Board, 1978).

The League for Adirondack Citizens' Rights was organized in 1975 by a wealthy landowner, a real estate developer, and others. It has relied on emotional appeals, denounced the APA for destroying private property rights, and developed an organization of "Minute Men," who staged demonstrations in Albany and disrupted town and village meetings throughout the park to discourage cooperation with the APA (D'Elia, 1979). Other opponents include the *Adirondack Daily Enterprise* of Saranac Lake, various developers and individual landowners who have taken legal action against the APA, and individual local governments.

Reasons for local opposition include basic social and philosophical differences between many Adirondack residents and the APA's state-level supporters. The latter were viewed as "rabid environmentalists" lacking compassion for local residents. The APA was considered unnecessary at best, and, more often, an unconstitutional invasion of property rights and denial of local self-government.

These inherent conflicts were aggravated by specific practices of the APA: inconvenient and lengthy project review procedures; APA jurisdiction over minor as well as major projects (that is, in the widespread absence of APA-approved local planning programs); a young and often insensitive and rigid staff; and the availability, originally of only criminal penalties for violations of the APA Act.

Every year from 1971 to 1977, bills were introduced in the state legislature to abolish or weaken the APA. Harris and Stafford led the fight. In 1973, legislation to delay implementation of the private land use plan for one year was vetoed by Governor Rockefeller. The LGRB was created in the same year, however. In 1976, legislation to give the LGRB more influence in selection of APA commissioners was vetoed by Governor Hugh Carey.

Other legislative changes in 1976—ones advocated by the APA itself—substituted civil for criminal penalties, facilitated APA approval of local planning programs, and provided state legal assistance for local governments attempting to implement APA-approved regulations (*Laws of New York,* 1976, Chaps. 898, 899). In 1977, Harris and Stafford introduced a bill to replace the APA with state agency regulation of "critical environmental areas," and a locally controlled agency to handle all other private land use control. The bill was approved by the state senate, but only with the knowledge that it stood no chance at all in the assembly, and would certainly be vetoed by the governor (Lewis, 1976; Nichols, 1977a and 1977b). By that time, especially with the revisions adopted the previous year, it seemed that much of the steam had gone out of the anti-APA lobby.

In addition to legislative challenges, legal actions against the APA resulted in some minor victories. However, major decisions rejected arguments 1) that the APA Act was an unconstitutional infringement on local government home rule (*Wambat Realty Corp.* v. *State of New York et al.,* 85 Misc. 2d 489 (1976), 41 N.Y. 2d 490 (1977)), and 2) that the agency's land use controls constituted a "de facto appropriation of private property," requiring just compensation (*Horizon Adirondack Corp.* v. *State of New York*, 88 Misc. 2d. 619 (1977)).

By 1977, local attitudes toward the APA appeared to be changing. Agency chairman Robert Flacke said, "It now appears we have turned a corner, and the controversy is largely behind us" (Adirondack Park Agency, 1978). The LGRB's executive director said, "People get worn down and figure, 'The hell with it; if it's reasonable, we'll live with it' " (personal interview with the authors).

Factors in these changes included the passage of time, the realization that the APA wasn't likely to go away, and evidence that its presence was not as devastating as originally predicted. In addition, the agency itself changed. It acquired a more locally acceptable chairman in 1975, streamlined its project review procedures, developed a more experienced and flexible staff, shifted its focus from developing regulations to providing planning assistance to local governments, and gave increasing attention to economic development.

By mid-1979, two-thirds of the park area's local governments had requested and received APA planning assistance, and nine town planning programs had received final agency approval (Anonymous, 1979). Agency personnel were satisfied that the laws were being obeyed, that most infractions were unintentional, and that a "regional consciousness" of being "part of the park" was growing (personal communication with the authors).[3]

CATSKILL STUDY COMMISSION

The 675,000-acre Catskill Park, though smaller than the Adirondack Park, is similar in other respects. The regional boundaries for the Temporary State Commission on the Catskills, in fact, extended well beyond the park, encompassing 4 million acres and eight counties (reduced to six and one-half counties in 1973). Agricultural and other traditional economic bases in the region have been declining, while absentee landownership, second-home development, recreation, and tourism have caused increasing environmental pressures.[4]

The recommendation for a study commission appears to have come exclusively from the Catskill Center for Conservation and Development, a nonprofit citizens' organization formed in 1969 by representatives of several prominent Catskill families (Borelli, 1974). Legislation to create the commission was introduced by two Catskill area legislators in the spring of 1971. Tentative support was offered by several Catskill area county governing boards and by Republican Party leaders, and there was state-level support from environmental groups, an influential state senator who represented two of the region's counties, and Governor Rockefeller.

---

[3] Zinser (1980)—drawing on interviews with local officials, realtors, businessmen, developers—concludes that, over its first three years, the private land use and development plan had a modest negative impact on the Adirondack economy. But Zinser found more opposition to the way the APA administered the plan than to its planning in itself.

Liroff and Davis (1981) are generally positive in their assessment of the agency's protection of open space in the Adirondacks, but note the following potential problems: excessive agency attention to small-scale, one- and two-dwelling-unit developments; insufficient conditions attached to some permits, and a degree of noncompliance with those conditions that were imposed; a danger of too much compromise on open space protection, in return for local adoption of APA-approved planning programs; and the potential impossibility of agency enforcement of the plan, in the absence of local cooperation.

[4] For a history and description of the Catskills, see Evers (1972) and Catskill Commission (1975). On the history of the Catskill Commission, See Anonymous (1972–1973); DeCelle (1973–1974); and Brock (1975).

The legislation was justified in terms of strong state interests in the Catskill area: state land ownership, recreation opportunities for a statewide population, and the region's role as a watershed for New York City drinking water. In addition, the proposed commission appéared nonthreatening, and the mood in Albany was positive toward environmental issues and substate regionalism. The legislation passed easily in both houses and was signed by the governor on June 22, 1971.

The commission was given a broad charge to study the region's natural resources, social and economic development of its communities, recreational development, and the need for development controls (*Laws of New York*, 1971, Chap. 688). Nine commissioners were appointed in May 1972, three each by the governor and the senate and assembly leaders; six were required to be region residents. An executive director was hired, and a staff assembled in 1973.

The commmission delivered an interim report to the state in 1974, and a preliminary final report in February 1975. The latter was the subject of eight public hearings, seven in the region and one in New York City. A final report was submitted to the state in April 1975 (Catskill Commission, 1975). The commission recommended a two-year extension for itself, and establishment of a permanent, state-funded, regional agency to implement land use and economic development programs.

In the spring of 1975, a variety of bills to extend the commission or to create a permanent agency were introduced in the state legislature (Kinney, 1975). By this time, however, hostility to continuation of the commission had been expressed in many portions of the Catskill region by resort owners, agricultural interests, the development industry, a number of "citizens' rights" groups, and county and local governments.

Some of the earliest and most significant opposition came from Sullivan County, center of the Catskill resort industry. One incident that alienated many strong local interests was the December 1974 release of a commission study of the resort industry (Kalish et al., 1974). The report emphasized the economic decline of Catskill area resorts at a time when county governments were heavily promoting the region as a vacation area.

Agricultural interests were concerned about landowner rights, and real estate and development interests, about restrictions on economic opportunities. County and local governments, at a minimum, were apprehensive about commission restrictions and wanted more input in commission deliberations. There were also widespread fears of "another APA."

The Catskill Center, meanwhile, remained supportive—but even it was not completely satisfied with the commission's approach, staff, or recommendations. At the state level, support remained from state agencies, especially the department of environmental conservation (DEC) and, of course, the commission and its staff. The governor's office—under Republican Malcolm Wilson and Democrat Hugh Carey—was visibly supportive, but environmental and recreation groups, while still supportive, were not highly unified and often took issue with specific commission recommendations.

Only one bill reached a floor vote in the legislature—a compromise sponsored by the assembly's rules committee, at the request of two Catskill area legislators, Maurice D. Hinchey and Jean Amatucci. By the time of the floor vote, only Hinchey—a staunch supporter of many environmental causes—remained in support. Amatucci's reversal caused a great erosion of Democratic support, and a 67–67 vote on June 27 defeated the bill. The senate took no action, and on July 1, 1975, the commission expired.

Principal factors in the commission's demise included:

● The fact that, aside from the Catskill Park, the Catskills are perceived as a meaningful region only by outsiders;

- The absence of a regional crisis to unify the region;
- The commission's inability to find or generate sufficient common identity or interest in common issues;
- The failure to overcome or alter region residents' perception of the commission as elitist, and representative only of the state's interests, those of absentee landowners, and those of downstate recreation and preservation groups; and
- The inability of the commission to convince regional residents that its extensive public involvement efforts—meetings, hearings, newsletters, etc.—were anything but sales jobs and one-way communications.

The commission apparently saw its own emphasis on economic development, as well as on natural resource protection, as evidence of responsiveness to regional concerns. However, it did not cater to any specific interests, and apparently ended up pleasing no one group sufficiently to mobilize its wholehearted support.

Later in the summer of 1975, the DEC picked up the commission's work, but, with limited funding, had to focus primarily on state lands and natural resource protection. The department issued a series of reports in September 1976, and strongly urged creation of a permanent regional agency (Department of Environmental Conservation, 1976).

In 1976, 1977, and 1978, Hinchey sponsored legislation to reinstate the Catskill Commission. These bills sought to satisfy the commission's opponents largely by increasing local representation on the commission, or by strengthening local government control over the selection of commissioners. However, opposition remained forceful and sometimes almost violent. Hinchey was tarred and feathered in effigy at one public hearing in 1977. Only one of Hinchey's bills moved out of committee during these years, and even it failed to reach a floor vote. In 1979 and 1980, Hinchey proposed a commission confined to the Catskill Park, with all voting members required to be full-time residents of the four Catskill Park counties; but those bills also failed to move out of committee.

TUG HILL COMMISSION

The Tug Hill region encompasses 1.3 million acres and 39 towns in portions of four counties. It includes a core area of largely unbroken forest, a northeastern agricultural rim, and a southern rim experiencing some urban development. Forestry and agriculture have been the traditional economic bases, though both are declining. Second-home development, residential growth in the southern rim, and increasing recreational use are occurring (College of Environmental Science and Forestry, 1974; Institute of Man and Science, 1974; Bowman and Gross, 1974).

However, in contrast to the Adirondacks or Catskills, Tug Hill has not been the target of strong interest by outside environmental or preservationist groups; large recreational use by New York City area residents; or land ownership or other interest by influential individuals from other parts of the state.

The proposal for a study commission for Tug Hill was initiated by a few individuals and groups within the region, acting through Assemblyman Edward F. Crawford, who represented part of the region in the state legislature.[5] Two events in the early 1970s provided the impetus: a proposed rock music festival, and the purchase of an option on 63,000 acres of land by the Horizon Corporation for second-home development.

---

[5] Very little published information about the Tug Hill Commission exists. See Coe and Ware (1977); Coe (1979); and Dyballa, Raymond, and Hahn (1981).

While some regional residents were concerned about these proposals, only a few—some local political leaders, a citizens' environmental group, the regional office of the DEC, and Senator Crawford—were outspoken. The rock music festival was canceled in the face of a threatened lawsuit; Horizon decided its land was not suitable for development; but Crawford continued to explore alternatives. He was apparently motivated by desires to protect the region and to bring in state resources.

Legislation was introduced in the spring of 1972 by Crawford and Senator H. Douglas Barclay (who also represented part of the region). There was little reaction within the region. Several local governments provided low-key support, but many local officials now say they were never consulted. Except for the DEC's support, there was little interest of any kind at the state level. The legislation passed by large margins in both houses and was signed by Governor Rockefeller on June 8. Passage was viewed largely as a favor to Crawford, a long-term upstate legislator.

The Tug Hill legislation paralleled the act creating the Catskill Commission, giving the Tug Hill Commission a broad charge to study all aspects of the region's conservation and development (*Laws of New York,* 1972, Chap. 972). Only three of the nine commissioners were required to be regional residents, but only one outsider was appointed—and that was Assemblyman Crawford. The original reporting date, March 1973, was extended twice by the legislature.

The commission's original activities included contracting for a comprehensive natural resource inventory (College of Environmental Science and Forestry, 1974), hiring an executive director and a staff strongly committed to working with local governments and regional residents, and holding a series of public forums throughout the region in early 1974. The forums, though not required by law, nonetheless influenced the commission's initial findings, issued in March 1975. The proposed goals and recommendations were summarized in the first goal—"Keep Tug Hill the way it is."

A second series of forums was held in June 1975. Overall reaction was favorable. The revised recommendations, issued in November 1975, reflected responses to criticisms voiced at the June forums—for example, a proposed mandated regional planning program was changed to reflect greater local government responsibilities and a decreased role for the commission (Tug Hill Commission, 1976).

Subsequently, the commission has evolved a regional approach to planning and land use control from the town level up. In 1974, officials from several of the core-area towns met at the suggestion of one of the town supervisors, and, by October, with help from the commission and its staff, formed a nine-town Cooperative Tug Hill Planning Board (CTHPB) (Brown, 1977; Marsh, 1980). With continued assistance, the CTHPB conducted community inventories, drafted a resource management plan, and prepared a model rural development code. As of March 1980, seven of the nine towns had adopted the code, and a joint zoning board of appeals and enforcement program was in effect.

The formation of the CTHPB greatly influenced the commission's approach. The commission has encouraged and facilitated the formation of four more cooperative boards, with such boards now covering 26 of the region's 39 towns. The commission also provides training and technical and organizational assistance for local governments, citizen education programs, and regional research on various topics.

Not all towns are involved: the other cooperative planning boards have not shared the CTHPB's emphasis on land use control; and implementation and enforcement mechanisms have not yet been adequately tested. But towns in the most critical core area *are* involved, and planning and land use controls have been instituted in a region previously hostile to such activities.

Since 1975, the commission has survived, not through specific legislative extensions, but through annual appropriations in the state budget bill—a low-profile approach through which support by an influential legislator, and the absence of opposition or controversy, have permitted the addition of the commission to the governor's annual executive budget. Following Assemblyman Crawford's death in 1975, Senator Barclay has been the commission's leading proponent in Albany. Statewide interest has remained low, and, at least in the absence of opposition or of severe budget constraints, Barclay's wishes have been respected.[6]

Within the region, support has grown over the years, especially among local governments and interest groups served directly by the commission's programs. Opposition appears confined to a relatively few individuals and groups, most of whom have had little involvement with the commission anyway. The commission receives such support because it has not threatened local governments or economic interests; local officials have been actively involved in commission policy formation; and the commission provides tangible benefits in the form of planning services, technical and organizational assistance, and help in acquiring financial assistance.

The commission has also benefited from a citizenry apparently favoring preservation of their way of life, rather than exploitation of the region's resources; from a consequent lack of conflict with strong state-level interests; and from the contrast between the commission's approach and the highly publicized controversy in the nearby Adirondacks. In addition, while the rock-music festival threat and the Horizon Corporation's threat were apparently sufficient to get the commission established, development pressures in general are less immediate, and therefore have permitted the Tug Hill Commission to engage in its effective though time-consuming, noncoercive approach.

COMPARATIVE ANALYSIS

Figure 3 provides a diagrammatic summary of the case studies. The APA survived on the basis of overwhelming state-level support—sufficient to outweigh the preponderance of opposition on the local level. Of the three agencies, it most completely satisfied its state-level objectives.

The Tug Hill Commission also survived, but it did so on the basis of limited interest and modest support at the state level, in combination with a strategy of building local support by responding to local interests. Its accomplishment of state-level objectives was spotty, but possibly adequate in view of the lower degree of state-level interest in the region.

The Catskill Commission, by contrast, failed to survive or satisfy any of the state-level objectives. It generated strong local opposition that, except in its very early history, was counterbalanced by support that was neither forceful at the state level nor effective at the local.

The comparative analysis of these cases focuses on three questions: 1) whether the APA's success from the state-level perspective is transferable to other regions; 2) whether the Tug Hill Commission's more compatible reconciliation of potential state/local conflict would have worked in the Adirondacks; and 3) whether the case studies of the two agencies that survived hold any lessons that could have helped the Catskill Commission.

---

[6] In September 1977, the commission resolved to phase itself out by March 31, 1981. However, in August 1980, it accepted a committee report proposing legislation to establish a permanent commission (*Watertown Daily Times*, August 29, 1980).

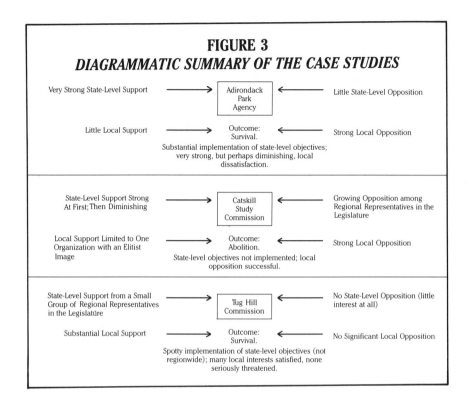

FIGURE 3

DIAGRAMMATIC SUMMARY OF THE CASE STUDIES

Very Strong State-Level Support ⟶ Adirondack Park Agency ⟵ Little State-Level Opposition

Little Local Support ⟶ Outcome: Survival. ⟵ Strong Local Opposition

Substantial implementation of state-level objectives; very strong, but perhaps diminishing, local dissatisfaction.

State-Level Support Strong At First; Then Diminishing ⟶ Catskill Study Commission ⟵ Growing Opposition among Regional Representatives in the Legislature

Local Support Limited to One Organization with an Elitist Image ⟶ Outcome: Abolition. ⟵ Strong Local Opposition

State-level objectives not implemented; local opposition successful.

State-Level Support from a Small Group of Regional Representatives in the Legislature ⟶ Tug Hill Commission ⟵ No State-Level Opposition (little interest at all)

Substantial Local Support ⟶ Outcome: Survival. ⟵ No Significant Local Opposition

Spotty implementation of state-level objectives (not regionwide); many local interests satisfied, none seriously threatened.

Figures 4 and 5 summarize the variables that are important in this analysis—that is, the main ones that shaped the patterns of support and opposition that emerged for each agency. They include aspects of the political environments faced by each agency, and strategies used by the agencies to alter or manipulate those environments.

The first conclusion is that the APA model would have been less likely to succeed in the Catskills or Tug Hill. The APA had several advantages contributing to its survival that were not present in either of the other cases:

- The APA had an overwhelming (and long-standing) degree of statewide interest, which was further solidified by a series of "crises" that appeared immediate and serious (the national park proposal and the threat of major second-home development). This led to strong statewide support for action.
- There was consensus on regional boundaries. While the Adirondacks are just as fragmented socially as either the Catskills or Tug Hill, the Adirondack Park itself was easily recognized as a meaningful region. By contrast, Tug Hill had no such unit, and the Catskill Commission's region extended far beyond the Catskill Park.
- There was no APA backlash. Established later, the other two commissions suffered from having to confront local populations already aware of the controversy over the APA, and hostile to any similar developments.
- The APA had the security of state legislative support. Because of its overwhelming statewide support, the APA did not have to worry much about the potential im-

FIGURE 4
ASPECTS OF AGENCY POLITICAL ENVIRONMENTS IN THE CASE STUDIES

Variables	APA	Catskill Commission	Tug Hill Commission
Nature of Perceived Crisis	Immediate and serious	None in particular	Immediate but short-lived
Expressed Local Values	Individualistic and prodevelopment	Individualistic and prodevelopment	Individualistic and opposed to exploitation of natural resources
Degree of Statewide Interest	Very high	High	Low
Consensus on Regional Boundaries	High	Low	Low
APA Backlash	None	Very strong	Strong, but effectively countered
Security of State Legislative Support	Considerable, because of strong statewide support	Limited	Possibly limited at first, but successfully expanded

pact of opposition on the state legislature. That, in turn, freed the agency from pressure to make accommodations with local interests and gave local people time to get used to the idea of having a regional agency in their midst.

To a considerable extent, the Catskill Commission did try to transfer the APA model, by proposing a centralized land use control agency for the Catskill region. It didn't work. The commission's political environment differed from the APA's in important ways: an APA backlash was underway, and there was serious disagreement over regional boundaries. Furthermore, while the Catskills were the target of considerable statewide interest, no specific crisis had occurred to create a sense of urgency. A crisis might have helped lessen opposition at the local level, as well as stimulate stronger statewide support. In addition, the loss of state legislative support occurred too soon to give the Catskill Commission much time to make accommodations with local interests, or to give local people much time to get used to the commission's presence.

The Tug Hill Commission also confronted an APA backlash, and disagreements over the definition of Tug Hill and its boundaries. Although it shared the APA's success in terms of survival, it did so through the use of very different methods and strategies. It had no strong statewide support, as the APA did. Instead, it concentrated on reassuring a suspicious local population and on building a local support base. If it had pursued a centralized, regulatory approach, such as the APA's, there can hardly be any doubt that it would have provoked considerable local opposition. Such opposition would surely have put pressure on the state legislature, and, in the absence of any significant statewide support, the Tug Hill Commission would have met the same fate as its Catskill counterpart.

The second conclusion is that the Tug Hill Commission's approach may not have worked in the Adirondacks. The Tug Hill Commission was the only one in the three case studies to have achieved a reasonably compatible accommodation of state and local interests. It overcame the APA backlash by quickly demonstrating an openess to local interests and then following up with visible results. Also, it dealt with the regional definition problem by adopting a "subregional approach," involving a number of different, locally organized cooperative planning boards. This approach produced a degree of local support for the commission that stands in sharp contrast to the other two agencies.

Of course, over the years, the APA has made a number of modifications in response to its local opponents. The degree of opposition appears to have lessened. However, one could argue, as at least one APA staff member did (Liroff and Davis, 1981), that compliance with the private land use and development plan might have been greater if the agency had been more accommodating with local governments and local residents from the beginning. For example, the APA could perhaps have reduced local opposition by being more lenient in regulating land use in certain areas, while still satisfying state-level interests with even stronger protection of the wilder and more fragile ones. Would such a strategy have been a viable alternative? The authors' judgment is that the answer is probably no.

In contrast, the Tug Hill Commission benefited from a set of interrelated advantages not present in the Adirondacks. These included:

- A lower degree of statewide interest in the region, leaving the Tug Hill Commission freer to respond to local interests;
- The presence—in the rock music festival and in the Horizon development proposals— of crises sufficient to trigger a degree of both local and statewide concern, but not persisting long enough to induce a strong call for a locally unpopular, centralized, regulatory approach; and
- A local population expressing values opposed to the exploitation of natural resources—"Keep Tug Hill the way it is."—and thereby reducing the likelihood of severe conflict with statewide interests.

As a result of these conditions, the Tug Hill Commission was able to operate with much more time and flexibility than the APA. This enabled the staff to learn local attitudes and preferences. Local people had time to assess the threats and opportunities the agency represented and to adapt to its presence. Citizen participation could be nurtured, and citizen recommendations built into the agency programs. The Tug Hill Commission had the flexibility it needed to develop programs that responded to a variety of interests within the region, and to work out compromises that incorporated local interests, as well as state-level ones.

The third conclusion is that aspects of the Tug Hill approach might have helped the Catskill Commission. In some respects, the Catskill Commission lacked the advantages of *both* of the other agencies. It lacked the APA's more coherent region; it lacked an APA backlash, a sense of crisis, and the security of state legislative support. At the same time, it also lacked the Tug Hill Commission's more compatible local value system, its freedom from strong statewide interests, and its opportunity to respond to local interests without generating strong statewide opposition. The Catskill Commission faced the same incompatibility of statewide and local interests that confronted the APA. The crucial difference was the comparative weakness of the Catskill Commission's state-level supporters.

That weakness should have made compromise more feasible in the Catskills than in the Adirondacks, as well as more obviously necessary. However, the commission's concessions to local interests—such as emphasizing a balance between resource protection and economic development—failed to satisfy the local opposition, and, at the same time, were too vague to solidify any state-level support.

Do the other two case studies suggest other compromises that might have been more effective? The authors' conclusion is that, though they would not have worked in the Adirondacks, some aspects of the Tug Hill Commission's approach might have worked in the Catskills.

Specifically, the Catskill Commission could have used the Tug Hill Commission's subregional approach. Instead of treating the entire region uniformly, the commission might have been able to satisfy statewide interests by applying centralized, regulatory policies to parts of the region of greatest interest to outsiders—chiefly the Catskill Park. With the most important statewide interests thereby satisfied, a more leisurely, locally responsive approach might have been possible in subregions of less statewide interest. Different policies and plans could have been developed for each subregion.

Making this work would have been more difficult than the Tug Hill Commission's job. But it is at least plausible that such an approach could have satisfied state-level interests (as well as the diversity of needs and interests within the region) to a degree sufficient to assure the commission's survival.

IMPLICATIONS AND GUIDELINES

These case studies have at least two broader implications. The most obvious one is the clear indication that rigorous, centralized, regulatory approaches to environmental planning on the APA model can be duplicated only in certain settings: they are likely to work only in the presence of strong statewide support, or in the absence of effective local opposition. These conditions are probably not very common.

The second implication is that, in the numerous situations where these conditions do not exist, agency survival, and the accomplishment of state-level objectives, require sensitivity to local values and preferences. They also require the ability to develop compromises that balance local and statewide interests. To some degree, this has even been true in the Adirondacks.

Alan J. Hahn is associate professor in the department of human service studies at Cornell University. A political scientist, he concentrates his work upon community decision making, intergovernmental relations, and citizen participation.

Cynthia D. Dyballa is regional community development specialist with the Massachusetts Cooperative Extension Service. Her previous work as a graduate student and research specialist at Cornell University focused on regional environmental planning and governmental decision making.

This article is excerpted from one that appeared in the *APA Journal* in July 1981. Use is by permission.

CREATIVE TENSIONS IN STATE/LOCAL RELATIONS

JOHN M. DeGROVE

T he states' acts to expland their roles in managing land development have, at
their best, forged a creative tension between local and state governments
and, at their worst, stimulated open warfare. In Florida, my home state, the
legislative initiatives undertaken to manage growth have been premised on the assumption that the state will continue to grow at a rapid rate. The questions arise of
how to provide infrastructure to support growth in a timely way, how to plan for it
in a sensible and orderly manner, and how to accommodate it without inadvertently
destroying natural resource systems or eating away at the state's quality of life.
Some people in Florida— environmentalists among them—would like to take a different tack and try to slow the growth. But state policy decrees accepting large-
scale growth and concentrating on managing that growth effectively.

SEVERAL STATES' EXPERIENCES

Oregon

Some idea of the tension that can be built up by state assertion of responsibility
in land use matters may be gained by looking at Oregon's experience. In 1973,
Oregon began one of the more ambitious efforts to set state goals for land development and preservation. Local governments were required to reflect these goals in
their local comprehensive plans. To make sure the local plans did reflect these
goals, the state's land conservation and development commission (LCDC) had to
"acknowledge"— or approve—the plans. Only now, 12 years later, has Oregon acknowledged the plans of all 250 + local governments.

The period from 1973 to 1985 was filled with friction between the state and local
governments in Oregon. Worse, some local planners believe that the courts were
brought too much into the process. One group of counties, called by some the
"Dirty Dozen," has been particularly stubborn about preparing local plans consistent with state goals. These tensions have not been very creative.

To ease matters, substantial state and federal funds have been made available to help local governments with their planning efforts. Does putting the sugar coating of dollar bills on the bitter pill of state oversight make it easier to swallow? The answer, in Oregon and elsewhere, is yes.

California

California offers an even more striking example of the tension that can emerge from the exercise of state authority in land use decisions. When efforts to pass state coastal legislation failed in 1970, 1971, and 1972, an initiative placed Proposition 20 on the ballot, and it subsequently became law. Because the law had not been subject to legislative give-and-take, it was stringent in its requirements, which mandated state planning and extensive permitting in the coastal zone.

A 1976 California law was aimed at turning planning and permitting authority over to local governments. However, until local governments passed their own coastal programs consistent with state goals and criteria, the state continued to administer the regulations and issue the permits. Now, 10 years later, only about one-third of the 68 local governments in California's coastal zone have completed the painful process of complying with state policies. Again, hassles between the state and local governments have proved less than productive.

Hawaii

A state one might expect to be free of such problems—Hawaii—has, in fact, reached something of a stalemate in state/local relations. Hawaii has only four local governments, all consolidated city/counties. After a state land use law was passed in 1961, the local governments became more and more hostile to the idea that the state should retain ultimate authority over land use, particularly along the coasts. According to knowledgeable observers, the confusion and conflict over how to share responsibilities has made it virtually impossible to implement the Hawaii State Plan adopted in 1978.

North Carolina

On the other hand, a success story can be found in North Carolina, which adopted a coastal program in 1974 that was widely believed to be impracticable because of political resistance. Gradualism, however, provided the key to making it work, thanks to the state's beginning with fairly general requirements for local plans. Five years later, by the time the state requested more detailed plans, state and local officials had become accustomed to working together, and revisions were carried out with relatively little fuss.

This North Carolina state/local combination has produced one of the most effective planning, implementation, and monitoring systems of any coastal program. State and local governments have evolved a very strong program to protect coastal dunes and estuaries: a 60-year erosion line, for instance, will prevent any construction in coastal areas likely to wash away within 60 years. Lot owners faced with this likelihood can be assisted in a number of ways, including through an acquisition fund. This kind of sensible approach to problems of private owners helps to make the program work. Now, twelve years after the Coastal Area Management Act (CAMA) passed, the state and its local governments are working in comparative harmony.

Why have state governments begun to take an interest in land use? Mostly because their citizens have perceived that local governments could not or would not handle growth management problems well, or even at all. This was certainly the case in California, where, in the 1960s and 1970s, the citizens acquired a widespread distrust of local governments. In Florida, in the 1985 legislative session, there was a general consensus that the Local Government Planning Act of 1975, which mandated a plan for every city and county, had largely failed. Although some local governments had been willing and able to plan effectively, others had not, and it was clear to most legislators that the state had to exert a stronger impact.

FLORIDA'S EXPERIENCE

To return to Florida, one of the ways in which it could have wielded more responsibility over local government's growth planning would have been by helping to fund that planning. In 1975, when the Local Government Planning Act was passed, estimates held that $50 million would be needed by local governments to implement the planning called for by the act. The legislature, however, never appropriated the funds; the local jurisdictions resented the lack of follow-through; and this, in turn, certainly led to some foot-dragging on their part in carrying out the mandate. Other states that had legislated local planning, such as Oregon, California, and North Carolina, had provided some funding assistance. But Florida never did until the new act was passed in 1985. The 1985 law requires local governments to reshape their comprehensive plans, in order to make them consistent with state criteria; it also appropriates $2 to $3 million to get started on the job. In addition, about $7 million more will probably be appropriated each year for the next three years, until this cycle of replanning comes to an end.

A New Plan

Florida's new legislation sets up an integrated policy framework for growth management. The foundation is a new state plan passed by the legislature that lays out, in simple English, goals and policies to guide the plans of state agencies, regional planning councils, and local governments. This statement of policy will help everyone, including the development community, to learn the rules of the game.

The state plan contains three major policies that will affect the way development can be carried out in Florida. One is to move development back off the coast, landward of the 30-year erosion line, and away from high-hazard areas and barrier islands. This policy will be carried out through local plans, and through prohibitions on state funds now being used to gain access, for example, to barrier islands.

The second major policy will bar development of any area, unless infrastructure capacities are available or can be made available as development proceeds. In effect, this is an adequate facilities ordinance at the state level— a revolutionary act in this and most other states.

The third policy— to encourage more compact urban development by encouraging infill, redevelopment, and the use of existing infrastructure—aims to protect open space, wetlands, groundwater recharge areas, well fields, and important farmlands.

Infrastructure Funding

The big question now is how to provide funds to support these policies— especially the provision that infrastructure be in place coincident with the impacts of new development. Without funding, policy implementation will be very difficult. Both private and public sources are being evaluated to arrive at a funding program. The private source being considered, and already in widespread use, is fees and exactions from new development—namely, impact fees. The new law requires that, in imposing impact fees, such exactions be applied to all development in a given jurisdiction, not just to large developments, as had often been the case in the past.

Even a full use of impact fees, however, still leaves a shortfall in funding of about $30 billion for the existing backlog, to which impact fees on new development cannot and should not be allocated. Other funding sources being considered include closing loopholes in the sales tax laws, adding to the sales taxes, increasing the corporate profits tax, and eliminating the homestead exemption. The state must come up with some kind of funding package that will make it credible in asserting its new responsibility for growth management. A special commission appointed jointly by the governor and by each legislative house—the comprehensive plan commission—has been struggling with this problem, and will make recommendations to the 1986 and 1987 sessions of the legislature.

A PREDICTION

As Florida has moved to expand significantly the state's role in growth management, a strong commitment has apparently arisen to providing the funds to do the job. If this proves to be the case, then the inevitable state/local tensions will probably be creative rather than destructive. From the perspective of the development community, the new planning system for Florida should mean more certainty for the private sector.

John M. DeGrove is director of the Joint Center for Environmental and Urban Problems at Florida Atlantic University, Boca Raton, Florida.

DeGrove's contribution to this book is drawn from an address he made at the ULI/Lincoln Institute seminar on growth management.

PART V.

ECONOMIC AND EQUITY ISSUES

F rom the very first applications of growth management techniques, strong concerns have been voiced about their potential impacts on private property rights, on various population groups in the regional community, and on such economic aspects as land and housing prices. Over the years, a number of studies have shown that growth management techniques exert some negative impacts on communities and on the development process—depending on such factors as the growth rate and the amount of market competition among regional jurisdictions.

Three articles in this part of the book discuss one of the major controversies raised by growth management programs—their exclusionary effects on certain income and population groups, either through raised land and housing costs, or through mandated selectivity in choices of housing types.

David Dowall discusses the former, and John Rahenkamp and Peter Buchsbaum examine the latter problem, as it is being approached in New Jersey in the context of the famous Mount Laurel cases. First, however, Robert Ellickson looks at the even more basic question of whether growth management by public entities can ever really prove effective.

Douglas R. Porter

PRIVATE MARKET AND PUBLIC INTEREST

ROBERT C. ELLICKSON

S hould we rely mostly on markets or on political processes to determine patterns of urban growth? Subversively, I suggest that growth management efforts tend to go off-target, not because of minor, correctable program flaws, but because, inherently, governments are inefficient and unfair growth managers.

Twenty years ago, when policy analysts debated any issue of government regulation, they would typically ask, "Is there a market failure present for government to correct?" They thought that the presence of a market failure was conclusive evidence that government intervention would improve upon market performance. Today, policy analysts are not so naively optimistic about the performance of government. Governments can also fail, and fail worse than markets. Both planning agencies and developers are, to some extent, untrustworthy agents. The relevant question is, which is the less incompetent?

In the United States, urban growth has always involved some interactive cooperation between the private and public sectors. Under the market-oriented approach dominant throughout most of U.S. history, and still alive today in places such as Houston, governments are essentially reactive. They respond to developers' initiatives in laying out streets, coordinating utilities, and perhaps assuring that projects meet mandatory performance criteria governing front-yard setbacks, parking, and the like. Basically, this reactive approach allows market forces to determine the amount and location of development.

By contrast, the recent growth management policies have involved proactive government efforts to control when and where development occurs. The planners who instinctively favor this approach have yet to develop a persuasive justification for government management of growth. They will be pleased to learn that microeconomic theory does suggest that markets may, in fact, imperfectly decide questions of city size, and, thus, that it is at least possible that planners could do a better job.

TWO ROADS TO BOULDER

"The Case of the Two Roads"—an example posed over one-half century ago by economist Frank Knight—illustrates how market actors can fail to allocate urban space efficiently. Knight's example involved two distant cities linked by two roads. One road, infinitely wide but in abysmal condition, can accommodate an infinite number of vehicles at a speed of 25 miles per hour. The second road is a superb express highway that allows vehicles to travel at speeds of 55 miles per hour. But this second highway is narrow and highly congestible. Knight asked, "If many vehicles travel between the two cities, how fast will traffic flow on the congestible expressway?"

His gloomy answer was: "Twenty-five miles per hour." He reasoned that motorists would use the express highway, so long as it was faster than the first highway. A market imperfection is present because motorists would consider only the average congestion costs they would impose on other drivers, not the marginal congestion costs. The individual decisions of drivers would, thus, result in the total waste of the expressway, because the first road alone had always provided intercity travel at 25 miles per hour.

Paul Danish and the other growth managers in Boulder, Colorado, can take heart from "The Case of the Two Roads." They should assert that Denver is like the first road, and Boulder like the expressway. If so, if people were allowed freely to migrate from Denver to Boulder in search of a nicer place to live, they would eventually ruin Boulder, and yet Denver itself would not be improved. In short, the basic economic rationale for growth management is that households (and developers who market urban life to households) consider only the average costs, not the marginal costs of growth.

THE BENEFITS OF GROWTH

This analysis is suspect, however, because it assumes that urban growth imposes steadily increasing net marginal costs. There is no solid evidence that this is true. Urban growth confers benefits as well as costs. With growth come more and various career opportunities, more cultural events, greater social variety. If enough growth occurs around Denver, for instance, a major league baseball team may move there. Law school graduates who have multiple job offers tend to flock to the biggest metropolitan areas.

There have been a number of empirical studies on the marginal costs and benefits of urban growth. (See Harry Richardson, *The Economics of City Size* [1973], and sources cited on pages 854 – 855 of Ellickson and Tarlock, *Land-Use Controls* [1981].) The authors of these studies examine wage rates for comparable jobs in different urban centers. They hypothesize that workers are willing to accept lower wages in return for being able to live in nicer environments; conversely, employers in harsh environments, such as Alaska, must pay premium wages to attract workers. Using econometric analysis to control other variables, these investigators thus learn from market wages how people assess the attractiveness of different living situations. Although the findings vary, much of the evidence suggests that workers actually prefer big cities and dense population concentrations.

Nevertheless, growth controls are popular with the current residents of growing areas. I see three main reasons for their popularity. First, most people are environmentally conservative; they oppose change of any kind. They would, thus, be as upset by depopulation as by rapid growth. Second, the costs of growth are more tangible than the benefits of growth. It is easier to see that a new subdivision will cause additional traffic congestion than to see that it may enrich cultural opportunities. Third, growth management may be financially rewarding to existing residents; growth controls can drive up housing prices and enable local governments to exact greater contributions from developers. (For a more detailed discussion, see

Ellickson, "Suburban Growth Controls," *Yale Law Journal,* Vol. 86, pp. 385–511 [1977].)

FOR BETTER OR WORSE?

Although developers working with passive, reactive governments cannot be counted upon to allocate urban growth "perfectly," I have yet to observe a metropolitan area where I would applaud government embrace of proactive growth management policies. Growth managers face two inherent hurdles. The first hurdle is the processing costs of running a growth management program. A central coordinator must have an enormous amount of information to do the job well. Growth management plans often work out to be mostly job-creating programs for planners and lawyers.

The second hurdle is that local political forces are stacked in favor of existing residents, who, history shows, are likely to use growth management policies to serve their own interests at the expense of new housing consumers, landowners, and residents of neighboring areas. In short, although a reactive, market-oriented government policy toward growth may not be perfect, recent experience suggests that proactive government management of growth is inherently likely to be worse—often, much worse.

Robert C. Ellickson is professor of natural resources law at Stanford Law School, Stanford University, Palo Alto, California.

Ellickson's article is drawn from his presentation at the ULI/Lincoln Institute seminar on growth management.

REDUCING THE COST EFFECTS OF LOCAL LAND USE CONTROLS (Excerpts)

DAVID E. DOWALL

T o date, little systematic effort has been made to make land use regulations more efficient and cost-effective. Most studies do not rigorously evaluate specific land use control devices, nor do they consider the benefits produced by them. Such incomplete assessments do not provide a basis for improving the effectiveness of land controls—such suggestions must be based on detailed determinations of how to increase the benefits and decrease the costs produced by land use control mechanisms.

This article attempts to aid efforts to improve the effectiveness of land use regulation by outlining a land market monitoring program that can be used for designing and evaluating the performance of local land use control systems.

HOW LAND USE AND ENVIRONMENTAL REGULATIONS AFFECT LAND AND HOUSING COSTS

Local land use controls directly affect the costs of land and new housing. By restricting the supply of developable land through the use of open space acquisition and agricultural zoning, or by limiting the extension of public facilities, a locality makes its land prices and new housing costs rise. Local regulations can also affect housing costs by placing onerous subdivison requirements on builders. Extensive review procedures, subdivision requirements, and limited land supplies may greatly affect the operation of many communities' land and housing markets. Figure 1 presents the various ways land use controls can affect land and housing markets.

Reductions in the supply of land are most often created by zoning ordinances that limit the amount of land available for residential development by placing lands in agriculture or open-space zones, or by overzoning other land uses (particularly industrial and commercial uses in urban "enclave" municipalities). With the widespread adoption of growth management controls, many communities have created urban-limit lines (Salem, Oregon), or have tied capital budgeting programs to devel-

179

FIGURE 1
EFFECTS OF LAND USE CONTROLS ON LAND AND HOUSING MARKETS

Effect	Land Use and Environmental Controls Most Responsible for Effect
Reduction in the supply of raw land	Zoning; urban limit lines; capital budgeting and timing ordinances; siting and environmental review and permit processes
Limitations on the level of development intensity	Zoning; height and bulk regulations
Qualitative changes in residential lots, housing, or development	Capital budgeting and timing ordinances; siting and permitting procedures; subdivision regulations
Shifting development costs from public to project	Capital budgeting and timing ordinances; service pricing and development charges; siting and permitting procedures; subdivision regulations
Administrative and delay costs	*All*, to various degrees, but most prevalent with siting and permitting procedures and with subdivision regulation compliance

Sources: Dowall (1979), and Dowall and Mingilton (1979).

opment timing ordinances (Ramapo, New York; Boulder, Colorado; Petaluma, California). Urban-limit lines restrict development to areas inside the designated boundary. If the program is strictly adhered to, all land outside the line is eliminated from the supply of potentially developable land.

Capital budgeting and timing ordinances can also have the same impact; they restrict development to areas in a community that have local services. Siting and permitting procedures, to the extent that they operate to restrict development to areas that will generate a minimum of fiscal and environmental impacts, can limit the supply of developable residential land. Also, since the development review process is often lengthy, the supply of land available for development can be restricted by bottlenecks in the siting and permitting program.

Besides regulating the physical stock of residential land, zoning ordinances directly affect the number of residential lots. Density and lot size requirements implicitly determine the supply of developable lots. Changes in local zoning ordinances, minimum lot size requirements, and other policies that affect the density of residential development, translate directly into lot supply changes.

In recent years, many growing communities have changed subdivison ordinances to require developers to provide more and more public facilities. Due to more sophisticated fiscal impact assessment models, and to higher development charges and fees, development is shifting to areas with existing public services. While such shifts are desirable for controlling urban sprawl, they can limit the supply of residential land.

The proliferation of sophisticated land use control and growth management systems has made development review processes more lengthy and costly. For example, in a telephone survey of homebuilders, Seidel (1978) found that the time required for development approval had increased dramatically between 1970 and 1975. Surveys show that the development review process can be very lengthy. Delays can cause bottlenecks, and inhibit housing and land supplies from meeting market demand.

Many of the unanticipated and undesirable land and housing market effects discussed above can be largely avoided or lessened. If the supplies of developable residential land and of new and exisiting housing units are monitored over time, and matched with anticipated land and housing demand, land and housing price inflation effects can be avoided. The next section of this article outlines a method for developing a local system to monitor land and housing supply.

MONITORING LAND AND HOUSING SUPPLY

Compiling Data

Assessing land supply should begin with a complete inventory of land uses in the community. Raw land and vacant parcels should be identified. Physical constraints to development, such as excessive slopes, floodplains, and environmentally sensitive areas, should be identified. Raw land should be categorized as developable or undevelopable according to these criteria. Next, the number of acres of developable land should be determined. This inventory of land should be classified according to the availability of public services. Land prices of raw land at various locations within the community should be determined by sampling land transactions annually.

Map overlays of zoning and density regulations should be used to determine the potential supply of developable residential lots or building sites. The supply of lots should be categorized by the availability of services. Using local capital budgeting projections, planners can estimate the number of lots that can be serviced each year for at least five years ahead. Local developers should be interviewed to determine the costs of lot preparation. Spot prices for finished lots should be obtained. A measure of the administrative performance is needed to assess the likelihood of land policy compliance and efficiency. The length of the approval process, and the ratio of the number of lots in approved projects to the total number of units contained in all proposed projects can be used to estimate the potential supply of lots likely to be approved for development per year.

Comparable measures for the housing markets should be assembled. The total housing stock should be inventoried and categorized by location and type of unit. Housing prices by type and location should be monitored for both new and existing units. Building permits should be monitored, and used to calculate future additions to the housing supply. The turnover rate of the stock should be estimated; this can be computed by dividing the total number of sales in a year by the number of total stock. Finally, vacancy rates for housing units should be estimated by type and location. (These data are often obtainable from the U.S. Postal Service or from utilities.)

Defining the Submarkets

So far, reference has been made to classifying information by location of land parcels and of housing units, and by the types of the housing units. Ideally, the monitoring of land and housing markets should be spatially disaggregated, according to distinct land or housing submarkets. Since the concern is with anticipating potential inflationary effects of land use and environmental policy, the demand for and supply of both land and housing within each submarket must be known. The problem with identifying precise submarkets for land and housing is that submarkets are multidimensional; that is, they vary by location, lot type, housing unit type, and the socioeconomic characteristics of the neighborhoods. Since land policy has effects that can only be meaningfully assessed along spatial lines, the submarket designations must be spatial.

One of the most important findings of research on the effects of land use and environmental controls on land and housing market operations is the role that controls have in segmenting land markets. Regulations differentiate land into submarkets, based on the degree of development restriction. The effect of land use controls on housing markets depends on how each submarket within a jurisdiction is affected. If the imposition of land use controls is not uniform over a region, then the excess demand created by excessive controls in one submarket will shift to other submarkets, as consumers search out substitute housing. To the extent that other, unrestricted submarkets provide alternative development opportunities, the aggregate price effects of land use restrictions may be minimized. To determine whether these substitutions can and do occur, localities must monitor their land and housing markets on a spatially disaggregated basis.

Using Census Tracts

Data availability should be given primary consideration when developing submarkets. In communities over 50,000 in population, census tracts should serve as the basic building blocks for submarkets. Clustering tracts can be accomplished by two methods: judgmental and empirical.

On intuitive grounds, community tracts can be aggregated into groups judged to be relatively homogeneous. Discussions with knowledgeable real estate brokers will prove valuable.

Empirically, on the grounds of census data, tracts can be combined into submarkets by using multivariate analytical techniques (cluster analysis, numerical taxonomy, etc.). Another promising approach is using telephone directories to trace houshold movements by spotting address changes from previous year's directories. The movement data can serve as the basis for grouping tracts, when coupled with socioeconomic data. This approach has been used by Adams in the Twin Cities (Adams, 1978).

Tracts can usually be categorized into broad types. A research project studying land and housing markets in Alameda and Contra Costa Counties, California, has identified 22 central-city, 70 inner-urban, 100 suburban, and 10 exurban submarkets. While these categories are purely locational, they differentiate well between housing types: single-family in suburban and exurban areas; mixed single-family and multifamily in inner-urban areas; and multifamily units in central-city locations (Dowall, 1979). Also, this kind of category does a good job of isolating types of development pressures, such as infill pressures in central cities and inner-urban areas, and large-scale development pressures in suburban and exurban areas. As a consequence, because land use and environmental policies are quite different in each area, these broad distinctions are useful for assessing policy impacts.

Land and housing market attributes would be collected and disaggregated, according to these submarket designations. If collected annually, these data could be used to monitor land development and land policy for the community. In a manner analogous to that of the preparation of a housing element, planners can use the data to generate a land element to assess the state of land market operation for the jurisdiction.

ASSESSING LAND POLICY

Projections of supply and demand for land and housing by submarket can be used to assess the potential spatial and price effects of various land use policies. Policies that restrict the supply of land for development, so that excess demand is created in all comparable submarkets, are likely to generate significant inflationary pressures. On the other hand, spatial development policies that shift the supply of developable land from one set of similar submarkets to others are not likely to generate significant inflationary tendencies.

If submarkets are readily substitutable within their broad categories (central-city, inner-urban, suburban, exurban), then estimates of demand need not be broken down by more than these broad categories. Land policies by submarkets can then be assessed to determine whether they are adequate to meet aggregate demand. Efforts to shift development from, say, suburban to inner-urban submarkets may be difficult, due to the limited substitutability perceived by housing consumers. In situations where land policy attempts to achieve this objective, the land and housing supply and price data should be monitored closely, in order to determine whether market forces are being redirected, or whether considerable land price inflation is occurring.

The land and housing monitoring system can be used to develop an offset or trade-off policy for land use and environmental regulation. The systematic monitoring of land and housing supply, and of prices, can serve as the basis for designing land use control programs that are less inflationary than those that limit land development in some submarkets without encouraging it in others. The intent of the land and housing monitoring system is not to equalize land prices between submarkets (inner-city and suburban ones, for example), or to alter all the relative prices of land in a city's land markets. Rather, the system is intended to help land use planners design land use control programs that do not cause massive price inflation in land markets—and this is best done, of course, by providing land market information that can be used to develop trade-offs between restricted and growth-targeted submarkets.

The land supply monitoring system will not eliminate the windfall and wipe-out problem. Unlucky landowners holding land that is restricted from development will still be wiped out. However, windfalls will be much less concentrated on landowners in particular submarkets, if the monitoring system is used to develop a program that opens other submarkets to development.

The land monitoring system is supply-oriented because it does not attempt to affect the level of demand for land. The advantage of the land monitoring system is that it can tell planners how much land is available where, and whether it is sufficient to meet anticipated demand. If the supply of land is limited to a point below that which is necessary to meet demand, the price of land will rise.

The land monitoring system can be expanded, however, to determine how much the demand for growth should be restricted, so that the level of housing demand will match the desired supply of developable residential land. Instead of applying land use policies that restrict growth by limiting housing supply, the monitoring system can be used to determine the amount of employment growth that can be accommodated, given the desired level of land supply. This approach would generate much less land and housing price inflation than traditional growth management approaches.

The above outline of a land monitoring system was based on the simplifying assumption of independence from other communities. In settings where other communities are in close proximity, such as in suburban portions of metropolitan areas, the land use policies and employment growth of other communities can greatly affect both the demand for land and housing, and the delineation and performance of land and housing submarkets. These spillover effects have important implications for the design of a land use monitoring system.

In communities that are in close proximity to one another, a single land use monitoring system must be developed for all interdependent communities. Housing and land submarkets should be identified as suggested above. In some instances, the submarkets may straddle several communities. It would be futile for one community to develop a land monitoring system that was based only on submarkets that were coterminous with community political boundaries—the land use and economic development policies of other communities could greatly affect the supply of and the demand for land and housing.

However, it does not seem necessary that the land use monitoring system be developed exclusively at the regional level. While the Association of Bay Area Governments could competently develop a regional land monitoring system, it would be reasonable and perhaps more efficient for Santa Clara and Marin Counties each to develop its own system. Each system could be tied into the efforts of both counties to restrict development in unincorporated areas; it could be used by the included cities to balance employment and housing growth. The only limitation on developing multijurisdictional land monitoring systems is that the communities together constitute a land and housing market area that is relatively unaffected by other communities.

BALANCING SUPPLY AND DEMAND IN LAND USE POLICY

While the monitoring of land and housing supply and prices may prove valuable for evaluating local land use policy, it provides no incentive for communities to balance the supply of developable land with the demand for it. A possible way of balancing land supply and demand is to use the land use monitoring system to develop land use plans and policies that equalize the supply of and demand for land. The demand for housing and land would be estimated annually, and housing approval targets established. Land policy would be formulated to meet environmental objectives, but would provide for an adequate supply of land to meet housing demand over time.

The review of development proposals would proceed as is now the case, except that the process would be required to approve enough projects to meet targeted housing production goals. These targets would be classified according to price range and type. Establishment of a required number of approvals would eliminate the tendency of organized special interest groups to oppose all development projects. Since a minimum number of units would be guaranteed approval each year, projects would be scrutinized as to their relative costs and benefits; those projects with the best benefit/cost ratios in terms of environmental, fiscal, and social attributes within each price range and category would be given development permission.

Though this housing target system may seem similar to the popular growth management schemes of Ramapo, Petaluma, and Boulder, there are several fundamental differences. First, the targets are minimums, not maximums. There is no reason why the target cannot be exceeded.

Second, in contrast to the situation in Petaluma, where the maximum quota of annual housing production is often not met (O'Donnell, 1978), here the proposed minimum automatically guarantees that as long as projects are proposed, they will be granted permits. In this case, developers can operate under a greater certainty, and hence are more likely to propose projects.

Third, many growth control quotas (Boulder, Petaluma, Davis) seem to set a target arbitrarily. The proposed housing target system, however, is based on demand projections and is subject to change. As projections of demand are altered by employment growth and net in-migration, the target will change.

Fourth, many current growth control programs regulate only residential development, but the suggested target system would increase housing quotas as new growth increased housing demand.[1]

Finally, the target system encourages the approval of development, while other growth management programs do not reduce the tendency to reject development because of citizen opposition to it. While Petaluma and Boulder can advocate compact development, or the development of designated areas, their systems of growth management offer no guarantee that actual development will occur.

Stopping sprawl, or, as in the case of Petaluma, shifting development from the east side to the west side of town, does not guarantee that development will occur either. But although the policy proposed here does not provide for explicit incentives to encourage development yet, given the automatic guarantee of a certain level of development *regardless of location,* the system will still implicitly encourage planners to promote growth in the "right" areas.

This last feature seems to be particularly important, given the increasing advocacy of infill development to offset the containment of sprawl. As Frieden has pointed out, environmental groups ostensibly in favor of such policies have frequently attempted to block infill development in several areas of the San Francisco Bay Area (Frieden, 1979). While planners can promote compact development (infill instead of sprawl), given the present design of land use and enviromental regulations, it seems likely that sprawl will be contained, but that infill will not occur to offset the restrictions of outward metropolitan expansion.

By guaranteeing development, a land use policy attempting to promote compact development is likely to facilitate infill activity, if infill is required to offset containment restrictions. Whether this will generate substantial adverse housing market effects is another issue, but at least the targeting approach guarantees that suburban restrictions be offset with development in vacant and underused urban areas on a one-for-one basis.

The proposed land use policy guarantees the production of a minimum number of housing units in local areas. As suggested, it will reduce the consistent tendency of citizen opposition to all development proposals. Instead, a given development project would be evaluated on its environmental merit relative to other projects. And by guaranteeing the production of a minimum number of units, land policy that attempts to restrict sprawl would be required, in any case, to promote offsetting development in other locations. Although significant housing market impacts are still likely to exist under this approach, the price effects of such a policy may be less— depending on the substitutability of the offset housing for the unrestricted units.

---

[1]Most growth management programs focus entirely on residential development. Construction of housing requires a special permit, and the application for the permit starts the growth management system. Requests for other types of uses are not subjected to this review process.

David E. Dowall is assistant professor in the department of city and regional planning, and a researcher at the Institute of Urban and Regional Development, at the University of California, Berkeley. For the past two years, he has been analyzing the effects of local land use controls on the development of the San Francisco Bay Area.

This article is excerpted from one that appeared in the *APA Journal* in April 1981. Use is by permission.

FAIR SHARE HOUSING IN NEW JERSEY

JOHN RAHENKAMP AND CREIGH RAHENKAMP

One of the major issues for communities adopting growth management techniques is the degree to which such techniques may act to exclude people with certain levels of income. Communities such as Boca Raton, for example, have effectively prohibited all but higher-income people from residing in the community, by restricting the range of housing types to those that require a good deal of high-priced land. On the other hand, New Jersey communities have been told by the state supreme court (in the famous *Mount Laurel I* and *Mount Laurel II* decisions, among others) that they may not regulate land use in a way that excludes a "fair share" of the region's cross-section of population.

"Fair share," as a concept, is not at all well defined. The opaqueness is in many ways intentional, as it allows a disparate group of individuals and ideologies to stand as one against a common foe, while at the same time blurring the differences that divide them. In general, "fair share" is the banner for those who oppose no-growth attitudes and concomitant policies that are grounded at the municipal level. The common root of the concept is the recognition of burgeoning regional responsibilities to participate in the production of housing for expanding numbers of households, due both to new household formations and to significant movements of current population.

Underlying all of our efforts as planners are two dynamic trends that continuously affect whether our chosen regulatory approaches succeed, and how we collectively define "success."

FORCES ECONOMIC AND DEMOGRAPHIC

One major trend is the restructuring of our economy, both with regard to the production process and to regional location. Many medium-sized cities in the Midwest and East have simply lost their economic purposes. Whether major metropolitan centers will survive in the long run is an ongoing debate. Most central cores continue to decline numerically, if not qualitatively, with new households and employment formation occurring on the fringes. The inescapable conclusion is that our nation is "suburbanizing."

Second, our household structures are changing as dramatically as our economic structure. At the end of World War II, about 70 percent of the families in the country had children present in the home; by now, that figure has dropped to less than 30 percent. The result is that more than 70 percent of the households contain three or fewer persons; yet, the majority of our suburban zoning is still for large-lot, large houses with many bedrooms. Unfortunately, that is the wrong product to bring forward for the majority of the current population.

In addition, if we ignore issues of affordability and of "effective demand," it is still clear that housing production has severely lagged behind demand. The "baby boomers" have squarely hit the prime homebuying ages, and have found tight competition for the homes provided.

MISTAKES WE HAVE MADE IN THE PAST

These crises of availability and affordability have many roots beyond the reach of planners, including higher interest rates, shifts in relative prices that have made construction more expensive, and the simple fact that by the 1980s, there was less available ground in premium locations than in the 1950s, 1960s, or 1970s. Unfortunately, rather than protecting our citizens from the crises, planning and land use control have frequently exacerbated the magnitude of the problems, primarily through four mechanisms, including: disproportionately taxing new construction, reducing the supply of buildable ground, lengthening review processes, and setting up cost-generative site design controls. To protect the broad public interest, we've got to balance the cost of housing against whatever land use techniques are currently being used.

Our regulatory structures for the management of land use have been exceedingly rudimentary. For example, growth management plans that focus on locational issues compound real estate speculation, and become forces in themselves against many of the goals sought. We must recognize that few uses in the modern suburb are sufficiently onerous to require the specificity and immensity of a "zone." We are not usually planning for development that occurs at the rate of one lot at a time. The building industry is maturing, and the sizes of projects are expanding. The moderate incompatibility between uses within some larger-scale projects, for instance, can be treated as an issue of project edges—resolvable with performance standards, including setbacks and buffers, rather than with zoning.

All too often, legitimate environmental concerns have become excuses for absurd regulatory constraints. From an environmental standpoint, there is no defense for establishing fixed densities. There is simply no scientifically defensible correlation between density on a given piece of ground and environmental criteria. In essence, we've been using "density" as a shorthand for the things we really care about, like percolation, soil stabilization, vehicle trips, etc. The inescapable fact is that you can't establish a fixed density on a given piece of ground, and have it defensible in terms of health, safety, or welfare.

We must stop forcing market demand into predefined pigeonholes of types and locations. There are techniques through which we can positively influence the development market—predominantly through performance standards tied closely to health, safety, and welfare. For example, we can permit more traffic generation in area "A," or require fewer off-site improvements, or contribute public funds to enhance capacity. In controlling where public monies are spent, and in allocating scarce capacities, we can influence the form that the public demand takes, stopping short of fixing exact growth patterns: a subtle but critical distinction.

On the local level, we have allowed our design codes and other criteria to become technologically outdated and procedurally complex. The time delays in the review of projects are extraordinarily costly. A year of delay costs between $1,500 and $4,000 per unit. We must move projects through the process faster. That is only possible if we have done our homework as planners.

Moreover, we need to eliminate all the excessive subdivision standards, which cost on the order of $5,000 to $7,000 per unit. Most of these standards do not relate to health, safety, or welfare, and many of them compound environmental problems.

Finally, we need to reduce, or at least closely monitor, all site exactions. How much should be asked for impact fees? Is it fair to lay all of the impact fees against the newcomers in town? What is a fair exaction, and where is it an inequitable newcomers' tax? For example, all too often, the public review and application fees exceed the actual costs to prepare the application and to design the entire project.

All of these trends and past failings had become self-evident in New Jersey by the early 1970s. When I [John Rahenkamp] was chairman of the planning board in Mount Laurel, New Jersey, we had approved several planned unit developments and started a program to build some low-cost units as a means of providing housing for employees in the emerging office and commercial developments. A new regime, however, once voted into office, proceeded to wipe out the low-cost housing program, as well as any additional planned unit developments. When the National Association for the Advancement of Colored People and the housing advocacy office of the state attorney general teamed up to challenge these decisions, they began the 15-year history of litigation against Mount Laurel.

THE LONG HISTORY OF MOUNT LAUREL, NEW JERSEY, IN THE COURTS

Mount Laurel was chosen as the battleground, not because it was the worst example, but because it represented a middle-of-the-road community that had made some, but insufficient, moves to allow development of reasonably priced housing. It was thought that the case made against Mount Laurel would be widely applicable to other communities, which has turned out to be the case.

The history of judicial involvement in New Jersey clearly demonstrates the various meanings of "fair share."

The first ruling from the state supreme court, in *Southern Burlington County NAACP v. Township of Mt. Laurel* 67 *N.J.* 151 (1975) (*Mount Laurel I*), decreed that the constitutional rights of New Jersey's citizens prevented a municipality from enforcing land use regulations that excluded households on the basis of income. The court required that a developing municipality must accept a fair share of the regional housing need.

In *Oakwood at Madison, Inc. v. Township of Madison* 72 *N.J.* 481 (1977), the court dealt more specifically with the need to provide "least-cost" housing through design deregulation, and identified a checklist of exactions that contributed to higher housing costs.

Mount Laurel II [*Southern Burlington County NAACP v. Township of Mt. Laurel* 92 *N.J.* 158 (1983)] responded to the lack of state legislation that could prod communities still resisting the concept of fair share housing. This decision, and trial court decisions implementing the fair share doctrine, assigned to each municipality a strict numerical allocation of needed residential units, specifically targeted at low- and moderate-income households. As an enforcement mechanism, the court enlisted the aid of the development community. A developer could undertake litigation to prove that a town's ordinances did not allow a reasonable opportunity for the provision of the allocated units, in exchange for the right to go forward with a particular development.

And, in a subsequent case [*Urban League of Essex County* v. *Township of Mahwah, et al.,* N.J. Super. L. Div.—Bergen County, Docket No. L-17112-71 (Smith, Harvey, J.S.C., August 1, 1984)], the court established a 90-day limit on processing periods for the issuance of building permits to developers.

No longer was it necessary to litigate for seven or eight years to get permission to develop, nor to win in the courts, only to be faced with bureaucratic shuffling. The cost of litigation, therefore, had proved a sound investment. For around $100,000 to $150,000, a suit could be brought to prove a recalcitrant town exclusionary, with the settlement likely to reduce exactions and the costs of delays by $5,000 to $7,000 per unit.

Conventional standards for roads, water and sewer lines, setbacks, and other building and subdivision code requirements are being reduced to those related to definable health, safety, and welfare criteria. Curbless roads with 22-foot pavement widths, storm drainage on the surface rather than through pipes, and 25-foot maximum setbacks are fairly common resolutions. By corollary litigation, standards' requirements that housing units have at least 1,200 and 1,600 square feet of floor space are also being significantly reduced [*Homebuilders League of South Jersey, Inc.* v. *Berlin Township,* 385 A.2d 295 (N.J. Supr. 1., 1978)].

HOW TO APPROACH FAIR SHARE HOUSING: TECHNIQUES AND PROBLEMS

Three types of questions must be addressed when dealing with the issue of fair share housing. The first is the notion of the regional responsibility of every community. The first Mount Laurel decision required that every community calculate its fair share of the regional market for various types of housing, both now and in the future, and then plan actively for that housing in the future development. The calculation required that estimates be made of the characteristics of the population segments who would be drawn to the area, either as prospective local employees or as commuters to jobs in other communities. Obviously, these estimates are difficult to make; but almost every region contains a university or a state agency that has made or will make these kinds of projections. Furthermore, in the absence of a decade-long history of municipal failure, such as that in New Jersey, the courts almost always accept the calculations, if they have been done in a reasonable manner. Even coming up with a crude approximation is better than ignoring the exercise altogether, and leaving the community vulnerable to litigation, or the majority of its population prospectively unhoused.

The second approach to the fair share housing issue analyzes the current regulatory structure to determine the effects of local development policies and regulations. The first test is whether the policies and regulations are legally based on valid public purposes. Standards for road rights-of-way, for example, may require wide roads because they are supposedly safer (although that is arguable). But then the secondary effects of that standard must be examined: a wide road costs more, adds to the price of housing, and therefore makes the adjoining housing too expensive for some numbers of people. These policy cross-checks are indispensable to finding resolutions of the issue of affordable housing.

A focus on the role of the community as an instrument of state policy distinguishes the third approach. Local governments, despite the grants of home rule charters, are still creatures of the state, and therefore constitute policy instruments that should regulate in a way that is consistent with state policies. *Mount Laurel II* stressed the responsibility of municipalities to regulate land use and development, so as to give added effect to statewide public policy.

The solutions sought in New Jersey still entail a number of problems. One problem is that builders are tending to sell, rather than to rent, the price-controlled housing they are providing, and the truly needy poor get left out of the picture. By and large, *Mount Laurel II* housing is being occupied by schoolteachers, firemen, municipal workers, and other people in lower-middle income brackets. Builders are encouraged to follow this path by the communities, and by neighbors who want the new residents to be as similar to themselves as possible.

A second problem is that the builders' remedy calls for 20 percent of the housing to be aimed at lower-income persons, and actually, the percentage of the population needing that kind of housing is much higher.

Then there is the allocation process, in which the court negotiates a settlement, rather than handing down a fixed number. This takes time and delays housing production that much more. The advantage of the negotiations, however, is that, usually, they reduce the normal exactions made by the community, to the point where builders' housing subsidies are practically made up by reductions in the cost of exactions. Indeed, a principle guiding the trial courts has been that the developer not be the scapegoat of the subsidy cost, but that the subsidy come from deregulation and from relief from exactions.

Another problem for builders with the Mount Laurel process relates to the circumstances under which they may obtain building approvals. Under the procedures created by *Mount Laurel II,* once a town has a settlement accepted by a trial court, no one can sue that town for six years to change the agreement. In some municipalities, a "public interest" plaintiff, such as a lawyer for a public interest group, has successfully challenged a municipality's zoning and obtained a settlement, only to find that the subdivision controls do not allow the type of low-cost construction that would now be both feasible and marketable. In effect, this outcome blocks development of affordable housing for six years.

The other side of the coin is seen in the case of the first builder who challenges the zoning, obtains a settlement, and is able to build to a higher density and make a profit. The second builder to come to the town, however, finds landowners who already perceive the increased value of their land under the higher density standards. The result for the second builder is a lengthy haggling process, simply in order to obtain land at a reasonable price.

EPILOGUE

In late 1985, the New Jersey legislature finally responded to the state supreme court's call for action. The legislature adopted two acts, one calling for the creation of the New Jersey Council on Affordable Housing, and the second creating a state planning commission. In conjunction with overseeing the new requirements in the municipal land use law, the council now has the responsibility to review and approve housing elements in all municipal comprehensive plans. As part of this review process, the council must affirm that the element under review conforms to the allocation of low- and moderate-income housing, as determined by the council. This allocation must itself be consistent with the state development and redevelopment plan, which the state planning commission is required to complete.

In *Mount Laurel III* (*The Hills Development Co.* v. *Township of Bernards, N.J.,* slip op. A-122-133 and related cases, February 20, 1986), all of the pending cases in the trial courts have been referred to the council for disposition. The trial courts are allowed to attach conditions to the transfer, protecting to some extent the rights of existing plaintiffs; however, it is too soon to estimate if any conditions will be applied.

Unfortunately, this abrupt change in the regulatory process has had a severe impact on the building industry. With the council and commission just beginning to organize, these cases are placed virtually on hold for up to two years—not a welcome reprieve for developers with options and large legal bills. The court has decided that the legislation is generally constitutional, and has placed its faith in the earnestness of the attempt. The language of *Mount Laurel III*, however, is clear in warning the state that failure to deal administratively with the affordability crisis will again trigger judicial management.

The bottom line is that the state may well be on the path to solving a most complex social problem of national significance. The courts have served well to focus the issue and to force resolution. All those concerned hope that the housing council will continue on the road toward statesmanlike policy choices.

John Rahenkamp is president of John Rahenkamp and Associates, Inc., planning and development consultants in Philadelphia. Creigh Rahenkamp is a member of the same firm.

The Rahenkamps' contribution to this part of the book has been drawn from an address given at the ULI/Lincoln Institute seminar on growth management issues.

NO WRONG WITHOUT A REMEDY:
The New Jersey Supreme Court's Effort to Bar Exclusionary Zoning

PETER A. BUCHSBAUM

INTRODUCTION

The unanimous New Jersey Supreme Court ruling in *Southern Burlington County NAACP v. Township of Mount Laurel[1] (Mount Laurel II)* is likely to have national as well as statewide ramifications. These impacts will result from the remedial innovations in the decision.

The ruling by Chief Justice Wilentz essentially reinforced the court's earlier insistence, in *Mount Laurel I,[2]* that the due process clause of the New Jersey State Constitution requires communities to allow construction of needed low-cost housing. Thus, the constitutional underpinning for prohibiting exclusionary zoning remains unchanged. The opinion has established, however, new ways to measure and enforce the obligation to zone equitably. First, the growth regions designated by a state planning document known as the state development guide plan have become the presumptive bases for determining judicially whether a community has an obligation to the region, or whether it need only zone to take care of its own. Second, municipal zoning must provide for a specific numerical fair share of low- and moderate-income housing. Third, municipal land use activity now must seek to promote lower-income development through specific affirmative steps, such as density bonuses, mandatory set asides, tax abatement, and participation in federal housing programs. Removal of restrictive provisions is no longer enough. Fourth, more drastic sanctions will be imposed for noncompliance with the constitutional standards. Builders who sue and win will usually get building permits. They will be allowed to construct four market-rate housing units for each lower-income unit they

---

[1]92 N.J. 158, 456 A.2d 390 (1983).
[2]Southern Burlington County NAACP v. Township of Mt. Laurel, 67 N.J. 151, 336 A.2d 713 (1975).

Reprinted by permission of *The Urban Lawyer,* the national quarterly journal of the American Bar Association, Section of Urban, State, and Local Government Law, as it appeared in Volume 17, Number 1 (Winter 1985).

provide. Communities that fail to zone validly after once being directed to do so in the courts may, in effect, forfeit their right to zone.

The implications of these innovations for New Jersey are just beginning to be felt. Most notably, in Mount Laurel itself, a 456-unit mobile home park will finally be built after a dozen years of litigation.[3] While the opinion's effect on the national scene is harder to gauge, it will almost certainly reinforce a discernible but not overwhelming trend to more centralized state control over local land use decisions that affect the housing supply.[4] While other courts may not go as far as New Jersey's, the *Mount Laurel II* opinion may well serve as a benchmark against which courts in other jurisdictions will measure their willingness to intervene in local housing and planning decisions.

THE COURT'S UNDERLYING GOAL: COMPLIANCE WITH EXCLUSIONARY ZONING MANDATES

The New Jersey court plainly acted as definitively as it did out of frustration with municipal indifference to its initial effort to prohibit exclusionary zoning. A scathing denunciation of Mount Laurel Township's reaction to *Mount Laurel I* is set forth in the first lines of the opinion:

> This is the return, eight years later, of Southern Burlington County NAACP v. Township of Mount Laurel, 67 N.J. 151 (1975) (Mount Laurel I). We set forth in that case, for the first time, the doctrine requiring that municipalities' land use regulations provide a realistic opportunity for low- and moderate-income housing. The doctrine has become famous. The Mount Laurel case itself threatens to become infamous. After all this time, 10 years after the trial court's initial order invalidating its zoning ordinance, Mount Laurel remains afflicted with a blatantly exclusionary ordinance. Papered over with studies, rationalized by hired experts, the ordinance at its core is true to nothing but Mount Laurel's determination to exclude the poor. Mount Laurel is not alone; we believe that there is widespread noncompliance with the constitutional mandate of our original opinion in this case.[3]

The court's conclusion recapitulates this theme: "We intend here only to make sure that if the poor remain locked into urban slums, it will not be because we failed to enforce the constitution."[6]

THE RULINGS

General Welfare

The court first reaffirmed the state constitutional basis for its curtailment of exclusionary zoning. Chief Justice Wilentz reasserted the constitutional requirement

---

[3]Other cases are being settled with provisions being made for substantial amounts of lower-income housing. *See, e.g.,* Hills Development Co. v. Township of Bedminster, No. L-36896-70 P.W. (N.J. Super. Ct. Law Div.) (260 units); Centex Corp. v. Township of East Windsor, No. L-51177-80 P.W. (N.J. Super. Ct. Law Div.) (50 units). Hundreds of additional units are in the offing. *See* Newark Star Ledger, Jan. 9, 1984, at 1.

[4]This trend is visible in the legislative as well as the judicial arena. *See* CAL. GOV'T CODE §§65580 to 65589.8 (West 1983 & Supp. 1984); Barton, *California Legislature Prohibits Exclusionary Zoning, Mandates Fair Share: Inclusionary Housing Programs a Likely Response,* 9 SAN. FERN. V. L. REV. 19 (1981). *See also* OR. REV. STAT. §§ 197.175–.190, 197.225–.265 (1983); Comment, *LCDC Goal 10: Oregon's Solution to Exclusionary Zoning,* 16 WILLAMETTE L.J. 873 (1980).

[5]92 N.J. at 198–99, 456 A.2d at 490–510.

[6]92 N.J. at 352, 456 A.2d at 490.

that local laws reflect regional welfare, and not respond solely to local interests:

> When the exercise of [police power] by a municipality affects something as fundamental as housing, the general welfare includes more than the welfare of that municipality and its citizens. . . . Municipal land use regulations that conflict with the general welfare, thus defined, abuse the police power and are unconstitutional.[7]

This mandate to further the regional general welfare was derived from "the state constitutional requirements of substantive due process and equal protection."[8]

In further explaining its constitutional holding, the court held that the state is responsible for the ultimate results of local zoning. It declared that the delegation of land use power to municipalities cannot shield the state's political subdivisions from responsibilities for the regional land use patterns that result from decentralized decision making:

> The basis for the constitutional obligation is simple: the state controls the use of the land, *all* of the land. In exercising that control, it cannot favor rich over poor. It cannot legislatively set aside dilapidated housing in urban ghettos for the poor, and decent housing elsewhere for everyone else. The government that controls this land represents everyone.[9]

This regional welfare analysis is not new.[10] But its strong restatement in a highly significant case is important. It enhances the place of states in our federal system. It declares that state governments cannot merely pass political power to municipal governments and disclaim the ensuing results. Rather, they will be judicially accountable for the results.

This view of state responsibility will enhance the state's role in land use policy making. This is true even though the state was not a defendant in *Mount Laurel II*. It can be presumed that over a period of time, the entity that is held responsible for the consequences of regulations in a given area is more likely to act in this area. Certainly, had the court permitted the state to delegate land use powers to municipalities that were only responsible for the welfare of their own residents, it would be unlikely that any state would respond to regional housing needs.

This general view of state responsibility also sharply contrasts with that taken by the Burger court in *Milliken v. Bradley*.[11] In that case, plaintiffs argued that the state should be held responsible for the disparity in percentages of blacks attending urban versus suburban schools. It was contended that there was a cause of action against the state for these disparities, since the state knowingly tolerated them, notwithstanding its ultimate responsibility for devising school district borders and regulating schools. The Supreme Court rejected this argument. It held that regional interdistrict racial disparities did not offend the U.S. Constitution, so long as the districts had not been initially established or later manipulated to achieve certain racial results.[12] Had the New Jersey Supreme Court adopted an analogous view of regional housing responsibilities, it would have been required to sustain municipal exclusionary zoning, except where such zoning adversely affected the resident poor. However, the New Jersey court ruled that localities do have to respond to regional needs.

---

[7]92 N.J. at 208, 456 A.2d at 415.

[8]92 N.J. at 209, 456 A.2d at 415 (citing 67 N.J. at 178, 181, 336 A.2d at 725).

[9]92 N.J. at 209, 456 A.2d at 415.

[10]Duffcon Concrete Products v. Borough of Cresskill, 1 N.J. 509 (1949).

[11]418 U.S. 717 (1974).

[12]In fact, the initial *Mount Laurel* case could have been decided on this narrow ground, since the trial court in that case found that its zoning was unfair to residents in certain semirural, low-income minority neighborhoods. *See* 119 N.J. Super. 164, 166–69, 209 A.2d 465, 473 (1972).

Defining the Municipality's Responsibility: Fair Share and the State Development Guide Plan

Having reasserted that municipalities did have a constitutional obligation to respond to regional housing needs, the court next set out to define that obligation. Its initial approach to this task was to resolve two preliminary issues. First, the court decided that municipalities would be required to provide for a specific number of low- and moderate-income housing units, that is, a numerical fair share. Second, the court held that to meet these goals, housing had to be affordable specifically to low- and moderate-income families—those with income no greater than 80 percent of the median income of the region. While other courts have employed fair share terminology, none have made the attainment of a fair share number a key constitutional requirement, and none have stated that the needs to be addressed must be those of persons whose incomes make them eligible for subsidized housing.[13]

The New Jersey court's determination in this respect was deliberate, particularly as it concerned fair share. Chief Justice Wilentz recognized that the court's 1977 opinion in *Oakwood at Madison* v. *Township of Madison,*[14] had stated that specific fair share quotas would not be required, although *Mount Laurel I* had indicated they were essential. The court in *Mount Laurel II* returned to fair share because it concluded that the lack of numerical standards was one of the reasons the constitutional requirements of *Mount Laurel I* were not being enforced. It firmly rejected the *Madison* test, which eschewed fair share in favor of an evaluation of the substance of challenged ordinances, and in favor of the existence of bona fide efforts to meet housing needs:

> It was hoped that this test would be adequate to protect the rights of low-income persons, while at the same time minimizing the role of the courts in this area. Unfortunately, experience has taught us that this formulation is too vague to provide adequate guidance for either the trial courts or the municipalities.[15]

The court also cited the trial court rulings in *Mount Laurel II* and *Mahwah,*[16] which had approved zoning ordinances with minimal actual provision for lower-income housing, as evidencing the need for a more definitive approach than one that deferred to bona fide efforts and good faith.[17] Moreover, in ruling on *Urban League,*[18] which involved seven Middlesex County municipalities, the court went so far as to condemn severely the prior nonnumerical approach of its *Madison* ruling, stating that it delivered "a clear message to the trial bench in *Mount Laurel* cases, and the message is 'hands off'."[19]

---

[13]*See, e.g.,* Surrick v. Zoning Hearing Bd., 476 Pa. 182, 382 A.2d 105, 110 n. 10 (1977); Associated Home Builders of Greater East Bay v. City of Livermore, 18 Cal. 3d 583, 557 P.2d 473, 135 Cal. Rptr. 41 (1976). Although Roberts, J., concurring in *Surrick,* objected to inclusion of the fair share concept in the majority opinion, it is quite apparent, from the absence of any mention of specific numbers in the majority opinion, that the Pennsylvania court was not adopting the formula approach approved in *Mount Laurel II.* Further, that the apartment units approved in the Pennsylvania cases were designed for middle-, rather than low- or moderate-income persons, has appeared not to bother the Pennsylvania courts at all. *See Surrick,* 476 Pa. 182, 382 A.2d 105 (1977); *In re* Appeal of Girsh, 437 Pa. 237, 263 A.2d 395 (1970).

[14]472 N.J. at 481, 499, 371 A.2d at 1200.

[15]592 N.J. at 220, 456 A.2d at 421.

[16]Urban League of Essex County v. Township of Mahwah, *decided sub nom.* Southern Burlington County NAACP v. Township of Mt. Laurel, 92 N.J. 158, 456 A.2d 390 (1983).

[17]92 N.J. at 220, 304, 456 A.2d at 421, 483.

[18]Urban League of Greater New Brunswick v. Mayor of Borough of Carteret, *decided sub nom.* Southern Burlington County NAACP v. Township of Mount Laurel, 92 N.J. 158, 456 A.2d 390 (1983).

[19]92 N.J. at 340, 456 A.2d at 484.

The court dealt with the crucial issue of targeting fair share housing to particular income groups in a lengthy footnote.[20] It defined low- and moderate-income families in accordance with the HUD standards for subsidized housing.[21] It also stated that affordability to such persons meant that no more than 25 percent of their income could be devoted to housing.[22] Elsewhere in its decision, the court reemphasized its requirement that the housing be affordable to lower-income persons by stating that even least-cost housing, which is a term referring to no-frills housing that may be more expensive than moderate-income housing, "does not mean $50,000-plus single-family homes and very expensive apartments."[23]

The court's choice of the fair share approach to crystallize municipal obligations to the region did not solve by itself the issue of the clarity of such obligations. The fair share concept itself is susceptible to many applications that have widely varying results in terms of housing obligations. Recognizing this, the court took a series of remarkable procedural steps designed to ensure that fair share obligations could be assessed with reasonable clarity and consistency.

The State Development Guide Plan. The most surprising of these steps was the court's reliance on New Jersey's state development guide plan[24] as the means to determine which communities in New Jersey had an obligation to provide in their zoning ordinances for the prospective low- and moderate-income housing needs of their region. The guide plan divided New Jersey into six basic areas, including growth, limited-growth, agricultural, conservation, pinelands, and coastal zone areas.[25] The court held that future low- and moderate-income housing needs should be met in municipalities made up substantially of the growth areas depicted on the guide plan.[26] It found that the guide plan, while not specifically directed to low- and moderate-income housing, was being used to guide state investment policies, capital growth strategies, and program policies, and to determine in general "where growth should be encouraged and discouraged."[27] These uses, in the court's view, made it an appropriate guide for the regional distribution of higher-density housing.

This branch of the opinion, though couched in the language of judicial deference to executive growth determinations,[28] gave the guide plan an unexpected importance. In effect, the court went beyond the usual, and usually ignored, invitation for legislative or executive consideration of a social problem that is being cast in judicial form. Rather, it told the legislature, which had simply authorized the development of a guide plan, and the New Jersey Byrne and Kean administrations (whose enthusiasm, for low-income housing, especially in the Kean years, was marginal), that they had made a policy choice as to which New Jersey townships should bear

---

[20]92 N.J. at 221–22 n.8, 456 A.2d at 421–22.

[21]42 U.S.C. § 1437A(b)(2) (1982).

[22]92 N.J. at 221–22, n.8, 456 A.2d at 421–22. The court indicated that it might be willing on occasion to alter these standards, but it did not indicate what facts would induce it to do so.

[23]92 N.J. at 277, 456 A.2d at 451.

[24]The state development guide plan was prepared pursuant to state planning legislation, N.J. STAT. ANN. § 13:1B–15.52a(2) (West 1979).

[25]92 N.J. at 226, 456 A.2d at 424.

[26]92 N.J. at 227, 456 A.2d at 425.

[27]92 N.J. at 226–35, 456 A.2d at 424–29. The court's reliance on the guide plan was limited to future housing needs. As to present housing needs, it held that "every municipality's land use regulation should provide a realistic opportunity for decent housing for at least some part of its resident poor who now occupy dilapidated housing," except in urban areas where such poor represent disproportionately large segments of the population. 92 N.J. at 214–15, 456 A.2d at 418.

[28]92 N.J. at 241, 456 A.2d at 432.

the responsibility for providing low-income housing opportunities.[29] Nonetheless, by thus using the guide plan, the New Jersey Supreme Court gave state planning in New Jersey a constitutional status that is probably unmatched in any other state, and that is equaled legislatively, particularly with respect to housing, perhaps only in California and Oregon.[30]

While the court's use of the guide plan may principally have been motivated by a desire for the kind of clarity that only reliance on its maps could provide, the court also stressed that low- and moderate-income housing obligations should be met in a manner consistent with such sound regional planning as the guide plan envisioned. Perhaps, in part, seeking to allay fears of an unbridled spread of lower-income housing, the court stated, with respect to its determination to limit the *Mount Laurel* obligation to state-designated growth areas:

> The Constitution of the State of New Jersey does not require bad planning. It does not require suburban spread. It does not require rural municipalities to encourage large-scale housing developments. It does not require wasteful extension of roads, and needless construction of sewer and water facilities for the out-migration of people from the cities and the suburbs. There is nothing in our constitution that says we cannot satisfy our constitutional obligation to provide lower-income housing and, at the same time, plan the future of the state intelligently.[31]

Determining Fair Share and the Three Judges. Having thus settled that growth area communities must respond to prospective housing needs, the court then described how those needs were to be assessed and allocated.[32] The court indicated that this task involved three steps: determination of a region, assessment of the housing need in the region, and an allocation of that need.[33] It gave only general substantive guidelines for making these three determinations, stating for instance, that a region should be defined as "that general area that constitutes, more or less, the housing market area of which the subject municipality is a part, and from

---

[29]The actual importance the Kean administration attached to the guide plan was demonstrated by its original 1984 budget. Prepared just a few weeks before *Mount Laurel* came down, this budget contemplated the abolition of the division of state and regional planning, which had prepared the guide plan and was responsible for its maintenance. *See* Buchsbaum, *Unlocking the Door to the House in the Suburbs,* 12 New Jersey Rep. 30, 32 (1983).

[30]*See* Comment, *LCDC Goal 10: Oregon's Solution to Exclusionary Zoning,* 16 Willamette L.J. 873 (1980); Burton, *California Legislature Prohibits Exclusionary Zoning, Mandates Fair Share: Inclusionary Housing Programs a Likely Response,* 9 San Fern. V. L. Rev. 19 (1981). The California legislative provisions are found at Cal. Gov't Code §§ 65580–65589. As to Oregon, *see* 1983 Or. Rev. Stat. § 197.225–.245 and Or. Admin. R. 660–15–000.

[31]92 N.J. at 238, 456 A.2d 430–31. As support for this statement, the court cited, interestingly, Duffcon Concrete Products v. Borough of Cresskill, 1 N.J. 509 (1949), one of the first cases to rely on regional considerations to justify local exclusion of certain otherwise lawful uses, if they were provided for elsewhere. 92 N.J. at 239. *Mount Laurel* turns *Duffcon* on its head by requiring *inclusion* of uses that are *not* elsewhere permitted.

[32]92 N.J. at 241–42, 456 A.2d at 432. It is to be noted that the use of the guide plan is subject to qualification where: (a) a party demonstrates that a growth area boundary zone was drawn in an arbitrary and capricious fashion; (b) a municipality in a no-growth category has undergone a substantial change; and (c) the guide plan, which was released in 1980, is not updated by January 1, 1985. This last item has become the focus of a statewide debate, which has included hearings by an oversight committee of the New Jersey State Senate and a resolution by the New Jersey State Bar Association, calling upon the governor to update the guide plan in order to avoid a constitutional confrontation with the court. Governor Kean's 1984 "State of the State" message contained the first executive commitment to provide for an updated plan. More recently, a bill, S. 1464, which would provide for updating the guide plan, has been passed by the state senate and awaits action in the assembly.

[33]92 N.J. at 251, 456 A.2d at 438.

which the prospective population of the municipality would substantially be drawn, in the absence of exclusionary zoning."[34] It provided no further guidance for determination of regional housing need. As to fair share methodology, it only indicated that formulas relying on new employment and ratables would be favored, while formulas that rewarded population projections based on successful past exclusion, or that relied on the presence of vacant land not suitable for development, were to be disfavored.[35]

This generality surely must have been the product of a conscious decision on the part of the court. The discussion in the opinion makes it clear that the detailed record on fair share issues in some of the six *Mount Laurel II* cases would have enabled the court to give more refined direction regarding the determination of region, need, and an acceptable fair allocation formula.[36] However, the court apparently chose to rely on a procedural innovation to produce clear and consistent fair share allocations. This innovation was the selection of three specially designated judges who would hear all the *Mount Laurel II* litigation that arose throughout the state.[37] The court expected that this centralization of decision making in three judges, each responsible for a different section of the state, would result in the relatively early and "fairly consistent determination" of regions and regional needs.[38] Further, these determinations are to carry presumptive validity in future zoning cases, even as to municipalities and developers that are not parties to the cases in which the determinations are initially formulated.[39] As a result, the court expected that all the litigation on fair share would soon be confined to the allocation issue, since the state plan would settle who has the obligation, and the initial determinations of region and regional housing need would be presumptively valid as to all covered municipalities.[40] Even as to allocations, the court expected that the centralization of decision making in three judges and their endorsement of certain allocation methodologies in the initial cases should simplify subsequent litigation considerably.[41]

The effectiveness of this unusual technique remains to be tested. To date, there have been several trial court determinations of region, need, or allocation. Most notable is the opinion of the trial court in *AMG Realty* v. *Township of Warren*.[42] These opinions show that the potential for quick achievement of uniformity clearly exists. The complex fair share formula utilized in the *Warren* case resulted from the deliberations of a group of approximately 20 planners involved with various cases and brought together by one of the three judges, the Honorable Eugene D. Serpentelli. It

---

[34]92 N.J. at 256, 456 A.2d at 440 (quoting *Madison,* 72 N.J. at 537, 371 A.2d at 1192).

[35]92 N.J. at 256, 258, 300–301, 456 A.2d at 440, 441, 463.

[36]*See* 92 N.J. at 300, 302, 343, 349–50, 456 A.2d at 463–64, 486, 489.

[37]92 N.J. at 253, 456 A.2d 439. These judges were, in fact, designated in June 1983. Moreover, the court also issued a highly unusual notice requesting that attorneys who had filed or who were intending to file *Mount Laurel II* litigation contact the administrative office of the courts to ensure that the cases were allocated to the three judges. *See Notice to the Bar Re: Mount Laurel II,* 111 NEW JERSEY L.J. 109 (1983).

[38]92 N.J. at 254, 456 A.2d at 439.

[39]*Id.*

[40]92 N.J. at 255, 456 A.2d at 439.

[41]*Id.* The court did note that its presumptive-validity holding as to region and regional need might justify intervention by a number of municipalities in the initial cases, but it left the decision on such intervention to the discretion of the three judges. In fact, Judge Skillman did invite participation by a large number of municipalities in a suit against 25 Morris County communities brought by the New Jersey Department of Public Advocate. However, as the New Jersey Supreme Court predicted, 92 N.J. at 254, 456 A.2d at 439, few of these municipalities have chosen to become actively involved.

[42]No. L-23277-80 P.W. (N.J. Super.Ct. July 16, 1984).

now appears that this formula, or a variant on it, will be utilized in most of the *Mount Laurel II* suits.[43] In any event, the court's use of its extensive supervisory powers over the trial judiciary in New Jersey to deal with a complex socioeconomic factual issue is certainly a unique technique that may have relevant application to other states and other problems.

Requirements for Municipal Action

Ordinance Changes. Having restated the underlying constitutional theory, and having held that municipalities in growth areas must respond to fair share requirements, the court then discussed what ordinance changes and other actions municipalities had to take, in order to demonstrate that they had provided the requisite "realistic opportunity for lower-income housing."[44] First, to the extent necessary to meet fair share requirements and the needs of its indigenous poor, each municipality is obligated to remove cost-generating ordinance restrictions and subdivision exactions.[45] However, the court added a very significant qualification to this mandate: once a municipality has taken sufficient steps to make construction of the fair share reasonably possible, it may then impose more restrictive zoning in the balance of the community:

> For instance, a municipality having thus complied, the fact that its land use regulations contain restrictive provisions incompatible with lower-income housing, such as bedroom restrictions, large-lot zoning, prohibition against mobile homes, and the like, does not render those provisions invalid under *Mount Laurel*. . . . *Mount Laurel* is not an indiscriminate broom designed to sweep away all distinctions in the use of land. Municipalities may continue to reserve areas for upper-income housing, may continue to require certain community amenities in certain areas, may continue to zone with some regard to their fiscal obligations; they may do all of this, provided that they have otherwise complied with their *Mount Laurel* obligations.[46]

This reaffirmation of municipal police power, except to the extent that *Mount Laurel* needs must be addressed, is an important concession to home rule. It limits judicial supervision of ordinances to provisions that have negative external impacts on the regional supply of moderately priced housing. Once having responded to the regional housing situation, however, the municipality under *Mount Laurel II* is free to follow its own notions of appropriate public policy.[47]

Affirmative Action. In addition to the removal of cost-generating requirements, municipalities have to take affirmative steps to make housing opportunities realistic.[48] Mere upzoning will not suffice, unless there is some basis for believing that the owners of land so zoned will provide inexpensive housing and not just luxury townhouses. Such affirmative steps to secure construction of lower-income housing

---

[43]This formula could, however, be superseded by alternatives approved by a state commission, if a widely discussed pending bill, S-2046, is adopted.

[44]92 N.J. at 260, 456 A.2d at 442.

[45]The court cited the U.S. Department of Housing and Urban Development *Minimum Property Standards,* and such texts as S. SEIDEL, HOUSING COSTS AND GOVERNMENT REGULATIONS (1978), as helpful, although not conclusive, sources of minimum building and zoning standards that reduce housing costs while adequately protecting health and safety. 92 N.J. at 259, 456 A.2d at 441.

[46]92 N.J. at 260, 456 A.2d at 442.

[47]92 N.J. at 219–20, 456 A.2d at 420–21. This emphasis on sound planning is characteristic of the opinion. Thus, the court specifically upheld five-acre zoning, where it was justified by environmental and open space needs. 92 N.J. at 315, 456 A.2d at 471.

[48]This affirmative obligation had been generally mentioned in *Mount Laurel I,* 67 N.J. at 174, 336 A.2d at 713, but its impact was never clarified in that opinion, and its scope was apparently curtailed in Oakwood at Madison, Inc. v. Township of Madison, 72 N.J. 481, 517–18, 546, 371 A.2d 1192 at 1200.

may be loosely grouped into two groups: ordinance requirements and other municipal actions.

The ordinance requirements include density bonuses, mandatory set asides, and mobile home zoning.[49] The discussion of density housing and mandatory set asides broke new doctrinal ground. The *Madison* court had actually questioned the validity of density bonuses specifically keyed to the production of lower-income housing.[50] In *Mount Laurel II,* both density bonuses and the more drastic mandatory set asides were approved.[51] Such provisions were attacked by the defendants, both as a taking and as an impermissible socioeconomic use of the zoning power because they regulated occupants, not structures.

The court squarely rejected these contentions,[52] accurately stating that traditional zoning for single-family residences, research and development zones, recreation, and agriculture all had a substantial socioeconomic impact "and, in some cases, a socioeconomic motivation."[53] The court also noted that such traditional zoning had helped create the socioeconomic problem of inadequate housing opportunity.[54] Under those circumstances, the court could find no impediment to zoning that sought to remedy a socioeconomic problem by specifically addressing the housing needs of a particular class of disadvantaged persons.

The court also drew support from its decision in *Taxpayers Association of Weymouth Township* v. *Weymouth Township,*[55] which approved zoning for senior-citizen mobile home parks. It reasoned that the special housing needs of lower-income persons were no less deserving of recognition than the special housing needs of the elderly, which the Weymouth ordinance sought to address.[56] In addition, the court noted an irony: since mandatory set asides in some towns might be essential to make low-cost housing possible, such set asides could be constitutionally required to meet *Mount Laurel* obligations. The court could not believe that, at the same time, such essential set asides could be constitutionally forbidden, absent some compelling statement in the constitution itself.[57]

The court's discussion of mandatory set asides addresses the even more difficult problem of maintaining the low-income character of units whose low sales prices and low rents were achieved by a concession under which the developer sold or rented the unit below its market value. The court suggested that rent controls or re-sale price controls might be constitutionally mandated to ensure that the low-income character of the units is maintained.[58] Whatever technique is selected, the

---

[49] 92 N.J. at 266, 277, 456 A.2d at 445, 451.

[50] Oakwood at Madison, Inc., *supra,* 72 N.J. at 518–19, 371 A.2d at 1224–25.

[51] Mandatory set asides, as described by the court, would require a developer to reserve a certain number of units for low- and moderate-income housing; bonuses give a developer additional market units, if he constructs a given number of lower-income units.

[52] 92 N.J. at 270–71, 456 A.2d 447–48.

[53] 92 N.J. at 273, 456 A.2d at 449.

[54] *Id.*

[55] 80 N.J. 6, 364 A.2d 1016 (1976).

[56] 92 N.J. at 271–72, 456 A.2d at 448–49. The court specifically recognized the contrary Virginia decision in Board of Supervisors v. DeGroff Enterprises, Inc., 214 Va. 235, 198 S.E.2d 600 (1973), finding that mandatory set asides were constitutionally invalid. However, it rejected the *DeGroff* holding. This summary treatment of *DeGroff* is appropriate. That decision, although only 10 years old, belongs to an earlier stage of thinking about zoning, which predated the present expansive notions of the police power inherent in such cases as Village of Belle Terre v. Boraas, 416 U.S. 1 (1974). For an overview of the expansion of zoning powers from the traditional mold of cases like *DeGroff,* see R. FREILICH & E. STUHLER, THE LAND USE AWAKENING (1980).

[57] 92 N.J. at 273, 456 A.2d at 449.

[58] 92 N.J. at 269, 456 A.2d at 447.

court stressed that price control is a problem "which municipalities *must* address in order to ensure that they continue to meet their fair share obligations."[59]

The discussion of mobile homes also broke new doctrinal ground. The court overruled *Vickers* v. *Township of Gloucester,*[60] which had provoked the famous exclusionary zoning dissent from Justice Hall. That ruling had allowed municipalities to ban mobile homes.

In *Mount Laurel II,* the New Jersey Supreme Court relied on the factual findings of the trial judge as to the enhanced quality of mobile homes, and on the existence of new federal regulatory mechanisms for ensuring the safety and soundness of such dwellings.[61] The court ruled that mobile homes in New Jersey must be treated as any other residences. Thus, as the court stated, future attempts to justify total exclusions of mobile homes will be evaluated in accordance with the same standards applicable to bans on apartment houses, townhouses, or even single-family residences.[62]

Not specified in the court's opinion is its attitude toward mobile home parks, as distinguished from the placement of mobile homes on ordinary building lots. However, the classification of mobile home zoning as an affirmative device indicates an intent to require mobile home park zoning, at least where other zoning devices are unlikely to work. The mere toleration of mobile homes, along with other types of structures, on large lots, would seem to be less an affirmative measure to attract low-cost housing than a removal of an undue restriction. In fact, it has been persuasively argued that the mere placement of mobile homes on single-family homesites will not do much to reduce housing costs.[63] Thus, mobile homes would appear to constitute an affirmative housing remedy only if parks are required.

Further, in the *Mount Laurel* appeal, the court determined that a developer who proposes a mobile home park in a community that has not otherwise provided for low- and moderate-income housing will be allowed to build—at least if there are no other prospective producers of low- and moderate-income housing on the horizon. Thus, Davis Enterprises was given the right to construct a 456-unit (20 percent low- and moderate-income), 107-acre mobile home park in Mount Laurel, which had done nothing meaningful to provide for low- and moderate-income housing despite 10 years of litigation.[64] The court's treatment of Davis demonstrates that mobile home parks will, in some circumstances, be treated as a required component of a municipal zoning ordinance.

The consequences of this one holding alone could be revolutionary for New Jersey. Mobile home production, especially for non–senior citizens, has been al-

---

[59]*Id.* (Emphasis in original).

[60]37 N.J. 232, 181 A.2d 129 (1962).

[61]92 N.J. at 274, 456 A.2d at 450, *citing* 161 N.J. Super. at 357 and 42 U.S.C. § 5401 (1974).

[62]92 N.J. at 277, 456 A.2d at 451. Other states have split on the propriety of mobile home exclusions. *Compare* Robinson Township v. Knoll, 410 Mich. 293, 302 N.W.2d 146 (1981) (voiding exclusion of mobile homes) *with* City of Brookside Village v. Comeau, 633 S.W.2d 790 (Tex. 1982)(sustaining such a ban). *See also* Cal. Gov't Code § 65852.3 (West 1983), which prohibits exclusion of mobile homes on single-family lots.

[63]Comment, *California Government Code Section 65852.3: Legislature Prohibits Exclusion of Mobile Homes on Single-Family Lots,* 16 U.C.D.L. Rev. 167, 178 (1982).

[64]92 N.J. at 308, 456 A.2d at 467.

most nonexistent, even though mobile home starts have consituted almost 15 percent of new residential construction nationally.[65] Production could now boom.[66]

Besides incentive zoning, the court indicated that "other municipal action inextricably related to land use regulations" would also be required in appropriate cases.[67] Thus, a municipality might be required to pass resolutions needed by a developer in order to obtain tax-exempt, financed housing under the New Jersey Housing and Mortgage Finance Agency Law.[68] Participation in the federal community development block grant program might also be required.[69] Finally, in one of its most controversial pronouncements, the court declared that a municipality might be required to grant a tax abatement for a project, where such abatement was required as a prerequisite for a housing subsidy, as long as municipal interests of greater importance were not affected.[70] The court justified this requirement on the ground that the fiscal impact of a tax abatement might be minimal, in comparison with the other financial impacts of *Mount Laurel II* housing.[71]

This tax concession requirement poses a dilemma. New Jersey, like most states, has a constitutional requirement for uniform taxation. The only constitutionally recognized limit relates to the development of blighted areas.[72] It may be that the constitutional imperative of *Mount Laurel* would be utilized by the court to add a second exception to the uniformity rule, one which would allow abatements where imposition of the uniformity requirement would impede fulfilling the constitutional obligation to provide housing opportunities for lower-income persons. The point remains unresolved as yet.[73] In any event, the court has raised a state constitutional tax issue with a potential national impact.

Another unresolved affirmative action measure is the extent to which municipalities must waive connection fees or provide infrastructure to low- and moderate-income housing. The court dealt only obliquely with this subject, stating that federal community development block grant monies could be used "to fund the necessary infrastructure" for subsidized housing.[74] Mandatory municipal contributions for infrastructure were not clearly before the court in the six specific cases it had to decide. The issue of municipal obligations to build sewers for low- and moderate-income development is thus still open.

The stakes are enormous. The funds required to extend the sewer line through a *Mount Laurel* development could dwarf the impact of any tax abatement, especially since even tax-abated improvements always produce more revenue than was pre-

---

[65]92 N.J. at 276. *See* R. Burchell, W. Beaton & D. Listokin, Mount Laurel II Challenge and Delivery of Low-Cost Housing 358 (1983).

[66]The mobile home ruling, like the mandatory set aside holdings in *Mount Laurel II*, demonstrates the remarkable scope of the decision. These two issues, considered separately, each could well have been the basis for significant and nationally recognized court decisions. Yet they take up less than 10 percent of the *Mount Laurel II* decision.

[67]92 N.J. at 264, 456 A.2d at 444.

[68]N.J. Stat. Ann. § 55:14K-6(b) (West Supp. 1984–85).

[69]92 N.J. at 264 n. 27, 456 A.2d at 264–65.

[70]92 N.J. at 265, 456 A.2d at 445.

[71]The court cited no factual authority for its conclusion with respect to either branch of this tax comparison.

[72]*Cf.* N.J. Const. art. VIII, § 3.

[73]There has been some indication that the New Jersey courts might have accepted differential taxation for blighted areas, even in the absence of a specific constitutional amendment providing the same. McClintock v. City of Trenton, 47 N.J. 102, 219 A.2d 510 (1966).

[74]92 N.J. at 264, 456 A.2d at 444.

viously derived from the vacant land on which the improvements have been constructed.[75] The court's reference to the fiscal impacts of tax abatements suggests that it would pay attention to the fiscal impact of infrastructure contribution. Its silence on a requirement to build infrastructure most likely reflects an awareness of the complexities of the problem, and a determination to defer resolution of these complexities until the presentation of a case squarely raising the issue.

Least-Cost Housing. The court concluded its discussion of municipal actions with an analysis of what communities must do if no combination of ordinance provisions and other actions proves successful in providing housing that could actually be afforded by low- and moderate-income people. In such cases, the court stated it would allow fair share requirements to be met with the "least-cost housing" that could be constructed after removal of "all excessive restrictions and exactions, and after a thorough use by a municipality of all affirmative devices that might lower costs."[76] However, some kinds of middle-income housing, "including $50,000-plus single-family homes and very expensive apartments," could not be least-cost housing, since presumably, less expensive apartments and mobile homes would be available at lower prices.[77]

This least-cost ruling is a clear rejection of that part of the *Madison* opinion that allowed municipalities to meet their *Mount Laurel* obligations by providing least-cost housing. That approach had been justified on the ground that least-cost housing would eventually filter down to lower-income persons. The Chief Justice apparently took judicial notice of the fact that suburban housing appreciates, and suburban units not immediately made available to lower-income persons are very unlikely to filter down to them later.[78] The court also asserted that use of middle-income housing to satisfy *Mount Laurel* obligations would only exacerbate inner-city segregation by providing additional housing that would allow more of the middle class to leave the cities.[79] This rejection of least-cost housing is, as mentioned above, a crucial point in the decision, and one that distinguishes the Pennsylvania cases, which employ much of the same fair share rhetoric. It demonstrates that the court's concern is not with a general rationalization of zoning requirements applicable to housing, or with the establishment of a free housing market, but with assuring an adequate opportunity for the poor, who, in the court's phrase, "remain locked in urban slums,"[80] and who are subject to "two societies, one black, one white—separate and unequal."[81]

Remedies for Invalid Zoning

The court went far beyond *Mount Laurel I* and *Madison,* and indeed beyond any zoning case ever decided, in specifying the remedies for unconstitutional zoning. The remedies fall into three categories. With respect to the first category, the "builder's remedy," the New Jersey court utilized the concept approved by the Pennsylvania courts for approximately a decade, by holding that a builder who wins a constitutional lawsuit should ordinarily be allowed to construct his project.[82] No

---

[75]N.J. Stat. Ann. § 40:55C–65 (West Supp. 1968–1983).
[76]92 N.J. at 277, 456 A.2d at 451. (Emphasis in original).
[77]92 N.J. at 277, 456 A.2d at 451.
[78]92 N.J. at 278, 456 A.2d at 452.
[79]*Id.*
[80]92 N.J. at 352, 456 A.2d at 490.
[81]92 N.J. at 210 n.5, 456 A.2d at 416 (quoting Kerner Commission, 1968).
[82]*Compare* 92 N.J. at 279–81, 456 A.2d at 452–53, *with Surrick,* 476 Pa. 182, 382 A.2d 105 (1977).

longer would such builder's remedies "ordinarily be rare," as described in the cryptic phrase employed in the *Madison* opinion.[83]

This change of expectation is drastic. It gives builders the whip hand in dealing with the great majority of suburban communities whose ordinances presently do not comply with *Mount Laurel II*. In exchange for the promise to build a substantial amount of low- and moderate-income housing, the developer obtains the significant right to build four standard units for each lower-income unit. This step incentive lends a potentially enormous impact to the builder's remedy. However, there are several important limitations to the builder's remedy. First, the builder/plaintiff must agree to construct a substantial amount of low- and moderate-income housing. Least-cost housing, while justifiable in some circumstances as a municipal zoning technique, is "*no* substitute for low- and moderate-income housing" as a prerequisite to a builder's remedy.[84] As to the crucial question of how much low-income housing is substantial, the court, in a footnote, suggested 20 percent as a reasonable minimum.[85] It also indicated that the amount of lower-income housing required in particular cases might be influenced by the amount of least-cost housing proposed. A developer might be allowed to build somewhat less lower-income housing, if the balance of his project consisted principally of no-frills rather than luxury housing.[86] This proportion is obviously a key element for builder/plaintiffs who challenge local zoning and seek a builder's remedy. In fact, the attorney for the New Jersey Home Builders, Stewart Hutt, has remarked that for builders, *Mount Laurel* is a case whose entire holding is wrapped up in two footnotes. These are footnote 8, which sets forth price ranges that qualify as lower-income housing, and footnote 37, which indicates how much of such housing must be constructed to obtain a builder's remedy.

Second, if the municipality established that environmental or other substantial planning concerns render the project unsound, the court should deny the builder's remedy. But these concerns must be substantial; a mere preference for another site, even if it is a better one, will not suffice in the absence of some serious environmental concern or planning problem.[87]

Third, the good faith of the builder and the community may also be relevant to granting the builder's remedy. The court stated that builders who plan no lower-income housing, but who instead use *Mount Laurel* litigation only as a club to obtain project approvals, will not be granted the builder's remedy.[88] There is also some obligation to attempt to obtain relief without litigation.[89] Not as clearly stated, but implied in the decision, is the proposition that a municipality whose zoning ordinance is essentially sound may also defeat a builder's remedy if only minor amendments to the ordinance are required to bring it into compliance with *Mount Laurel.* While the court stated that good or bad faith is irrelevant in determining whether fair share needs are realistically met,[90] it did imply that good faith was relevant to the issue of remedies in general, which indicates that it could be relevant to the builder's remedy in particular.[91] This suggests that the court wished to give the trial judiciary at least some flexibility in selecting builder's remedies to be imposed on communities whose efforts are reasonable, although not fully satisfactory.

---

[83]72 N.J. at 551–52 n.50, 371 A.2d at 1227.
[84]92 N.J. at 330, 456 A.2d at 478.
[85]92 N.J. 279 n.37, 456 A.2d at 452.
[86]92 N.J. at 330–31, 456 A.2d at 478.
[87]92 N.J. at 280, 456 A.2d at 452.
[88]*Id.*
[89]92 N.J. at 218, 456 A.2d at 418.
[90]92 N.J. at 222, 456 A.2d at 422.
[91]92 N.J. at 306, 456 A.2d at 465.

The court did not define what "substantial planning concerns" would justify the denial of the builder's remedy. However, it is probable that the court was referring to substantial incompatibility of uses. The court's discussion of mobile homes provides a set of potential examples of how sound planning considerations can rule out a particular low- and moderate-income use. In this section of the opinion, the court stated that the otherwise inoffensive appearance of a mobile home might be quite offensive in the context of a development in particular municipalities. Thus, in this situation, the court endorsed a legitimate allotment of particular land for uses other than mobile homes.[92] These comments appear to involve incompatible uses. However, it remains to be seen when the phrase "substantial planning concerns" will be clear enough to further the court's objectives of facilitating housing approval, while retaining some local planning discretion.[93] In addition to the above, the court held that builder's remedies could be phased or timed to guard against the sudden and radical transformation of the municipality.[94]

The second remedial device described by the court was the appointment of a master. Such appointment will occur after a trial in which a zoning ordinance is declared invalid. The major purpose of the master will be to work with the municipal officials to develop constitutional zoning and land use regulations.[95] The master's fee is, in fact, to be entirely paid by the municipality.[96]

The effectiveness of a master would be enhanced by the compressed time period in which he or she will be operating. Municipalities will, as a rule, have only 90 days to zone.[97] During this period, the master will work, not only with the governing body, but also with plaintiffs, the board of adjustment, the planning board, and other interested developers, in negotiating the requirements of the new ordinance. Further, the new ordinance must be submitted to the master for his or her review and recommendations prior to its submission to the court.[98]

At the end of the 90-day period, the master will give, under oath, his or her opinion as to the validity of the revised zoning ordinance.[99]

Like the builder's remedy, the use of the master has substantial prior judicial roots. Although infrequently found in zoning litigation, special masters have been judicially used for years to help courts formulate equitable decrees. Moreover, their role has expanded in recent years, as the courts have become more involved in litigation that requires them to reform and to oversee agencies and institutions, such as jails or schools.[100] The analogous complexity of zoning ordinance changes makes these equitable and institutional litigation precedents well applicable to *Mount Laurel* litigation.[101] Therefore, the court's reliance on the special master

---

[92]92 N.J. at 276, 456 A.2d at 450.

[93]Of course, the existence of environmental hazards on the site in question would justify denial of a builder's remedy. *See* 92 N.J. at 316, 456 A.2d at 474, where the court, in discussing Caputo v. Township of Chester, No. L-42857-74 (Law Div. Oct. 4, 1978), one of the six cases before it, indicated that projects in environmentally sensitive lands could be found to be unsuitable for lower-income housing. *See* 92 N.J. at 279, 456 A.2d at 452.

[94]92 N.J. at 280, 456 A.2d at 453.

[95]92 N.J. at 281, 456 A.2d at 453–54.

[96]92 N.J. at 281 n. 38, 456 A.2d at 453 n. 38.

[97]92 N.J. at 281, 456 A.2d at 453–54.

[98]92 N.J. at 284, 456 A.2d at 454.

[99]92 N.J. at 284, 456 A.2d at 455.

[100]*See, e.g., Special Project, the Remedial Process in Institutional Reform Litigation,* 78 Coɪ.uм. L. Rev. 784, 794 (1978).

[101]*See, e.g.,* Fidelity Union Trust Co. v. Ritz Holding Co., 126 N.J. Eq. 148 (Chancery 1939), *cited* in *Mount Laurel II,* 92 N.J. at 284, 456 A.2d at 455.

technique is not only consistent with judicial tradition, but conceptually appropriate in zoning cases. Moreover, the courts will almost certainly be helped by the advice of a neutral expert.[102] In fact, as a practical matter, the three *Mount Laurel* judges have already appointed masters well before the remedial stage, in order to provide an independent source of facts and expert opinion as to such issues as region, housing need, and fair share.[103] Thus, there is every reason to believe that the use of a master for remedial and fact-finding purposes will be a useful and significant legacy of the *Mount Laurel II* opinion.

The court's third remedial category concerns a municipality that fails to produce a valid zoning ordinance, even after an initial judgment of invalidity by a trial court and the subsequent advice of a remedial master. The remedies for such noncompliance are drastic. They include any one or more of the following orders by the court:

(1) That the municipality adopt such resolutions and ordinances, including particular amendments to its zoning ordinance and other land use regulations, as will enable it to meet its *Mount Laurel* obligation;

(2) That certain types of projects or construction, as may be specified by the trial court, be delayed within the municipality until its ordinance is satisfactorily revised, or until all or part of a fair share of lower-income housing is constructed and/or firm commitments for its construction have been made by responsible developers;

(3) That the zoning ordinance and other land use regulations of the municipality be deemed void in whole or in part, so as to relax or eliminate building and use restrictions in all or selected portions of the municipality (the court may condition this remedy upon failure of the municipality to adopt resolutions or ordinances mentioned in (1) above); and

(4) That particular applications to construct housing and included lower income units be approved by the municipality, or any officer, board, agency, authority (independent or otherwise), or division thereof.[104]

These remedies amount to direct judicial supervision of the community's zoning. Yet they are to be invoked only after the municipality has been found to have violated the constitution and then, notwithstanding the advice of a court-appointed master, to have refused to bring itself into compliance with the constitutional mandate. Moreover, the municipality's good faith will be relevant to these remedies. Courts will not require a municipality to be unzoned simply because it had made an honest mistake in determining, for example, whether a certain building height restriction or setback would impermissibly raise housing construction costs.[105]

Moreover, the need for such remedies is already evident. The clearest remedial order issued by the court in *Mount Laurel II* was its direction to Mount Laurel Township to approve the mobile home park proposed by Intervenor Davis. Yet, after 10 years, two New Jersey Supreme Court decisions, and denunciation of its efforts by the New Jersey Supreme Court,[106] Mount Laurel persisted in obstructing this development. After *Mount Laurel II* was decided, the township claimed that there was no sewer capacity for the Davis mobile homes. This claim was mysteriously but quickly overcome when the trial judge, responding to *Mount Laurel II*'s mandate, ordered that all sewer hookups in the township be enjoined.[107] The municipality's latest gambit—an attempt to deny final site plan approval to Davis—was more recently overcome when the trial judge now sitting on the case refused to remand the matter

---

[102]92 N.J. at 282, 456 A.2d at 454.

[103]*See* Order of Honorable Eugene Serpentelli dated July 25, 1983, in Urban League of Greater New Brunswick v. Mayor of Borough of Carteret, No. C-4122-73 (Super. Ct. N.J. 1983).

[104]92 N.J. at 285, 456 A.2d at 455.

[105]*See* 92 N.J. at 306, 456 A.2d at 465.

[106]*See* 92 N.J. at 198–99, 456 A.2d 410–11.

[107]Conversation with Gerald Haughey, attorney for Intervenor Davis (December 3, 1983).

to further planning board action and, instead, issued the site plan approval himself.[108]

These incidents demonstrate very simply the occasional need for the drastic remedies described by the *Mount Laurel II* court. The court's perception that rights may never achieve fruition in the absence of an expansive remedial arsenal is clearly correct. As the United States Supreme Court stated in *Swann v. Charlotte-Mecklenberg School District*,[109] the scope of the remedy must be equivalent to the constitutional wrong. The remedies described by the court clearly come within this constitutional standard.

Time of Decision, Finality, and Repose

The court found that the complexity of the *Mount Laurel* cases requires an alteration of the usual procedure for responding to adjudications of validity. No longer will municipalities be able to delay the ultimate decision by enacting new zoning ordinances while appealing initial judgments of invalidity. Rather, a matter will stay before the trial court after such an initial judgment. The municipality will have one further opportunity in 90 days to revise its ordinance by consultation with the master.[110] No further new ordinances will be considered; the new ordinance must pass the test of compliance. As the court stated in connection with Mount Laurel Township, no longer will a municipality be allowed to block the use of land by continually adopting new ordinances, one just as invalid as the next.[111]

However, municipalities have the right to revise their ordinances under protest, so that they can continue their disagreement with an initial judgment of invalidity, as well as appeal from a final judgment declaring the revised ordinance to be invalid. A municipality, under such circumstances, may also win a stay of the effectiveness of any revised ordinance, pending the appellate determination of a claim that they should not have been required to revise the ordinance in the first place.[112]

These arrangements for appeals recognize that *Mount Laurel*–style litigation has lasted, in some cases, 10 years or more because each ordinance revision has been subject to a separate judgment that can be individually appealed. For example, the *Mount Laurel* plaintiffs have gone through two rounds of trial decisions and appeals. The township's attitude, as described above, might clearly have resulted in a third and fourth round. The court's goal of providing effective means for relief to *Mount Laurel* plaintiffs requires an alternative to such a merry-go-round. The court's solution, allowing one revision and a consolidated appeal from the initial judgment and judgment as to the revision, gives the municipality a sufficient opportunity to review its ordinance, while providing an expeditious mechanism for appellate determination of the issues. It is hard to see how a court, determined to provide an effective remedy, could have solved the problem of successive appeals in any other fashion.

Finally, the municipality gains a significant benefit from adopting a complying ordinance. A community that obtains either an initial judgment of validity, or a judgment of compliance after revision of its ordinance to satisfy fair share requirements, will be rendered immune from *Mount Laurel* litigation for six years, in the absence of a substantial transformation of the community. This six-year period is

---

[108]Remarks of Honorable Anthony Gibson, one of the three specially appointed judges, at the Second Annual Land Use Law Section of the New Jersey State Bar Association (December 3, 1983).

[109]402 U.S. 1 (1971).

[110]92 N.J. at 290, 456 A.2d at 460.

[111]92 N.J. at 306, 456 A.2d at 466.

[112]92 N.J. at 285, 456 A.2d at 455.

derived from the New Jersey Municipal Land Use Law, which requires the examination and amendment of a master plan and land use regulations every six years.[113]

CONCLUSION: WILL IT WORK? IS IT JUST?

The foregoing analysis demonstrates that the New Jersey Supreme Court went to extraordinary lengths to provide a legal basis for the encouragement of suburban low- and moderate-income housing. Will the court be successful in this effort? If so, will the results be just—to the poor, to the builders, and to the suburban communities?

The answer to the first question appears more likely than not to be "yes." Developers have been rising to the bait provided by the builder's remedy. According to the New Jersey Administrative Office of the Courts, which is keeping special statistics on *Mount Laurel II* litigation, over 70 exclusionary zoning cases have been filed since *Mount Laurel II*.[114] All, or almost all, of these were by developers, who have promised, as required by footnote 37,[115] to set aside a substantial number of housing units for low- and moderate-income homebuyers. Several cases have already been settled with remedies granted to builders. Construction has begun on the Bedminster condominium and *Mount Laurel II* mobile home project, for a total of over 400 low- and moderate-income units without external subsidy. The number will undoubtedly swell over time.

This is not to say that there has been a resolution of all the practical problems of administering *Mount Laurel II* housing. For example, the price or rent control methods for ensuring that lower-income units remain so are still being threshed out. Potential legal structures vary from elaborate tenant screening specifications in detailed condominium documents to simple delegation to the title company to determine, by appropriate affidavit of title, the qualification of the buyer.[116] Further, lending institutions must be assured that a mortgage loan on a price-controlled unit represents a reasonable investment.

However, these difficulties do not appear to be insuperable obstacles. Therefore, it appears likely that the initial blush of enthusiasm on the part of developers will ripen into the actual production of units over the next few years.

Nor does the opinion seem likely to lead to the morass that some observers have deemed to be associated with the use of fair share methodologies to determine housing obligations.[117] In fact, the planning experts involved in the litigation have appeared to acquiesce in most aspects of the so-called consensus fair share methodology adopted by the 20 or so planners from whom Judge Serpentelli sought to obtain agreement. Reportedly, the other *Mount Laurel* judges are making use of that methodology as well. Thus, the potential for endless debates over a fair share formula appears to have been avoided by the special three-judge procedure required by the New Jersey Supreme Court, and by the initiative of one of those judges in meeting informally with the experts involved in the cases, and in encouraging them to develop a consensus approach to fair share.[118]

---

[113]N.J. Stat. Ann. § 40:55D–89 (West Supp. 1984–85).

[114]Memorandum from the administrative office of the courts, July 3, 1984.

[115]92 N.J. 279, 456 A.2d at 452.

[116]The author has reviewed a number of documents in his capacity as a trustee of the Bedminster Hills Housing Corporation, which is administering the 260 Mount Laurel II units in Bedminster.

[117]Lefcoe, *California's Land Planning Requirements: The Case for Deregulation*, 54 S. Cal. L. Rev. 447, 486–87 (1981).

[118]A decision by Judge Serpentelli on the validity of the consensus formula is expected imminently.

As can be seen, even though these practical questions are not free from doubt, they raise less difficult issues than the questions as to justness and fairness of the decision. One line of criticism in this regard claims that inclusionary zoning techniques mandated by the court present an undue imposition on builders, landowners, and middle-income housing consumers. It is urged that the costs of providing housing below market prices should not be imposed on the developer or landowner, who loses the profit from that part of the development that is devoted to low- and moderate-income housing, nor should it be imposed on the middle-income home purchaser, whose housing price is increased to offset the losses on these units.[119] The similar allegation is made that such internal subsidization constitutes a form of taxation of property owners and homebuyers that would more fairly be borne by the public at large, rather than only persons involved in the construction and purchase of new housing.[120]

These arguments have some appeal. However, they do not withstand analysis, especially given the broad police power accorded by the *Mount Laurel II* court to implement land use objectives that do not interfere with the provision of housing. Under the court's analysis, a municipality would have a perfect right, under its police powers, to continue large-lot zoning in order to conserve open space, preserve agriculture, or protect the environment.[121]

As a result, the court has narrowed the basis for voiding zoning ordinances on the grounds that they constitute a taking without just compensation, or arbitrary and unreasonable restriction in violation of the due process clause.

In the context of such potential regulatory latitude, a decision by a court to grant rezoning to a builder who promises to construct some low- and moderate-income housing constitutes a windfall that is given to that builder only on the strength of his or her promise to implement the social objective that is the justification for the windfall. The developer is thus being told that large-lot zoning is valid as a device to preserve open space or agriculture, unless the developer proposes to construct low- and moderate-income housing. If he makes that commitment, the court will grant a windfall profit, but require that some portion of this windfall be channeled to meeting a social goal.

Given this line of reasoning, imposition of an inclusionary requirement on developers who win lawsuits seems quite appropriate. The builder's remedy is, in effect, a density bonus for the achievement of certain goals. As such, the inclusionary requirement does not acutally constitute a tax on the present value of the land. It is, instead, a partial diversion of a windfall profit resulting from a relaxation of regulation.[122]

The same considerations apply to zoning granted by a municipality rather than by a court order. To the extent that the municipality is zoning to bring its ordinance into compliance with *Mount Laurel II*, it is granting developers and certain landowners a windfall in order to achieve the social end. As with the court order, the municipality's decision to divert part of this windfall to low- and moderate-income

---

[119]This line of criticism is set forth in Ellickson, *The Irony of Inclusionary Zoning,* 70 S. Cal. L. Rev. 1167 (1981) [hereinafter cited as *Irony*]; and Ellickson, *Suburban Growth Controls, An Economic and Legal Analysis,* 86 Yale L.J. 345 (1977).

[120]*See Irony, supra* note 119, at 1184.

[121]This was the essence of the court's ruling in the *Chester Township* case, one of the *Mount Laurel II* sextet in which the court upheld five-acre zoning in sweeping terms. Superior Ct. of N.J. Law Division, Hunterdon County, *See* 92 N.J. at 315, 456 A.2d at 71.

[122]Professor Ellickson appears to agree that density bonuses are not unfair, since they add value to a piece of land, at the same time that they convert part of its value to social ends. *Irony, supra* note 119, at 1188, 1192.

housing does not tax the landowner, but simply ensures that a part of his extra value is used to achieve the stated purpose of the rezoning.

Neither is this system unfair to the middle-class homeowner, who will be purchasing the market-rate units in a development with 20 percent low- and moderate-income housing. In the first place, it is not at all clear that such persons will actually pay more for their housing. In fact, they may actually pay less than in a market-rate development, since builders may feel that they have to lower the price of the market-rate units in order to ensure their salability in the mixed-income development context. Any extra revenues needed to subsidize the low-income units, in that situation, might come from increased densities, such as increased sales volume, rather than increased markup on individual homes.

Further, the impact of *Mount Laurel* should be an increase in the supply of middle-income housing. After all, under the standards set forth in footnote 37, up to 80 percent of the units contained in a *Mount Laurel II*-type development will be market units. Thus, in terms of actual numbers, *Mount Laurel II* will result in more middle-income housing than low- and moderate-income housing. The increased supply is bound to benefit middle-income home purchasers, as a class, by providing an enhanced amount of more reasonably priced townhouses and condominiums. Thus, even if a middle-income family has to pay $72,000 instead of $70,000 for a townhouse because of an internal subsidy, the result is still superior to the $100,000 or more that might be required to purchase a single-family home under large-lot zoning.

Thus, the system is unfair neither to the developer, whose profits increase, nor to the landowner, whose land still becomes more valuable, nor to the middle-income homeowner, whose housing choice has been expanded. It would appear that the unfairness argument, as applied to developer and purchasers against *Mount Laurel II*, is not persuasive. And, after all, if developers thought *Mount Laurel II* was unfair to them, they would not be bringing in the lawsuits.

Is *Mount Laurel II* actually fair to the poor, whom it purports to serve? The New Jersey Public Policy Research Institute, an organization of black public officials in the state, has argued that little *Mount Laurel II* housing will actually be acquired by urban households, unless special affirmative tenant selection efforts are made.[123] Apparently supporting this argument is the fact that most prospective *Mount Laurel II* households, low- and moderate-income households, are not black. Rather, according to a Rutgers Center for Urban Policy Research study, 80 percent of the prospective *Mount Laurel II* households are white, with 36 percent of the total being elderly.[124]

This concern, while valid, represents less a flaw in decision than a question of implementation. As noted above, the court indicated that resale price controls and rent controls will be necessary on occasion to maintain the low- and moderate-income character of the units. The court may be induced to impose similar requirements for affirmative marketing, should it appear that the problem reported by the Public Policy Research Institute is actually occurring. At this stage, it simply can be said that *Mount Laurel II* will make housing available where there was none before. Thus, it at least creates an opportunity for urbanites to seek housing elsewhere. Implementation of this opportunity may require further monitoring.

A similar concern has been expressed that the market-rate units constructed by *Mount Laurel* will result in a further migration of the middle class or working class

---

[123]Holmes, *A Black Perspective on Mount Laurel II: "Fair Share,"* 14 Seton Hall L. Rev. 944 (1984).

[124]R. Burchell, W. Beaton & D. Listokin, *Mount Laurel II Challenge and Delivery of Low-Cost Housing* 210 (1983).

from the cities, and will further depress the cities. The fallacy in this argument is its exaltation of place over people. For 30 years, upwardly mobile urban citizens have sought to obtain what were to them the advantages of suburbia. The vast majority of these citizens were white. No one told these persons that, by law, they should be required to remain inside the cities in order to preserve urban health.

However, now that a black middle class has emerged in the cities, such freedom is being contested. These black potential suburbanites supposedly must remain in the cities, whether they will it or not, in order to maintain the vastly depressed (in New Jersey, at least) economic and physical bases of the cities. In other words, it was fine for the past white, urban middle class to desert the cities, but not for the present, integrated middle class to do so.

Such an argument must be rejected. Economic discrimination cannot be a proper device for maintaining our cities. If our urban areas are to revive, they should do so on their own merits, rather than by the maintenance of legal restrictions on out-migration.

The final "fairness" issue may prove to be the most substantial of all. It relates to the question of *Mount Laurel II's* impact on communities, and on how they met their fair share. The problem is simply put. In several cases currently pending before the trial courts, expert reports have been submitted that recommend fair share allocations for particular communities in excess of 3,000 dwelling units.[125] In the absence of ongoing state or federal subsidy programs, many of these obligations must be satisfied by developments that include four market units to each low- or moderate-income unit. Accordingly, the provision of 3,000 low- and moderate-income units might require zoning to accommodate 15,000 dwelling units in total. However, this zoning was supposed to be implemented over a six-year period in the ordinary case.[126] This comes out to a rate of construction of units of 2,500 per year, which is enormous for New Jersey's communities.

Such a result is insupportable. Infrastructure costs associated with that level of expansion are bound to be enormous. For example, communities with volunteer fire departments may have to hire professionals. There will be a precipitous need for new roads, new schools, and new sewer and water lines to meet the need of 15,000 new families, or approximately 40,000 new residents. Moreover, the sheer volume of such population additions is beyond any that has existed in New Jersey, even during the 1960s, when zoning was a relatively mild constraint to housing expansion. Such a result also contravenes other aspects of *Mount Laurel II*, namely the New Jersey Supreme Court's clearly expressed desire to avoid a housing influx that sweeps away community character.[127]

Mount Laurel II does suggest one avenue of escape from this dilemma. In its opinion, the court does state that fair share obligation can be phased-in over a period longer than the usual six years, if the construction of so many units would result in the deluge that would overwhelm a community's character.[128] Unfortunately, the court did not specify with any precision the circumstances under which such phasing would be permitted. A number of factors would certainly be relevant. These would include the size of a community's infrastructure, and its capability to expand. The impact of a large influx of persons on a community's character, and its ability to accommodate the influx without altering the community character, would be other factors. In addition, the court should look to the historic market patterns in the community and in the region, to see whether there was any real likelihood

---

[125]This statement is based on this writer's involvement in several cases pending *Mount Laurel II* litigation, and his review of expert reports of such litigation.
[126]*See* 92 N.J. at 291, 456 A.2d at 459.
[127]*See* 92 N.J. at 219, 456 A.2d at 421.
[128]*Id.*

that the kind of expansion indicated by the fair share numbers would ever actually occur in the six-year time period. Upon proper proofs and similar factors, the court should allow phasing-in of the obligation.

Alternatively, the court should deem least-cost housing within the community to be a credit to the achievement of low- and moderate-income housing goals. The opinion already indicates that least-cost housing can be utilized to achieve low- and moderate-income housing goals, after all other means of attracting such housing have been tried and proven unsuccessful.[129] However, reliance on least-cost housing would seem to be at least as appropriate in those communities whose fair share numbers are so large that it can be predicted in advance that the market is going to produce the number of units required under reasonable planning constraint. In situations in which it can be predicted that low- and moderate-income housing cannot be built in required numbers, or where such production, even if technically feasible from a market standpoint, will produce severe distortions within the community, the court could credit least-cost housing as low- and moderate-income housing, on the theory that meeting the obligation through low- and moderate-income housing on an 80-to-20 basis alone might be impossible, or at least severely inappropriate from a planning standpoint.

This result seems far more consistent with the emphasis of opinion on sound planning to avoid suburban sprawl and alteration of suburbs only to the extent necessary to meet the opinion's goals.[130] The court that said suburban municipalities are not to become land banks for speculators,[131] could not realistically have intended to add 40,000 people to a community by court order in six years. As stated by the court in *Mount Laurel I*:

> There is no reason why developing municipalities like Mount Laurel, required by this opinion to afford the opportunity for all types of housing to meet the needs of various categories of people, may not become and remain attractive, viable communities, providing good living and adequate services for all their residents in the kind of atmosphere that a democracy and free institutions demand. They can have industrial sections, commercial sections, and sections for every kind of housing from low-cost and multifamily, to lots of more than an acre with very expensive homes. Proper planning and governmental cooperation can prevent overintensive and too-sudden development, ensure against future suburban sprawl and slums, and assure the preservation of open space and local beauty. We do not intend that developing municipalities shall be overwhelmed by voracious land speculators and developers, if they use the powers that they have intelligently and in the broad public interest. Under our holdings today, they can be better communities for all than they previously have been.[132]

This is the hope of *Mount Laurel II* as well.

---

[129]*See* 92 N.J. at 277–78, 456 A.2d at 451–52.
[130]*See* 92 N.J. at 220, 238, 456 A.2d at 426–27.
[131]*See* 92 N.J. at 211, 456 A.2d at 420.
[132]67 N.J. at 151, 336 A.2d at 733.

Peter A. Buchsbaum is an attorney with Sterns, Herbert & Weinroth. Buchsbaum acted as special counsel to Lawrence Township for *Mount Laurel II* litigation.

This article is excerpted from one that appeared in *Urban Lawyer,* a publication of the American Bar Association. Use is by permission.

Conclusion

THE SECOND GENERATION OF GROWTH MANAGEMENT

PAUL R. NIEBANCK

T here emerged at the seminar a remarkable clarity and degree of agreement on the advances that have been made and on the major challenges that lie ahead. In reviewing my notes and then reflecting on what happened, I was surprised at the amount of general clearsightedness and consensus. And others have pointed this out, too.

To summarize and paraphrase some of the observations made at the seminar: for one thing, there seem to have been four major advances made under growth management since its inception:

1) Growth management has resulted in a somewhat smoother development process—most notably, a more predictable and steadier pace, a context of information on public concerns, and a new personal acquaintance and fresh willingness to work together among the actors in the development process.

2) Growth management has contributed to a revitalization of the land use planning enterprise with enhanced elements of rationality, comprehensiveness, and responsiveness to the public will. Along with these has come a movement away from those regulations, restrictions, and inhibitions that characterized the earlier phase, and toward guidance and negotiation of specified ends.

3) Under growth management, public goals have begun to stand a better chance of accomplishment, through fees and dedications, through negotiations of exemptions and exceptions, and through decision-making processes that are more deliberative and that include more varied perspectives.

4) Growth management has helped to produce a development pattern that is more compact, more efficient, more convenient, and more livable—with a closer functional relationship to infrastructure and transportation, with improved site design, and with greater concern for environmental quality and natural processes.

Now, there is still work to be done, still challenges to be faced. The work left to do is associated with certain byproducts of the gains. The most important byproducts seem to be these:

1) The administrative complexity issue, and our overreliance on numerical, analytical methods of dubious worth. Generalized formulas have been misapplied to

specific situations, and administrators within this field have commonly taken unduly rigid approaches. These, it seems to me, are problems of professional competence, and they will only be solved through attention to them in these terms, through the course of time.

2) Occasional misuse of infrastructure prerogatives and of other public prerogatives to inhibit development. Ultimately, this is a problem for the courts. There are, in California just now, a couple of localities that are trying to put absolute moratoria on growth for indefinite periods, on the basis that there's no infrastructure available. The counterpart of this kind of action would be a suit—obviously on the part of the business enterprise community—to encourage the localities to extend infrastructure and, therefore, to provide for growth. These kinds of counterclaims need to go to the courts for resolution.

3) The frequency of knee-jerk popular initiatives that bypass good processes and interrupt good working relationships among actors. This—in some contradiction of what I just said—seems to me to be, for the most part, a residue from growth management, phase I. That is, communities no longer need to accommodate quite the intensity or frequency of governance by initiative for the next little while.

4) The absence of a supportive structure at regional, state, or national levels, offering, for example, infrastructure subsidies; housing incentives; programs of technical assistance, experimentation, and research; or, especially, cooperative approaches to regionwide problems.

5) Most dramatically, the decline in residential opportunity for poor people, for people of color, and, yes, for middle-class people, resulting from the decidedly negative effects of growth management on housing prices. Despite the exceptions to this rule, these effects have been proven and demonstrated over and over again. Too, the parsimonious programs of affordable housing, which do precious little to make up for the induced price increases that growth management brings about, have arisen over and over again. So have the difficulties of getting a share of the unearned increment accruing from growth management for public purposes, including housing. (My good friend Bob [Ellickson] has called the growth management reality a homeowner's cartel, and there's some truth in his allegation.) And also outstanding among the inequities is the contribution to a progressively bimodal distribution of income and opportunity. Assuredly, growth management has done its part toward this graceless outcome.

Now, phase I may well be on its way out—except for the last two items listed above: the combined matter of the housing prices and the resulting exclusion, which make for a formidable exception; and the need for a support structure for local growth management among higher government levels. Of course, this support structure will have to be standardized to recognize certain societal characteristics about which growth management can't do a damn thing—for example, the prevailing structure of wealth, the patterns of age and family composition, the tax structure, and similar data. Nonetheless, growth management seems to be emerging rapidly from its phase I.

The timing of the ULI/Lincoln Institute seminar was, in fact, remarkable in this regard. And good beginnings all across the country were provided with useful reinforcement by that seminar. Whether the threshold to phase II has actually been crossed is still an open question, but the vision of a vigorous future, full of accomplishment, seems now to be much closer at hand than it seemed a few years ago.

Afterword

GROWTH MANAGEMENT: KEEPING ON TARGET?

DOUGLAS R. PORTER, Editor

T his assemblage of papers and articles on growth management is intended to show how such techniques are being applied, as well as the issues they are raising in communities throughout the United States. Clearly, growth management has come a long way since the early days of "slow growth" and "no growth." Growth management techniques are being used selectively or comprehensively in many communities as a matter of course, rather than as a newsworthy exception.

Still, it is evident that adoption of development controls under the rubric of growth management fails to assure trouble-free growth and development. Virtually all of the communities that have enacted strict regulations to control the pace of growth, to match development with infrastructure capacity, and to improve the quality of development—with one or all of these aims—have encountered political, legal, technical, and economic difficulties along the way. Furthermore, these communities, as the reports in this publication attest, are constantly adjusting and adapting their practices to meet the new problems and perceptions.

Paul Niebanck's closing remarks indicate that he believes growth management to be entering a new phase: a second phase, in which more rational, responsible, and cooperative approaches are favored over knee-jerk reactions to popular demands, and over methods using inadequate data gathering and plan making. This may well be true in a number of communities, especially those with some history in the growth management field.

I am not so optimistic as Niebanck, however, about the general trend. News comes daily about local governments passing development moratoria, adopting large-lot zoning, setting new requirements for infrastructure, and such—without much evidence that they are truly coping with a growth problem in a sensible way. For that matter, some communities appear simply to be trying to avoid as much growth as possible. It seems that many communities have learned that restrictive or innovative land use regulations can be legally adopted if enough groundwork—in the way of studies, plans, detailed ordinances—has been laid.

Until now, apparently, the courts have treated these communities leniently, preferring to rest on the presumption of legislative validity: namely, that the local governing body knows best. Babcock and Siemon, however, in *The Zoning Game Revisited,* conclude their history of contemporary zoning by remarking that the courts are beginning to examine legislative acts more closely, especially for the rationales upon which they are based. If this is true, we can expect what Paul Niebanck prescribes: more reasonable applications of growth management techniques.

At present, however, much remains to be done toward understanding the real effects of various management techniques and their degrees of adaptability to particular communities and specific projects. And the hard choices—those by which localities must find ways to accommodate reasonable growth—will still be essentially political ones.